SUBURBAN YOUTH IN CULTURAL CRISIS

RALPH W. LARKIN

New York   Oxford
OXFORD UNIVERSITY PRESS
1979

Copyright © 1979 by Oxford University Press, Inc.

Printed in the United States of America

Library of Congress Cataloging in Publication Data
Larkin, Ralph W 1940-
    Suburban youth in cultural crisis.

    Bibliography: p.
    Includes index.
    1.   High school students—United States.
    2.   Youth—United States—Sexual behavior.
    3.   Drugs and youth—United States.   4.   Youth—
United States—Political activity.   I.   Title.
LA229.L3   373.1'8'0973   78-10742
ISBN 0-19-502522-9
ISBN 0-19-502523-7 pbk.

For Deb

FOREWORD

Many people will read this book, and many of them will say they dislike parts of it. In fact, if we could measure ambivalence, the "index of ambivalence" would probably be very high for Dr. Larkin's book. *Suburban Youth in Cultural Crisis* is interesting and rewarding if read as an *ethnography* of an American middle-class suburb and its high school. One sees the suburban youth culture reacting to economic and political events, first of the 1960s, and then of the contrasting 1970s.

However, chapter 2, "Youth in Post-Scarcity America," and chapter 7, "Youth and the Degradation of Everyday Life," will disturb many readers. Our affluent society contains 99 million persons who are employed or seeking work, but it has not found jobs for 5 million of those people and is unable to employ its youth under age twenty. Larkin sees *monopoly capitalism*, backed by dynamic technology, as the cause of our difficulties. American industry and business are profitable as long as improved technology makes labor increasingly productive and thus increases profits. But people must be taught to consume the goods and services that are produced, whether they need them or not. Schools and the media teach youth and adults to want degrading products.

Society must be restructured to make it a better place for people of all ages, and, in this process, education will be reformed. Larkin does not claim to have a map of the needed society, but he stimulates the reader to think about the problem and, perhaps, to work at it.

ROBERT J. HAVIGHURST
*Professor of Education
and Human Development,
University of Chicago*

November 1978

ACKNOWLEDGMENTS

I would like to express my appreciation for all those who helped me in this study: to all those at "Utopia" High School—the students for their confidence and openness, the faculty and staff for their help, and especially "Mr. Seraph," the principal, who allowed me free access, without interference, to the resources of the school and who trusted me under sometimes difficult circumstances; to Lydia Zmyj and her friends, Stephen Barr, and Paula Bender who had an intimate knowledge of the school and community and read early drafts of the manuscript; to Judy Barr, Saranne Boocock, Ray Calluori, Peter Freund, Edgar Friedenberg, Robert Havighurst, Ann Lieberman, Ernie Sheldon, and Norman Washburne, all of whom read the manuscript at various stages of preparation and gave me helpful comments; to Daniel Foss, who closely oversaw the preparation of the manuscript, worked with me on the theoretical sections, and was my toughest critic; to Jim Anderson and Dale Demy of Oxford for their salutory work on the editing of the manuscript; and to Mary Mitchell and Dorothy Jentz for typing the earlier drafts of this work. Finally, I would like to thank my wife Debra for commenting on the manuscript, giving me encouragement, and making the uncounted sacrifices in her time, energy, and money that contributed to this book.

CONTENTS

1

WELCOME TO THE GREAT AMERICAN DREAM

"Kathy, I'm lost," I said,
Though I knew she was sleeping.
"I'm empty and aching and
I don't know why."
Counting the cars
On the New Jersey Turnpike.
They've all come
To look for America,
All come to look for America,
All come to look for America.
Paul Simon, "America," 1968

PLEASANT VALLEY: AMERICA THE BEAUTIFUL

The town that I will call Pleasant Valley has a picture-book quality about it: tree-lined, quiet streets, some of which are lit with quaint gas lamps; rolling hills; spacious parks; public buildings built with care and splendor; sedate one- and two-story homes on large lots with flower beds and trellises that become riotous in spring with colors that would blind a Fauvist painter; and few sidewalks. Pleasant Valley is isolated, yet located within thirty minutes of a major metropolitan center. It is rustic, yet enjoys all the conveniences of the urban environment. It is the embodiment of the American dream: scenic, friendly, publicly spirited, family-oriented, affluent, historic; in short, a refuge from the problems that plague America today.

This book is a study of the lives of the children who are the products of the American dream, for Pleasant Valley provides them with all the necessities of life in a safe and beautiful environment. The schools they attend are well above any standard of adequacy and they are staffed with concerned teachers. This is an inquiry into the best America has to offer its children. In contrast to rural America, which is completing a depopulation phase created by the development of mechanized agribusiness, and to urban decay (especially in the Northeast), brought about by the abandonment of cities by the capitalist enterprises that built them, Pleasant Valley has been relatively untouched by the course of modern history, achieving the dream of most suburbanites who flee the problems of urban life.

Pleasant Valley can be characterized as having captured the myth of America: a relatively trouble-free community. The youth are well-schooled, crime is low, property rates are on the incline, there are enough blacks in the school district (approximately 4 percent) so that it can call itself integrated without being too hypocritical, city services have been delivered without serious problems, and the various racial and ethnic groups have harmonious relations.

Let us look at the community's political life for an example of this outward harmony. In an era of state and federal governments' having been exposed as deceitful, illegal, and immoral, Pleasant Valley has had an enlightened, public-spirited leadership. The state in which Pleasant Valley is located has a history of sending top government officials to the penitentiary for bribery, malfeasance, misappropriation of funds and perjury. One of the running jokes is that government leaders seem to go from the state house to the "Big House." Of course, from 1969 to 1973, the Nixon Administration took to copying the antics of this state's government with the Watergate burglary and cover-up, the FBI and CIA scandals, Spiro Agnew's bribery and downfall, the IT&T episode, and counterinsurgency against the Democrats. To this we can add the scandals which involved Lockheed, Gulf and Western, Northrup, and several other global corporations in international bribery; and the Congressional sex and Korean bribery scandals in 1976 and 1977.[1] Yet, Pleasant Valley, in the midst of all this, managed to maintain its purity. The town government has been dominated by Republicans who have the grudging admiration of the local Democrats for their efficient and honest administration.

> The governing body is comprised of fair and fairly selfless men. The sense of smugness is probably the only problem. But no problem has been ignored or pushed aside by the governing group. (The executive editor of the local paper as quoted by Martin Gansberg in *The New York Times*, August 26, 1973.)

In the beautiful Georgian town hall hangs a plaque awarded by the National Municipal League. In 1969, Pleasant Valley was chosen as an Honorable Mention All-American City. And why not? In addition to its government, it contains breathtakingly beautiful parks and one of the best school districts in the state. It seems far removed from the serious problems of the neighboring metropolis which was facing bankruptcy and a serious decline of services at the time of this study (1976).

Pleasant Valley is a stable community of well-kept older dwellings. According to the town's statistical summary produced in 1974, its major growth period was during the late 1920s and early 1930s. Since that time, the population figures have stabilized. The area was populated by Northern Europeans until the late 1950s, when upwardly mobile Italians, Eastern Europeans, and Jews settled in the area, giving it some ethnic diversity. Although Pleasant Valley is located in a county that is nearly 20 percent black, it is overwhelmingly white. This can be explained by the fact that its real estate values are prohibitive to most blacks who live ten miles away in one of the most economically depressed areas of the country.

A look at table 1 gives us a profile of the families that live in Pleasant Valley. Even the most cursory glance shows that they are an advantaged group. More than 25 percent of those age 25 and older are college graduates, compared to the national average of 11 percent. Nearly 75 percent of those living in Pleasant Valley are employed in white-collar positions—with 40 percent of them in professional, technical, managerial and administrative positions—compared to the national labor force in which nearly 50 percent are employed in white-collar positions, and approximately 23 percent are in the upper reaches of the white collar labor force. The median income of the community is nearly 2.8 times the national average. There is practically no poverty. Pleasant Valley has houses valued at 3 times the national average. Though it is not what might be called an elite town such as Grosse Pointe, Michigan; Short Hills, New Jersey; or Great Neck, New York; it is well-off by any standard.

Pleasant Valley is a suburban bedroom community. Although there are a few light industries in the area (e.g., a well-known map-making company), the vast majority of residents work outside the township in government and corporate bureaucracies in and around the neighboring urban core. Most (68 percent) own their single-family homes. Since the area is completely built-up, the possibility of the encroachment of high-rise buildings is remote. It is "America, the Beautiful."

UTOPIA HIGH SCHOOL: SOFT BUREAUCRACY

If Pleasant Valley is the embodiment of the American dream, then Utopia High School is a monument to the community's

TABLE 1. Major Demographic Characteristics

	Pleasant Valley	Its County	The Nation
	PERCENTAGE		
Persons 25 years old or older having four or more years of college	27.7	14.2	11.2
Total white-collar labor force	72.4	54.6	48.2
Professional or technical	24.3	17.1	14.8
Managerial or administrative	15.3	8.9	8.3
Sales	12.0	7.8	7.1
Clerical	20.8	20.8	18.0
Median income compared to national median income	278.0 ($17,921)	184.0 ($11,847)	100.0 ($6,446)
Families below the poverty line	2.8	6.8	10.7
Black population	2.6	18.8	11.1
Housing			
Owner occupied	76.8	51.8	62.9
Owner occupied, single family	68.0	42.3	....
Assessed value of $50,000 or more	10.9	4.1	3.1

SOURCES: 1970 Census of Population; 1970 Census of Housing; 1970 Census of Population and Housing: Census Tract Data for County (U.S. Department of Commerce).

faith in education as the instrument of success. Its imposing Gothic facade likens it to a church, symbolizing the seriousness of the pursuits within. Utopia High is housed in a three-story structure built with a mind to beauty and detail. In the center of the building, which was constructed in 1927, stands a seven-story bell tower representing the aspirations of the community. It is the tallest structure in the vicinity. Since the original building was constructed, two large additions have been made, both modern equivalents to the brick and cement original, with the pointed arch theme carried throughout. Upon arriving at the school, I was struck by its imposing beauty. The entrance is comprised of four massive golden oak doors. Behind the doors is a large foyer that empties into the main corridor through a Gothic archway. The foyer floor is laid with red, green, and brown flagstone, polished to a high shine. The entrances to the administrative offices are on the main corridor just off the entryway. The decor of the school combines the new and old. The desks and equipment are modern. The moldings, chair railings, and window fixtures are of darkly stained oak. All this is coordinated with the colors of autumn: browns, tans, umbers, and ochres. The office seems to communicate both tradition and modern efficiency. The principal's office is designed to emphasize the stateliness and authority of the position. The ceilings are approximately 14 feet high, and the office is 15 by 30 feet in area. The floor is covered with a forest green rug. The walls are panelled to a height of about five feet in darkly stained oak. Above the wainscot, gold and brown textured wallpaper in a sedate pattern reaches to a wooden molding at the intersection of the wall and ceiling. The principal's desk, though not antique, is old and looks as if it is constructed of mahogany, stained in somber reddish-brown. The desk is large enough to fit the room. Facing it are several overstuffed chairs with red leather upholstery. Off to one side of the chairs, not visible when one first enters the room, is a bank of metal file cabinets and a side table that is usually strewn with papers, giving the office an anomalous atmosphere, it seems as if the papers don't really belong there, but there is no other place to put them.

Mr. Seraph, the principal, is himself an unassuming person who seems almost embarrassed by the imposing nature of the room and its suggestion of stern, paternalistic hierarchy. He operates in a low-key style. He is very personable and likeable; his relationships with both faculty and students are casual and relaxed. Only if there is serious business is the door to his office closed. It is almost always open and Mr. Seraph is easily accessible not only to those who make appointments, but also to those who wander into his office with a question, a problem, or a desire to chat.

During my first visit to Utopia High, Mr. Seraph took me on a tour of the facilities. Walking through the corridors one could see the care with which the building was constructed. The hallways in the old building have tile to the height of five feet, above which was built a decorative ceramic molding. As we walked, I began to sense the ambiance of the school. There were no hall monitors. The security of the school was handled by one elderly retired police officer who was seen from time to time walking the premises. Although we were touring during class time, there were a number of students in the halls. They were walking from one place to another using the bathrooms, making phone calls, or occasionally stopping for short conversations with other students. There were no hall passes, no teachers quizzing students as to where they ought to be, no students making themselves scarce when they saw the principal coming.

On one occasion, I came upon a group of five students called the "greasers" after the fifties' stereotype of the black leather-jacketed heavies who rode around in 1949 chopped and lowered Mercurys or Lincolns; and who, according to legend, used grease to keep their duck-tail hairdos in place. These students were boisterous, loud, and supercilious. They tended to treat me in a good-hearted condescending manner. This particular time, they were playing dice in the hall, although no money was changing hands. As they were playing and jumping about, a teacher came out of a nearby classroom and requested that they keep the noise down and explained to them in a most reasonable voice that he was showing films and that the noise was disturbing the class's concentration. The reaction of the greasers was to immediately clam up and act as if they had been threatened by the exercise of authority. They assumed a mock deference that was right out of *West Side Story*. I told the teacher that I was interviewing one of them. My presence and intervention seemed to calm the teacher, who, after extracting a promise that there would be less noise, went back to the classroom. The "hard guys" (two female and three male students) turned to me with sighs of relief and one said, "You really saved us." Shortly thereafter, one of them wanted to smoke a cigarette. His friends admonished him since it was strictly against the rules. As a compromise, he held the unlit cigarette between his forefinger and middle finger. When two teachers walked by, the student, in an act of audacity, asked one of them if he had a match. The teacher scowled at him, said no, and walked on.

The authority pattern of Utopia High School might be termed indulgent, tolerant, liberal, permissive, or democratic, depending on one's ideological position. There is a reason for this, which we will explore in detail later. For the present, we must content ourselves with an overview of the school and its culture without involving ourselves in the issues raised by them.

The school, partly because of its non-authoritarian structure and partly because the students are mandated by law to attend, has become a place for a great deal of "hanging out," even by those who are skipping classes. Since "commons periods" in which students are expected to be in school but have no class to attend have supplanted study halls, much commons-period time is spent "hanging out." This adds to the informality of the place; at any time one can see students in various parts of the school sitting and talking, having a smoke, studying individually and in small groups, reading, or even driving off with a friend for an hour or two (which is forbidden).

Students will congregate at the front doors for a few minutes before classes start or, in the afternoon, a crowd will gather and then slowly dwindle away. Students get together in clusters of usually three to six; they smoke cigarettes, "shoot the bull," occasionally horse around or pull a prank, sell some pot, or wait for a friend or a ride.

However, there is one place that most people fear to tread. It is the first floor men's lavatory in the main building. Most of the men's lavatories have had the ventilation slats kicked out of the doors, but the first floor men's lavatory is missing the whole bottom panel. Attempts by the custodial staff to replace it have been futile; each new panel has been kicked out faster than it could be replaced. The custodians have stopped trying. Upon entering, one is immediately assailed by the smells of urine and stale cigarette smoke. Because of the unsavory atmosphere, only a certain "element" hangs out here. Few others venture in, especially during noontime. It is rumored that three pounds of marijuana were divided and cleaned in the lavatory without the knowledge of the faculty or administration. The lavatory is pervaded by a sense of purgatory: the walls are gray; the fixtures and floor tiles (little hexagons) are white, though both are showing signs of age and heavy use; the lighting is dim. At the far end of the bathroom was once a window, but now both panes are filled with plywood, and the plywood is painted the same gray as the walls and stalls. Every place the hand can reach is covered with graffiti: names, sexual epithets, pictures of human genitals, political slogans, initials, names of rock music groups, and comments about students, pot, and the sexual exploits of girls. Some examples: "Peanuts is a sap;" "Bad Company sucks cock;" "Tony strikes again;" "Give food to Nicaragua earthquake victims;" "Its hard to be a saint in [Utopia] where the Columbian grows wild;" "I want pussy;" "Mike, '75;" "Lyn D. gives head." The first floor men's lavatory stands as a reminder that all is not well at Utopia High School. Like the grease stain on the white tablecloth or the black dot on the symbol of the Tao, the lavatory alerts us to the fact that there are negative forces at work.

Utopia High has wonderful facilities. It has a beautiful, spacious, well-staffed library. There is a math lab that has its own IBM 1130 computer which is used for attendance and bookkeeping. For the student who wishes to explore the arts, there is a large, well-stocked art room, a graphics lab with photo-offset equipment, a photography lab, and a ceramics lab. The student newspaper is printed on the school's own press. In addition to the auditorium, there is a little theater for the drama department. The school has its own audio-visual department complete with previewing rooms and a film library. Lest one think that academic subjects are emphasized to the detriment of the vocational arts, Utopia High School sports one of the finest sets of shops in the state. The school has large, well-maintained wood, metal, electronics, and auto shops.

MR. SERAPH

Mr. Seraph, as the principal, is the educational leader of the school. He was hired three years prior to this study. The school district conducted an extensive search that lasted one-and-a-half years, and, according to Mr. Seraph, he was hired because he was experienced in setting up an alternative education program, which, in 1973, the district administration wanted to establish in their high school. He was chosen for the position over a graduate who studied with Dwight Allen at the University of Massachusetts. Mr. Seraph's name was submitted to the district by Teachers College of Columbia University as one of their three top candidates.

When Mr. Seraph accepted this job, he was thirty-five years old. This is the third administrative position in his career. His first was a vice-principal in charge of a "house" in another wealthy suburban school district. (Utopia High School also operates on a "house-plan" system, and houses will be described in detail below. For the present, a house is self-contained administrative jurisdiction within a high school, the school being divided up into several houses.) He occupied this position for three years until he was designated acting principal of the school. Following his year as acting principal, he took a leave of absence, fulfilling his year of residency at Teachers College, while working part-time as a teacher in that high school. Following his residency at Columbia, he took the position at Utopia High.

As one can see, Mr. Seraph is not the type of principal that occurs all too commonly in the field: the ex-football coach who returns to the local school of education to obtain an administrative credential, and, who upon assuming the position, is more concerned with the win-loss record of the major varsity teams than the content and process of the educational program. When accepting the position, Mr. Seraph was on the verge of receiving a doctorate from one of the top graduate schools of education in the country. Teachers College still maintains the aura and influence of its greatest professor, John Dewey. As a matter of fact, one can hear the echoes of Dewey in the voice of Mr. Seraph.

LARKIN. What do you see as the purpose of education?

SERAPH. The purpose, broadly speaking, I think is to do several things: to *allow* students to explore a whole range of areas so that they can make career selections as well as gain some fundamental background so that they can be better participants in *their* world that they're going to be involved in. I see the aspect of socialization is important also in school. You could conceivably do this sitting at home watching television and being fed the right information. But I don't think that would satisfy the day-to-day learning of how to get along with peers, people who are older than themselves, and people in different role relationships. (Recorded July 19, 1976.)

The focus of Mr. Seraph's comments is the student. The school should *allow* the students to make choices so they can effectively participate in *their* world. He sees the learning process as a social one and assumes an active role of the student who makes selections. Implicit in this statement is the notion that students may be more knowledgeable than adults about the world in which they are going to participate. This is an astounding admission on the part of an educator! His views on authority are every bit as liberal and egalitarian.

LARKIN. How do you feel about the use of, the development of the authority of the school? What kind of authority do you see as the ideal way of operating a school?

SERAPH. *(Pause)* Well, I don't know, that's so broad, I'm not sure. The *ideal way*, of course, would be to have a place like Walden Two [!] where *(laughs)* you'd have built upon the child's desire to learn from . . . age six onward. You look at my daughter who is just beginning school. You know, she's so enthusiastic about everything. I think if school could nurture that, I think we would have an ideal participatory democracy, and students would be involved.

Yet, I think more realistically, I think there is a need for strong student and faculty input into the decision-making processes. I also feel that there's a very, very strong need for planning. (Recorded July 19, 1976.)

Mr. Seraph espouses the ideal of participatory democracy at all levels of involvement. He sees students as active participants in their own education, primarily through the process of selection and providing input to decision makers. The participation that Seraph speaks of, though it includes committee participation (input to decision makers), emphasizes the student as a consumer of educational programs (selection). The desire for spontaneity and enthusiasm about education is the same goal of the advertisers of commodities. We shall return to the question of the hegemonic relationship between the educational system and commodity consumption in chapter 2.

The principalship at Utopia High is a professional plum. Pleasant Valley has a reputation for maintaining one of the finest school systems in the state. It maintains this reputation by paying its administration and faculty well above the state average: Mr. Seraph is the second highest paid school principal in the state. With only three years on the job, one can assume that his market value is extremely high.

THE HOUSE PLAN

Utopia High School is quite large. It has an enrollment of 2,000 students. Because of its size, it is divided into four semi-autonomous administrative units, called "houses," with each house containing about 500 students. In addition to the four houses, there is an alternative school which is designed to satisfy the needs of terminal students who have difficulty adapting to the normal school program. Unlike the alternative school, the houses are not differentiated by student orientations, achievement levels, or ability. Students are randomly assigned to a house upon entering school, and remain a part of the house until graduation. The purpose of the house plan is stated in a folder given each student at the beginning of the school year:

> In order to prevent some of the depersonalizing effects which are experienced in large high schools [Utopia] High School operates

under a house plan. The school is divided into four houses composed of an equal number of students, faculty, and guidance counselors under the supervision of a House Director. Dividing the school into four smaller bodies enables the student to have a greater opportunity to become familiar with his teachers, counselors, and classmates. (High school folder, n.d.)

Each house is organized around its own center, which consists of a large commons room, a suite of offices for counselors and the director, a reception area, a teachers' work room, and a conference room. The commons room resembles a lounge or a lunch room, depending on how the students fix it up. For example, the least used commons room contains a large mural, a large open space and a few tables and chairs in addition to the obligatory automatic vending machines that dispense soda, candy, pastry, and snacks. The most often used lounge is divided into two areas: a lunch area at one end of the room, where the machines, tables, and chairs are; and a slightly smaller carpeted area in which large pillows made of foam rubber are strewn, on which students would sprawl or sit. This particular lounge is one of the favorite hang-out places in the school.

Although the houses have their separate administrations and guidance personnel, the students spend progressively less time in their own houses as they come closer to graduation. It is estimated that 75 percent of the sophomore's time spent in school will be within the assigned house, 50 percent of the junior's, and 25 percent of the senior's. The rationale for this procedure is that the school will be able to provide a more supportive social atmosphere for the younger, inexperienced student who must adjust to a new and larger organization and make new friends that come from other feeder junior highs. It is hoped that the student will begin to find a subject of interest and will begin to specialize in the area, regardless of whether or not it is offered in the assigned house.

The guidance function is central to the house plan. The grouping of students in "mini-schools" is to provide a more personalized, supportive environment for the student. Administration and guidance are physically close to the students. Pleasant Valley is proud of the fact that it installed one of the first guidance programs in the state more than forty years ago. The administration claims that it is still one of the best guidance programs in the state.

The house plan is designed to increase student participation and involvement in school affairs. In addition to adding another level of administration, it also adds levels of opportunities for student leadership and governance. Each house has its own officers and organization which plan and sponsor social events. For example, one house conducted an art show in which there was musical accompaniment. The whole project was carried out by students.

Few schools provide the students the variety of opportunities for social and political participation as Utopia High. In addition to the school clubs and house organizations, there are the student body government and various administrative advisory committes in which students can participate.

The alternative school is for those students who have difficulty with the traditional high school program. Conceivably, the alternative school could be a dumping ground where those whom teachers cannot tolerate in the regular classroom could be placed. This does not seem to be the case at Utopia. The students enrolled in the program are self-selected and screened through the guidance counselors. They take a great deal of pride in their program even though they tend to feel somewhat isolated and different from the rest of the students. Unlike most others, alternative school students have decided that high school education is all the formal education they need and they plan to go directly into the labor force upon graduation. Their course work tends to be oriented toward the practical concerns of survival in the modern world: consumer education, human relationships, family economics, and so forth. The hope was that the program would use alternative teaching techniques such as simulation games, role play, and field trips; however, teachers have mostly relied on traditional methods.

THE STUDENTS

Finally, we come to the students, who are the subject of this study. We have already described them as upper middle class[2] with a minority (maybe 30 percent) of working-class backgrounds. They are overwhelmingly white, perhaps 96 to 97 percent of the total population. Most of them are from Protestant backgrounds, with a significant minority of Catholics from Italian and Polish descent. Approximately 15 to 20 percent of the students are Jewish, although most people will estimate higher, since the Jews are overrepresented in leadership positions.[3]

The vast majority of these students are college bound. According to school statistics, 63 percent of the class of 1975 went on to four year institutions, with 16 percent going on to two year institutions and non-degree granting schools. When we compare their aspirations with the class of 1970, in which 65 percent went on to four year institutions and 25 percent went to institutions of lesser status, we find that the declining value of higher education seems to have the greatest effect on marginal students' college plans. As a result, going on to work is becoming a respectable alternative to higher education for many students.

Table 2 indicates the mean SAT scores for Utopia High School students. Their scores show the same downward trend taking place across the United States. For the thirteen years between 1962 and 1976, there has been a steady decline in SAT scores, both nationally and among Utopia High School seniors. The Utopia High mean verbal score of 1975 is 57 points below that of 1962 and 68 points below the highest mean score which was established in 1965. The decline in the math scores is somewhat less precipitous: 1975 is down 53 points from the 1962 high. Even though Utopia High School students score consistently higher than the average college bound student, the alarm that has spread across the nation due to the declining academic abilities of its youth has struck a responsive chord in Pleasant Valley. The composition of the school board has swung from a majority of liberals who viewed the high school as an instrument of cultural pluralism to a conservative majority who are demanding that the three R's be reemphasized and that basic skills be included as the staple of the high school program.

Pleasant Valley with its Utopia High School has had to swallow some bitter medicine lately, even though in the seventies there are not the eruptive student protests that plagued the school during the late sixties. In 1969, for example, forty students were suspended from Utopia High for distributing leaflets for a march on the headquarters of a major automobile company to protest pollution. Along with the American Civil Liberties Union, the students and their families sued the school district for abridgement of their First Amendment rights of free speech and peaceable assembly. The State Supreme Court refused to hear the case in 1975, since all students had graduated and the case was moot. "Catch-22." Nor is there in the seventies the hippified cultural revolt against middle-class morality. Yet, there is cause for concern. Utopia High is experiencing perhaps more pernicious and disturbing problems than those of the sixties, although they are quieter and less spectacular.

TABLE 2. Mean SAT Scores for College Bound Seniors

Year	VERBAL		MATH	
	Utopia	Nation	Utopia	Nation
1962	507	473	542	498
1963	...	478	...	502
1964	515	475	538	498
1965	518	473	535	496
1966	501	471	532	496
1967	499	467	523	495
1968	510	466	534	494
1969	496	462	512	491
1970	491	460	530	488
1971	480	454	500	487
1972	485	450	500	482
1973	469	443	503	481
1974	475	440	516	478
1975	450	437	489	473

SOURCES: National Data, College Entrance Examination Board. Supplement to "National Report: College-Bound Seniors 1975–79."
School Data, Utopia High School. Mimeo, n.d.

EROSION IN PARADISE

The 1975–76 school year began with a crisis. The school district was facing a $230,000 cut in the state appropriation which had to be subtracted from the operating budget. In addition, the teachers were coming back to school without a contract and were threatening a strike unless they received an eight percent cost-of-living salary increase. The Board of Education had planned the budget assuming the teachers would accept a five percent increase in salary, reducing their real income by three percent. The school board was pushed against the wall and capitulated on the teacher demands, which added approximately $300,000 to the deficit. The original budget was $14.5 million dollars and now the Board was faced with the unpleasant task of cutting $500,000—a slash of nearly four percent of total operating costs. The budget crisis sent shudders through the school district all year. The superintendent was forced to make forty recommendations to the school board. Cuts were as follows: administrative costs, $4,900; educational supplies and equipment replacement and repair, $174,000; plant operations and repair, $110,000; community services, including assemblies, health care and building use, $28,000; teacher training and curriculum development, $68,000; and personnel cuts, $115,700.

The cuts hit the high school hardest. Class sizes were increased and course offerings were reduced. The math and language labs were temporarily closed and reopened with reduced staff. Custodial staff was cut. All teaching aides were dismissed. The audiovisual department, which was to be run through the high school for the whole district and which had been stocked with equipment, could no longer continue its search for a director. There were even threats that there would not be enough money to carry on an interscholastic sports program. The tennis coach resigned his position over lack of funds and the baseball coach was upset over the reduction of the team schedule by one-third. Because of the cutbacks in sports, a committee of citizens was established to raise funds for high school athletic activities and to put pressure on the school board and principal to develop a high quality sports program and to allocate an increasing amount of a diminishing budget for athletic activities.

Of course, one alternative to cutting a budget would be to raise local taxes. The school board did not even consider the possibility, since property taxes in Pleasant Valley were already quite high ($6.54 per $100 assessed valuation in 1976 with property being assessed at 100 percent market value), and the mere suggestion of raising taxes would have probably generated hysteria and recall petitions. As a matter of fact, in February 1976, some of the more troglodytic elements of the community had formed a committee which claimed that the school district could run efficiently on $12.25 million for the 1976–77 school year, instead of the $15 million the Board of Education claimed it needed. One of the provisions was that the teachers would receive a maximum pay raise of three percent. At an annual inflation rate of over seven percent, they essentially demanded that the teachers take a four percent cut in pay. The Board of Education approved a budget of $14.75 million for fiscal 1976–77, which would allow it to operate at the level of the previous year. There was still no audio-visual director at the high school and there was a staff reduction of thirty, including eleven professional lines, even though the high school population had dropped only forty students over the past three years.

In addition to the troubles with school financing, the township itself has had fiscal problems. Contract negotiations with the firemen and policemen in 1976 were long and bitterly fought. A walkout was threatened before the contract was settled. For Pleasant Valley, which had the reputation of a wonderful place in which to work and live, such employee strife was unprecedented. Although the town hall had just been refurbished, it seemed to house some embittered employees.

Yet coupled with the decline of police, fire, educational, and health services are some nasty statistics that reveal that the present services are being taxed with increased incidence of problems: crime is on the rise, and not just a little. Auto theft and robberies are up from the previous year; assaults are up 70 percent, and most of them are being done by juveniles; juvenile alcohol abuse is up; gonorrhea cases are up 300 percent over the previous year, again, most cases are among the young; vandalism is increasing at such an alarming rate that the town has organized a citizen's committee to study the problem. Damage caused by vandalism cost the township $30,000 in 1975; the cost is twice that in the schools—an estimate that was told to me before a group of boys threw a coke machine down a stairwell. And in addition, the football team had another losing season.

The problems of Pleasant Valley are being replicated all over America. The government payroll is being cut at the same time that the unemployment rate is higher than it has been in two generations. There is wealth, but it doesn't find itself in the production of government services. Besides, government services don't seem to work. The schools don't seem to educate. Welfare is hated by everybody: the social workers, the recipients, and the general public who provides the money. Policemen are believed to be either on the take, overly oppressive, or just plain lazy—the latter criticism is also made of firemen; and health care is a travesty, especially in public institutions.

Pleasant Valley, in its scenic beauty, was constructed by an economy based upon capital expansion and waste consumption. In the 1970s, capital has stagnated and America is choking in its own waste. American capitalism has sold itself a bill of goods it cannot afford, and Pleasant Valley is having an increasingly difficult time supporting itself. It is dedicated to waste consumption: single-family dwelling units, two-car garages, and the status race. In their attempt to escape the problems of urban living, suburbanites have generated problems of their own. In addition to the ecological disaster they exacerbate, they ghettoize their inhabitants along social-class, racial, and ethnic lines and cloister their young; the suburbs become unidimensional environments. Suburbanites' waste consumption patterns are extracted from the wealth of the urban core, immiserating cities and leaving them to house the poor with diminished resources. They are parasitic and wasteful. Suburban living is a privilege the upper middle class enjoys. As the American economy stagnates, such class privilege cannot be maintained without intensified conflict over utilization of social resources.

NOTES

1. Watergate was the biggest public scandal in the history of the nation. It began as the Nixon Administration planned the 1972 presidential campaign. The Committee to Re-elect the President was established and began collecting funds, much of which were secret and illegal. According to testimony, corporations' officials were approached by representatives of CREEP (Committee for the Re-Election of the President) who intimated that if they were not forthcoming with contributions, things wouldn't go well for their corporations in Washington. Other corporations, such as Hughes Aircraft and International Telephone and Telegraph Company were paying large amounts in bills of small denominations under the table. In the case of Hughes Aircraft, $100,000 dollars were found deposited in Nixon's best friend's, Bebe Rebozo, bank. Rebozo testified that he never touched the money, even though some of the bills were printed after the known deposit date. In the case of IT&T, a memo from Dita Beard, their Washington lobbyist, implicated Attorney General Richard Kleindienst in a fix whereby for $200,000 the Justice Department would drop an anti-trust suit against the company. Cash was used to finance a dirty tricks squad which set out to undermine the Democratic Party in their primary campaigns. They were successful in eliminating the leading and most popular contender, Edward Muskie, the senior senator from Maine, by spreading lies about his wife. He lost his temper and cried on national television. They were able to hand-select George McGovern as their opponent, resulting in a Nixon landslide in November 1972. Another undercover operation was the "Plumbers" who were supposedly trying to stop information leaks in the administration. However, they were involved in the burglaries of Daniel Ellsberg's psychiatrist's office, in an attempt to find damaging personal information about the man who released the Pentagon Papers, and of the Democratic National Committee headquarters, where they were caught. When the Plumbers Unit was arrested, the Nixon administration attempted to cover up their activities. However, Nixon had recorded the deliberations on tape; this was unknown to anyone but his own top advisors. Nixon avoided impeachment by resigning, his chief of staff, Robert Haldeman; his domestic advisor, John Erlichman; the Attorney General, John Mitchell; the Presidential Council, John Dean; and several other high-ranking members of the Nixon Administration were convicted of crimes related to Watergate. L. Patrick Gray, Nixon's appointee to succeed J. Edgar Hoover as head of the FBI, was implicated in the destruction of evidence.

   In 1976, it was discovered that the CIA had been surveilling United States citizens and had been opening incoming mail from abroad (including the correspondence of then Representative Bella Abzug). They were also discovered to have been reviewing income tax returns, committing burglaries, bugging Americans, experimenting with LSD and other drugs on unwitting subjects, and were even suspected of having agents in the Nixon administration itself. All of this was heaped on prior revelations of CIA dirty tricks on the international scene, such as the assasination of Massagadah of Iran and the "destabilization" program in Chile.

In the same year, it was discovered that the FBI had bugged Martin Luther King in his most intimate moments and had sent him tapes of his nocturnal exploits along with threatening letters. Under the freedom of information act, it was found that the FBI had 70,000 pages of information collected over a 25 year period on the Socialist Workers Party, even though they could not document a single indictable offense.

The international bribery scandel occurred as a result of an investigation by the Securities Exchange Commission and centered around the methods by which American-operated multinational corporations conducted business. It was discovered that Lockheed Aircraft, the company that received a $750 million loan guarantee by the federal government, had apparently used some of those funds to bribe foreign officials. Lockheed admitted to spending $25 million in bribes. This revelation led to the collapse of regimes that had received such bribes; namely, the Rumor government in Italy and the Tanaka administration in Japan. In addition, Prince Bernhard of the Netherlands was implicated in the bribery plots and was forced out of some of his official posts as a result. Although the Lockheed bribery was the most spectacular and extensive, other corporations admitted to international bribery, including Exxon, Northrup Aviation, United Brands, and Gulf Oil Company.

Gulf, part of the Gulf and Western conglomerate, was also implicated in a national scandal surrounding influence peddling in the form of corporate contributions to those Congressional office holders who could do them some good. This revelation led to the retirement of the Republican's "Mister Integrity," Hugh Scott of Pennsylvania, who received, apparently knowingly, some of Gulf and Western's largesse.

As long as influence peddling is being discussed, it seems that the government of Korea was also buying congresspersons. Dubbed "Koreagate," after Watergate, it was found that through Tongsun Park, a Korean businessman, the Park regime was funnelling millions of dollars to buy congressional good will. Over one-hundred congresspersons had received contributions that originated from the South Korean government. Unlike Watergate, the congress investigated itself. They hired Leon Jaworski, the principal investigator of Watergate, to take charge of the investigation. The result was that Tongsun Park was indicted on sixteen charges but never brought to trial because the Park regime refused to grant extradition. Two representatives, Richard Hanna and Otto Passman, were indicted as a result of the investigations. At the time of their indictment, they had already retired from public office.

Prior to these bicentennial revelations, Vice-president Agnew had been forced to resign his position in 1973 because he was prosecuted for income tax evasion as a result of his not declaring the bribes he received while sitting as vice-president. The bribes were a result of the good work he had done in previous years as governor of Maryland. He pleaded "nolo contendre," a middle-class way of stating one's guilt, and he was fined $10,000.

In 1977, Wayne Hays, a Democrat from Ohio was forced to resign from Congress when Elizabeth Ray claimed that she was on his payroll to render him sexual favors.

2. The 1970 census shows 72.4 percent of Pleasant Valley's residents as white collar. Whatever biases in the statistics equal out. Twenty percent of the white-collar occupations are clerical, which are most likely women supplementing husbands' incomes, lowering the percentage of upper middle-class families. However, there are a number of live-in domestic servants who, though residents of the community, are not contributors to the school population. Since we are concerned with the *culture* of the school, the most important fact is that children of upper middle-class, white-collar families are dominant.

3. The assessment of the Jewish population was done through the counting of Jewish surnames in the class yearbook. Since the research was done in a public school, questions of religious preference were not asked. The method of assessment, though rough, is probably accurate to within five percentage points. The biases work both ways: students of Jewish background with non-Jewish surnames would not be included and non-Jewish students with certain Germanic names were included.

All the people we used to know
They're an illusion to me now
Some are mathematicians
Some are carpenters' wives
Don't know how it all got started
I don't know what they're doin' with their lives
But me, I'm still on the road
Headin' for another joint
We always did feel the same
We just saw it from a different point
Of view
Tangled up in blue.

Bob Dylan, "Tangled Up in Blue," 1975

2

YOUTH IN POST-SCARCITY AMERICA

Come mothers and fathers,
Throughout the land
And don't criticize
What you don't understand.
Your sons and your daughters
Are beyond your command
Your old road is
Rapidly agein'
Please get out of the new one
If you can't lend your hand
For the times they are a-changin'.
Bob Dylan, "The Times They Are A-Changin'," 1963

I see the people of the world,
Where they are and what they could be.
Jefferson Airplane, "D.C.B.A.—25," 1967

I read the news today oh boy
About a lucky man who made the grade
And though the news was rather sad
Well I just had to laugh
I saw the photograph.
He blew his mind out in a car
He didn't notice that the lights had changed.
John Lennon and Paul McCartney,
"A Day in the Life," 1967

America in the mid-1970s was in the depths of a cultural crisis. The legitimacy of its institutions, which came under attack by the insurgencies of the 1960s by youth, blacks, and women, continues to be undermined. George Gallup (1973, 1975) has found declining faith in such dominant American institutions as the federal government, education, religion, the press, television, and big business. Daniel Yankelovich (1972) confirmed the Gallup findings and adds that the loss of faith is most acute among the young. In the 1976 presidential elections, despite early predictions of a heavy vote, the voter turnout decline that began in 1960 continued. Even though the election was one of the closest in modern history, participation dropped to 53.3 percent from 55 percent in the 1972 presidential election. A CBS-*New York Times* poll of voters ascertained that most of those who voted did so because they felt that it was their duty, as opposed to having any affinity for the candidates or having the desire to exercise their privilege in a free society. The poll also attributed the low turnout to a sense of powerlessness on the part of non-voters. Most disturbing to the pollsters was that 58 percent of those not voting agreed with the statement, "The country needs more radical change than is possible through the ballot box." In addition, 41 percent of those voting also agreed that more radical change was needed (*The New York Times*, November 16, 1976).

Perhaps the most puzzling aspect of this erosion of legitimacy is that it is occurring in a period of social quiescence.[1] There are no insurgencies as there were in the 1960s. Riots, sit-ins, insurrections, confrontations, violent strikes, school takeovers, and street-fighting are all faded memories of a bygone era. The problems of contemporary society seem to have altered in their symptomatology from overt conflict to a cancerous rotting from the inside out. In Pleasant Valley it is experienced in the form of declining social resources in the face of increasing social problems. Most of the problems are associated primarily with the youth in the community: alcoholism, venereal disease, vandalism, and delinquency.

In order to adequately examine what is happening to and

among the high school students in Pleasant Valley, we must analyze the larger society, especially trends in the economic and cultural spheres, since they touch so intimately on the lives of Utopia High School students. In addition, we must examine the recent history of youth culture which both serves as a background and shapes youths' experiences of the 1970s.

POST-SCARCITY SOCIETY

Post-World War II America has been characterized as an "affluent society" (Galbraith, 1958) dominated by a "consumerist" mentality (Bell, 1976) in which the culture of production has been supplanted by the culture of consumption. We must examine this characterization in greater depth—especially the economic and social structures that brought about material abundance and pollution, urban decay, sexism, racism, prejudice against youth, class privilege, economic discrimination, alienation, war, and the decline of the "quality of life."

It is a well-established social fact that the American economy is dominated by a few extremely large corporations which control vast sectors of the marketplace (see Galbraith, 1967; Baran and Sweezy, 1966; and Barnet and Miller, 1974). In 1948, the hundred largest corporations held 40.2 percent of the total assets of manufacturing enterprises. By 1972, their share had increased to 47.6 percent. Likewise, in the generation of value-added (i.e., the amount of value added to the raw material generated by the production of a commodity), the hundred largest corporations increased their share from 23 percent in 1947 to 33 percent in 1972 (U.S. Department of Commerce, 1975:502). The major sectors of the economy such as automobile production, steel, electrical equipment, communications, food processing, chemicals, home appliances, aerospace, building materials, petroleum, computers, personal care products, and tobacco are all dominated by a handful of corporate giants. These corporations act as price leaders in their field. Instead of price competition, prices are administered by the dominant corporation(s) in each field, with the smaller companies following suit.

> . . . Size allows General Motors as a seller to set prices for automobiles, diesels, trucks, refrigerators and the rest of its offering and be secure in the knowledge that no individual buyer, by withdrawing its custom, can force a change. The fact that GM is one of a few sellers adds to its control. Each seller shares the common interest in secure and certain prices; it is to the advantage of none to disrupt this mutual security system. Competitors of General Motors are especially unlikely to initiate price reductions that might provoke further and retributive price-cutting. No formal communication is necessary to prevent such actions; this is considered naive and arouses the professional wrath of company counsel. Everyone knows that the survivor of such a contest would be not the agressor but General Motors. Thus do size and small numbers of competitors lead to market regulation. (Galbraith, 1967:46.)

With the development of monopoly capitalism[2] has come increasing levels of industrial productivity brought about through technological innovation directed at greater profits by increasing the efficiency of the individual worker. Each new innovation allows capital to increase the ratio of surplus value to the wages of the labor. That is, as each individual laborer becomes more productive, that laborer produces greater amounts of wealth in a shorter period of time, of which an increasingly smaller fraction is returned to the worker in the form of a salary.[3] Nevertheless, the productive laborer experiences an absolute increase in personal wealth, even though this laborer receives a smaller share of the pie. It is through the mechanism of increased productivity that capitalism has been able to generate a post-scarcity society.[4]

What is meant by the term *post-scarcity society?* Murray Bookchin (1971:10) celebrates its arrival:

> We of this century have finally opened the prospect of material abundance for all to enjoy—a sufficiency in the means of life without the need for grinding, day-to-day toil. We have discovered resources, both for man and industry, that were totally unknown a generation ago. We have devised machines that automatically make machines. We have perfected devices that can execute onerous tasks more effectively than the strongest human muscles,

that can surpass the industrial skills of the deftest human hands, that can calculate with greater rapidity and precision than the most gifted human minds. Supported by this qualitatively new technology, we can begin to provide food, shelter, garments, and a broad spectrum of luxuries without devouring the precious time of humanity and without dissipating its invaluable reservoir of creative energy in mindless labor. In short, for the first time in history we stand on the threshold of a post-scarcity society.

Actually, Bookchin's heralding in of the new age of material abundance in which economic productivity has progressed to the point where society can adequately feed, house, and care for *all* of its members may be as much as twenty years tardy. We choose to define a post-scarcity society as one in which the economic surplus exceeds 50 percent of the gross national product. This indicator shows us at what point more labor is generated by the necessity to consume economic surplus than to produce it. According to Joseph Phillips (1966:369–91), this point was reached in the American economy between 1948 and 1950.[5]

The post-scarcity society is the child of monopoly capitalism. However, the major problem of a capitalist economy is stagnation. It is subject to boom and bust cycles as it produces more than can be consumed. Most theorists seem to agree that corporate monopoly capitalism was consolidated as a permanent feature of the economy in the years between 1900 and 1920 (see Baran and Sweezy, 1966; Bell, 1976; Ewen, 1976; and Bowles and Gintis, 1976). Since that time, the United States has experienced one major depression (1930–1941), one panic (1921–1922), and six recessions (1949–1950, 1954, 1958, 1961, 1969–1970, and 1973–1975).

The central contradiction of monopoly capitalism is that it literally produces more goods than it can easily consume; and the major problem of the American economy, ironically, is the absorption of economic surplus (Baran and Sweezy, 1966). The vast bureaucracies that have been built up since the turn of the century are living monuments to the attempts of capital to absorb ever-increasing amounts of surplus wealth. The expansion of capitalists' consumption and the reinvestment of profits into corporate expansion and world-building in the form of globalization of markets, the burgeoning of the sales effort and the precipitous rise of the advertising industry (from $360 million per annum in 1890 to $25 billion in 1973), the growth of public bureaucracy, and the expansion of the military and consequent development of economic imperialism are all testimonials to the attempts of capital to absorb economic surplus. Even though the growth of all these sectors has generated massive numbers of non-productive white collar positions, whose occupants' major economic function is consumption at work and at home, the level of stable unemployment has increased by about a half-percentage point per decade, from 4 percent in 1900 to 1910 to 8 percent in the 1970s.[6]

For youth, the most significant consequence of the expansion of capital was the economic necessity to delay their entry into the labor force. Population growth and the importation of a labor force by capital necessitated the exclusion of the young from the labor market. In addition, both capitalists and reformers saw the need to educate the young en masse. Though the reformers tended to view the process of education as a process of humanization and an aid in helping the young "maximize their potential," it functioned as an instrument to shape a docile and disciplined labor force. Samuel Bowles and Herbert Gintis (1976:199) summarize their analysis of the Progressive Education Movement as follows:

> The legacy of the urban school reform movement in this period [1890–1930] reflects both its strongly upper-class basis and its commitment to social control as the overriding objective of schooling. Social amelioration, open education, equalization of opportunity, and all the democratic forms could have been pursued only insofar as they contributed to—or at least did not contradict—the role of the school in reproducing the class system and extending the capitalist mode of production. The essence of *Progressivism* in education was the rationalization of the process of reproducing the social classes of modern industrial life. The Progressives viewed the growing corporatization of economic activity as desirable and forward-looking—indeed, the best antidote to the provincialism and elitism of U.S. culture. For some, Taylorism[7] in the schools was, in turn, seen as an ideal. For others, the unified

and centralized high school with the differentiated curriculum represented the most efficient accommodation to the new exigencies of economic life.

Though Bowles and Gintis focus on the *process* of education as the reason for its existence, socialization in the classroom was secondary to the educational institution's function of surplus absorption which required that money be spent to keep young people out of the labor force. Between 1910 and 1940, seventeen year olds who were high school graduates rapidly expanded over each decade. From 1910 to 1920, the increase was from 8.8 to 16.8 percent, an increase of 90 percent; in 1930, 29.0 percent were high school graduates, an increase of 73 percent over 1920; in 1940, 50.8 percent were high school graduates, an increase of 75 percent over 1930. By 1975, nearly three out of every four seventeen year olds were high school graduates. Higher education shows the same expansion, though the maximum rate occurred in the 1940s when college enrollment more than doubled. In 1900, 1.9 percent of all twenty-three year olds were college graduates; by 1973, that figure had reached 29.3 percent (Brookover and Gottlieb, 1964:51; and U.S. Department of Commerce, 1974 and 1975).

The consolidation of monopoly capitalism in the 1920s and the creation of a post-scarcity society in the 1950s has had tremendous ramifications for contemporary culture. As early as 1890, Thorsten Veblen (1899) had posited the existence of an elite leisure class. Stewart Ewen (1976) notes that with the development of the techniques of mass production and the institutionalization of the assembly line in the factory, a degradation of labor occurred which generated worker resistance. Capital attempted to deflect such dissidence through capitulation to worker demands for a shorter work week, and the development of consumer items and mass marketing techniques which acted as the carrot along with the stick of the lockout. With the emergence of advertising, the family automobile, and the radio began the attempt by capital to supplant folk culture (which was anti-capitalist and the source of worker resistance and truculence) with popular culture, controlled by capital and projecting a pro-capitalist ideology. With the cloistering of youth in age-graded institutions, a distinctly youth-oriented culture began to emerge. The social status of youth, then, is a direct consequence of the social relations of a corporate economy. Youth, always economically exploited in the past (with a few notable exceptions, see Gillis, 1974), had been rendered part of the industrial reserve army.

THE CULTURAL CONSEQUENCES
OF POST-SCARCITY

Perhaps the most visible consequence of the development of the corporate economy and the arrival of post-scarcity society has been the erosion and destruction of bourgeois culture. Bourgeois culture was the culture of productivity par excellence. It was the culture of Protestantism, stressing the virtues of economic productivity and capital accumulation: thrift, emotional restraint, rationality, rugged individualism, punctuality, sexual repressiveness, the patriarchal nuclear family, hierarchy, and most of all, the work ethic. Work, in bourgeois culture, was equivalent to a religious calling—the most important human activity. Thrift and saving were the mark of virtue and *eo ipso* the legitimation for the accumulation of wealth and for the moral superiority of those who had it. The cultural hero of bourgeois culture was the individual entrepreneur (Bell, 1976). Children were raised on the mythology of the Horatio Alger stories in which upward mobility was achieved by a combination of luck, pluck, and saving. The "masculine" virtues of emotional restraint and rugged individualism were tied to notions of "getting ahead" while "slovenliness" and "dissoluteness" were sure roads to perdition. ("Idle hands do the work of the devil.") The demands of the workplace, such as punctuality, deference to hierarchy, and rationality were used as the "measure of a man."

Bourgeois culture deified scarcity. Calvinist doctrine envisioned a heaven in which only the predestined elect could enter. Bourgeois institutions emphasized rationalized hierarchies in which "many are called, but few are chosen." The notion of the elect pervaded bourgeois conceptions of democracy. Jeffersonian democracy depended on an educated electorate whose choices would reflect the "natural" order of human superiority. All bourgeois institutions were imbued with scarcity assumptions. The bourgeoisie defended its economic and political dominance with the ideology of social Darwinism. The family socialized its members to deny themselves sexual pleasure and sensual indulgence. Education reinforced the rationalism of the family and acted as an allocation device in which the favored few would be selected from the many. Even the bourgeois God became vulgarized as the great accountant in the sky who records sins and good deeds in his heavenly ledger.

> . . . The . . . idea of God's bookkeeping is carried by Bunyan to the characteristically tasteless extreme of comparing the relation of a sinner to his God with that of customer and shopkeeper. One who has once got into debt may well, by the product of all his virtuous acts, succeed in paying off the accumulated interest but never the principal. (Weber, 1958:124.)

As the ideological superstructure of industrial capitalism in the accumulation phases during the eighteenth and nineteenth centuries, bourgeois culture served well in legitimating the dominance of capitalist elites and serving as a justification for the disciplining of the working classes. Yet, by the turn of the century, the individual entrepreneur was being eclipsed by the consolidation of capitalism into large corporations. With the centralization of capital and the consolidation of the economy, the era of monopoly capitalism had arrived. Local elites were either being incorporated into a national upper class or bypassed as merely local (Mills, 1956:39). Individual entrepreneurs were quickly being supplanted by employees (Reich, 1972).

Corporations increased their dominance of the economy through their unique ability to make huge capital investments in revolutionizing the means of production, thus allowing for greater exploitation of labor power. Yet the contradiction of capitalism is that greater productivity presupposes increased markets. If there are no consumers to buy the products produced by capital, then overproduction results in recession or depression. Thus, the demands of capital require the development of a consumer class that will buy more than they need and spend more than they earn. Bowles and Gintis (1976) suggest that contemporary capitalism can be likened to a bicycle: in order to keep it up, it must continually go forward. If the economy is not expanding, it is contracting.

Bourgeois culture, with its emphasis on thrift, saving, frugality, and fear of indebtedness, acted as a fetter on consumption. Throughout the progress of the twentieth century, it became increasingly undermined while capital assaulted bourgeois notions of "deferred gratification" through the introduction of installment buying, layaway plans, and, in the 1950s, the introduction of credit cards. Its ideological wing, the advertising industry, continually associated commodity consumption with the attainment of pleasure, especially sexual pleasure. In addition, the demands of corporate life which substituted skill in manipulating human relations for craftsmanship, became grounds for the cultivation of the social self adequate to the necessities of bureaucratic existence. Thus, fear of job loss, status loss, and the humiliation of personal inadequacy were manipulated by advertisers:

> The ads also indicated that where job-dissatisfaction occurred, it was often a result of personal inadequacies combined with insufficient consumption. Blue-Jay Corn Plasters told men about a fellow whose painful corn "cost him his job," even though he was generally "the best-natured man on the payroll. Nothing seemed to faze his good humor." Here, this man's body turns against him: a corn. And "then came the amazing blow-up," which got him fired. Here the Listerine dictum that people should "suspect themselves first" entered into the question of job conditions and satisfaction. To keep a job, people must love it; they must fight against those things *in themselves* which get in the way of job satisfaction. They must consume to keep healthy to keep their jobs. (Ewen, 1976:155.)

Yet bourgeois institutions such as Protestantism, education, and the nuclear family were necessary for the maintenance of the legitimacy of corporate capitalist hierarchy. By the 1950s, capital was on the one hand waging the most blatantly sexual and instant-gratificational sort of advertising campaigns, introducing credit cards, and spawning the *Playboy* and singles cultures; on the other, it was propagandizing on behalf of God, motherhood, and the family in the shrillest terms ("Togetherness"; "The family that prays together stays together").

Following World War II, the illusion of scarcity could be maintained through a distribution system which encouraged waste consumption at the upper levels of the status hierarchy and economic deprivation at the bottom. In addition, the Cold War allowed for increased expenditures on military waste which served as a surplus absorption device, while at the same time created an atmosphere of continual public sacrifice for military preparedness. Cynical observers (e.g., Baran and Sweezy, 1966) have said that if we hadn't had the Cold War, we (and the Russians) would have had to invent it. World War II ended the Great Depression and the continual increase in military expenditure that generated a consumer economy which expanded throughout the post-war period.

Even though mass consumption began in the 1920s, the Great Depression and World War II delayed the advance of the consumer society. By the early fifties, the cultural drift was chronicled by radical sociologist C. Wright Mills (1951:237):

> . . . Over the last forty years, Leo Lowenthal has shown, as the "idols of work" have declined, the "idols of leisure" have arisen. Now the selection of heroes for popular biography appearing in mass magazines has shifted from business, professional, and political figures—successful in the sphere of production—to those successful in entertainment, leisure, and consumption. The movie star and the baseball player have replaced the industrial magnate and the political man. Today, the displayed characteristics of popular idols "can all be integrated around the concept of the consumer." And the faculties of reflection, imagination, dream and desire, so far as they exist, do not now move in the sphere of concrete, practical work experience.

Four years later, the more conservative social theorist David Riesman (1955:243) similarly wrote:

In the focus of public attention the old captains of industry have been replaced by an entirely new type: the Captains of Non-industry, of Consumption and Leisure. Surveys of content in the mass media show a shift in the kinds of information about business and political leaders that audiences ask for. In an earlier day the audience was given a story of the hero's work-minded rise to success. Today, the ladder climbing is taken for granted or is seen in terms of the breaks, and the hero's tastes in dress, food, women, and recreation are emphasized. . . .

Along with the emergence of consumer culture came new techniques in child rearing, emphasizing the priorities of the newly emerging middle class. Schedule feeding was supplanted by demand feeding of babies. Toilet-training techniques were relaxed and weaning was delayed. Yet, at the same time organizational prerogatives were entering into the socialization process. As the new white-collar consumer class developed, its members' main foothold on security was organizational position. The paternalism of the industrial proletariat was supplanted by the organizational hierarchy as the source of discipline. Thus, white-collar children became socialized not to fear paternal dominance, but to manipulate themselves and others within a bureaucratic context. Riesman (1955) notes the passing of the "inner-directed" individual, who was instilled with an internalized sense of right and wrong who would stand against the violation of morality. This artifact of bourgeois culture, claimed Riesman, was supplanted by the "other-directed" personality which depended on situational morality and cued his or her behavior to the appropriateness of what everybody else was doing. The other-directed person used radar for his or her behavioral cues (although a television set might be used now), while the inner-directed personality was guided by an internal gyroscope.

Jules Henry (1963) put the capstone on the characterizations of American culture in the 1950s. He saw Americans driven to have more fun while awaiting the nuclear holocaust. Henry observed American culture generating a psychic revolution created by the demands of the corporate economy. First was the creation of needs by commodity producers. Second, was the unhinging of the old impulse controls. Herbert Marcuse (1963) reiterated Henry's thesis from a Marxian perspective. It became evident to observers of the 1950s that the "warfare-welfare" state embodied a huge contradiction in that people were being driven to produce more and consume more for the sole purpose of legitimating the existence of dominant economic and political elites. According to Marcuse, the system of technological production was legitimated because it "delivers the goods," while at the same time manipulating a docile population to want more than it needed. Both Marcuse and Henry thought that the "new people" of the era of monopoly capitalism are taught to be easily manipulable because of the total domination of the ideological apparatus by commodity producers. The "fun mentality" generated by the commodity producers created the volatile consumer. Noted Henry (1963:44):

> . . . Nowadays, as the Super Ego values of hard work, thrift, and abstemiousness no longer pay off, and technological drivenness presses the Self so hard; nowadays when the high-rising standard of living has become a moral ideal, the Id values of fun, relaxation, and impulse release are ascendant. *Only a people who have learned to decontrol their impulses can consume as we do.* (Emphasis mine.)

The flaw in the arguments of Marcuse and Henry rests in the motivation to consume. Commodity consumption has its grim side when people are spurred to consume out of fear. Interpersonal competition has spread from the arena of production to consumption as "life-style" has become an arena of intense competition. The sexual competitive struggle has become extended and intensified beyond the pre-marital selection phase with the creation of "open marriages," the increasing divorce rate, and the popularization of sex after sixty. In the wake of the 1960s' counterculture, has come the hip-competitive struggle in which one must consume the proper plays, books, television programs, houseplants, clothes, high-grade marijuana, etc., to "keep up with the Joneses."[8] Obviously, keeping up with the Joneses is nothing new. However, it has become intensified under the conditions of monopoly capitalism which necessitates volatile consumption. The problem raised by Henry and Marcuse is answered by them in positive terms. People consume more because they are hedonistic: they "have learned to decontrol their impulses" or capital has made a conquest of the "unhappy consciousness." Yet, a more sinister interpretation of consumption must be offered: People consume at astronomical levels because of the fear of what will happen if they don't. As we have seen, as early as the 1920s, men were told by advertisers that improper consumption could cost them their job. Today, one may be left behind in the status struggle.

Bourgeois culture contradicted the demands of monopoly capitalism and had to be destroyed in order to generate larger markets. Although Daniel Bell (1976) attributes its destruction to the "free market economy," he is mistaken. Monopoly capital depends on an administered economy in which markets must be maintained and expanded in order for the economy to remain healthy. The final burying of the bourgeois culture by the insurgencies of the 1960s was resisted by commodity producers on the symbolic and ideological levels. However, once "the wicked witch was dead," they danced on the grave. Many of the trappings of dissident youth culture have been adopted in commodity advertising in the 1970s: Buick is dedicated to the "free spirit" in just about everybody; a Salem ad uses sixties' subjectivism ("If it feels good, do it") in its ads, for example: "I don't analyze smoking, I enjoy it." *Cosmopolitan Magazine* blatantly advertises that its readers have had a number of lovers (something once defined as wantonness is now evidence of high value in the sexual marketplace), and Chrysler sponsored the "Dodge Rebellion" in the early 1970s.

THE ECLIPSE OF ADOLESCENCE

The social status of adolescence emerged with the nuclear family and the industrial revolution. It began in the cities and eventually spread to the countryside as the period of economic de-

pendence of the young on the adults in the family extended well
beyond puberty. As health care improved and the infant mor-
tality rate declined, young people, for the first time in history
had become a surplus rather than a scarce population (Gillis,
1974). With the onset of industrialization and the removal of
vast numbers of subsistence farmers from the land to urban areas
to form the industrial proletariat during the eighteenth and
nineteenth centuries, young members of the family were able to
participate in the labor force. However, as their numbers increased, the industrial labor force came to be dominated by adult
male workers. Reform legislation functioned to exclude the
young and female from the labor force, segregating the young
into schools to await their entry into the work force. Although
F. Musgrove (1965:33) claims that adolescence was invented by
Jean Jacques Rousseau in 1762 and John Gillis (1974) asserts
that it was discovered in 1870, it is clear that adolescence did not
become a widespread phenomenon until the twentieth century.
Thus, the social invention of the adolescent phase of life coin-
cides quite neatly with the advent of the corporate economy.
Paul Baran and Paul Sweezy (1966) note that by the turn of the
century capitalism was already showing problems of surplus
absorption. In order to control the labor market, capital requires
a massive reserve army that can be mobilized during periods of
economic expansion and laid off during periods of economic
decline without serious social disruption. Youth, blacks, and
women have been traditionally consigned to the ranks of the industrial reserve army. However, immiserization following prosperity often leads to social upheavel and insurgency (e.g., that of
the 1930s). For women, domesticity could be relied upon to
claim their labor, as in the period following their mobilization
for World War II. For blacks, outright oppression was used.
However, youth could be tantalized by the promise of future
opportunity. As the capitalist economy became dominated by
the large corporation, the entrepreneurial ladder of social mobility was reduced to insignificance, and schooling became the
prime mechanism for moving upward. The result has been that

throughout the twentieth century, dependency upon education has steadily increased.

Moreover, adolescence has its cultural side. Formerly confined to the children of capital during the eighteenth and nineteenth centuries, adolescence became democratized during the early twentieth century. Its major psychological characteristics serve the demands of bourgeois culture. Ideally, according to Erik Erikson (1950), adolescence is completed upon the resolution of the Oedipal complex. The young bourgeois male is supposed to do battle with his father over the affections of his mother and the conflict of "values." The intergenerational masculine rivalry functions to give the adolescent a sense of his own autonomy and identity. It is through the rejection of the "values" (itself a bourgeois term that reifies the market mentality) of the parental generation that the adolescent throws off the yoke of paternal authority and establishes his own internalized morality which guides him through life. As the battle unfolds, the adolescent male experiences an "identity crisis" as he attempts to define himself in autonomous terms. Finally, his sexual feelings are cathected to a female of his own peerage and he emerges from the Oedipal conflict with an independent, individuated, and autonomous sense of his own selfhood. He has arrived at adulthood.

The adolescent female, however, according to the Freudians, has a different set of problems.

> Girls have a fateful experience at this [the genital] stage in that they must comprehend the finality of the fact that although their locomotor, mental, and social intrusiveness is equally increased and as adequate as that of the boys, they lack one item: the penis. While the boy has this visible, erectable, and comprehensible organ to attach dreams of adult bigness to, the girl's clitoris cannot sustain dreams of sexual equality. (Erikson, 1950:88.)

The Freudians looked for the cause of female social inferiority in the physical construction of their own bodies. However, it is implicit in Freudian theory, itself a product of sexist bourgeois culture, that women were expected to be socialized into roles of subordination to the paternalistic dominance of the nuclear family and her dependency was expected to be merely transferred from father to husband.

Yet, almost as theories of adolescence were being formulated, they were being undermined. Most of the writers on adolescence appeared in the 1950s. Yet Gillis (1974), writing in the 1970s, sees adolescence as ending in the 1950s. Edgar Friedenberg heralded the end of adolescence in 1959. The silent generation of the 1950s with its isolated "rebel without a cause" signaled the end of the adolescent struggle for an autonomous identity:

> Adolescence is not simply a physical process; there is more to it than sexual maturation. It is also—and primarily—a social process, whose fundamental task is clear and stable self-identification.
>
> This process may be frustrated and emptied of meaning in a society which, like our own, is hostile to clarity and vividness. Our culture impedes the clear definition of any faithful self-image—indeed, of any clear image whatsoever. We do not break images; there are few iconoclasts among us. Instead, we blur and soften them. The resulting pliability gives life in our society its familiar, plastic texture. It also makes adolescence more difficult, more dangerous, and more troublesome to the adolescent and to society itself. And it makes adolescence rarer. Fewer youngsters really dare to go through with it; they merely undergo puberty and simulate maturity. (Friedenberg, 1959:17.)

Even Erikson, as he constructed his theory of adolescent identity considered the fact that, at least in the United States, something else was going on. In America, Erikson claimed, the adolescent was caught between the contradictions of independence and conformity, paternalism in the mother figure, and competition and cooperation. It was the very polarities in which the adolescent was caught that defined his or her existence.

> Thus the functioning American, as the heir of a history of extreme contrasts and abrupt changes, bases his final ego identity on some tentative combination of dynamic polarities such as migratory and sedentary, individualistic and standarized, competitive and cooperative, pious and freethinking, responsible and cynical, etc. (Erikson, 1950:286.)

As the modern economy demands an easily manipulated labor force in which operatives become interchangeable, those who have crystallized identities are not easily fit into a pre-set structure of interchangeable parts. In addition, the crystallized self is not easily manipulated in the consumptive sphere either. Therefore, adolescence as a psychological stage of development becomes obsolete as the necessities of flexibility and manipulation supercede the demands of individual morality. The "iron will" has been supplanted by "plastic people," and adolescence makes no sense as the emphasis on the reality principle declines in relation to the pleasure principle as the populace is manipulated by the creation of desire.

Let us review, then, the nature of adolescence. It is the product of both capitalist development and bourgeois culture. The progress of capitalism has made it necessary to increase the length of social and economic dependency beyond the onset of puberty. Gillis (1974) notes that not only has the period of dependency lengthened, but the onset of puberty has dropped five years since the beginning of the century. Psychologically, adolescence was the period in which the Oedipal complex would be overcome and the young male would establish an independent, autonomous sense of self. However, such a notion of psychological development presupposes the existence of a paternalistic family structure in which the father was the embodiment of the superego. By the 1950s, paternalism in the family was an artifact of working-class families (Kohn, 1969). White-collar families tended to be more matriarchal in their structure. Henry (1963) found that in a sample of predominantly upper middle-class children, mothers tended to administer punishment more than fathers. Fathers were more closely associated with fun than were mothers. If this is indeed the case, then how can the Oedipus conflict be resolved if there is no paternalistic authority within the family? The answer is found in the research of Kenneth Kenniston (1968). In his study of young radicals, he found that the New Left participants in the Vietnam Summer Project in 1967 had ambivalent feelings toward their fathers:

> In most young radicals the positive side of the paternal image is uppermost, and the negative side emerges only later; sometimes only in apologetic asides. Yet whichever side of the ambivalence is most stressed, there almost always seems to be a quite conscious split in the image of the father, involving the picture of him (and by extension his tradition and the older generation) as idealistic, sympathetic, honest, highly principled, warm, and admirable; but on the other hand, as dominated, humiliated, ineffectual, or unwilling to act on his perceptions of the world. (Kenniston, 1968: 59.)

Some authority figure! Young radicals saw their fathers as nice guys, but also as *chickens*. Rather than battling over convictions, young radicals were more likely to upbraid their fathers for their inability to act upon their beliefs. Kenniston's findings are substantiated on a larger scale by Armand Mauss and William Garland (1971) and Marshall Meyer (1971) whose work or intergenerational conflict indicated that the radicalism of youth in the 1960s seemed to be an extension of parental ideology.

If the most identifying characteristic of adolescence is the resolution of the identity crisis, then what happens to it as a stage of development when the self becomes a life-long project never to be completely solidified? Erikson (1950) claimed that society has become adolescentized since the Oedipal conflict is never resolved. Kenniston (1975) theorized that youth followed adolescence: once the identity crisis is solved, the age of youth is entered into in which accommodating oneself to the social order assumes dominance as the prime developmental task. However, as Edgar Friedenberg has noted, adolescence in our society has become obsolete and has gone the way of bourgeois culture. Kenniston's research shows that the revolt of the 1960s was based on the conditions of *youth*, not of adolescence. The youth insurgencies of the 1960s were not directed toward parents, but *authorities*. By the 1960s, paternalism had been divested from the middle-class family and instituted in bureaucratic structures. Thus, the attack was not so much against "Daddy" as it was against the "capitalist-fascist-pig-bureaucracy" which had much greater potency than Father. The family was more indulgent of insurgency in the 1960s than were the dominant bureaucratic structures. Youth rebelled against "the system," and, meanwhile, parents were doling out allowances that aided and abetted the revolt.

With the decline of sexual repressiveness, the reconceptualization of the self as a process, and the displacement of paternalism into rationalized bureaucratic structures, the significance of the Oedipal complex diminishes. Adolescence is supplanted by youth. *Youth is the consequence of the arrival of the post-scarcity society.* It is a stage in life where social and psychological issues merge. As youth is consigned to the reserve army and the young await such time that they can assume an adult career, the question of the relationship between self and society becomes paramount in the consciousness of the young. One does not merely assume an identity and then find a place to plug it in, as Kenniston assumes. Rather, the young exist in a continual struggle of polar opposites. We will now examine the nature of this struggle.

YOUTH IN POST-SCARCITY SOCIETY

The 1950s: Capital Expansion and the Postponed Life

The 1950s was a period of relative normalcy. There were no social movements that challenged the patterns of domination in society. The Cold War and the necessity for military preparedness fueled the corporate economy, which grew fitfully throughout the period. Korean War veterans flooded the colleges and universities in the mid- and late fifties, bent on pursuing white-collar careers. Television had just made its appearance and was quickly being installed in most American homes. With the expanding economy came the "affluent society": a house in the suburbs with a two-car garage. It was a time of both heady optimism and ritualized terror. Children were performing atomic bomb drills in schools to protect themselves from the nuclear holocaust when and if the Russians dropped the bomb. However, the infidel not only was an external threat, but agents of the "international Communist conspiracy" operating within the boundaries of "Fortress America." McCarthyism, red-baiting, black-listing, and the general oppression of left-leaning views were staples of popular culture. Julius and Ethel Rosenberg were executed for supposedly revealing atomic bomb secrets to the Russians, and Richard M. Nixon made political history by "proving" Alger Hiss was a Communist spy. One of the most popular television shows during this period was "I Led Three Lives," a fictionalized story of the life of FBI agent and professional anti-Communist, Herbert Philbrick.

Throughout the era, no one was sure which side the young were on. H. H. Remmers and D. H. Radler (1957) studied political attitudes of youth and found them vaguely reactionary and suspicious when asked to apply the Bill of Rights to specific situations. A majority felt that a Communist should not be allowed to speak at a public meeting. Yet they could hardly be called hard-line anti-Communists. The research seemed to indicate that their views were an agglomeration of contradictory notions without much coherence. For the youth of the 1950s, politics was an aspect of the adult world and an alien sort of endeavor. For most, politics was something one didn't really think much about. Fifties' youth was apolitical.

However, when it came to the cultural realm, adolescents had generated their own, centered around interests such as sex, violence, cars, and "fun." The two most important sociological studies of the adolescents of the 1950s (Gordon, 1957; Coleman, 1961) found a distinct adolescent culure in high schools that emphasized the non-intellectual aspects of life. C. Wayne Gordon found that male students' peer status was centered around sports achievement and female students' was focused on the attributes of the Yearbook Queen who was selected on the basis of dress, school service, open personality, leadership ability, and Puritan morality! Similarly, James Coleman found men valuing athletic prowess, dating success, and "fun," while women were concerned with good looks, clothes, personality, and extra-curricular activity. By the mid-fifties, youth had generated its own market. Because of increasing affluence, they could buy clothes, food, and records that reflected their own tastes. As the focus of youth switched from the city and small town to the suburbs, the necessity for an automobile increased and fifties' youth culture became akin to car culture with the spawning of car clubs all over America.

Yet, for all the hedonism and "fun" orientation of the 1950s, there was an underlying *angst* that pervaded 1950s' youth culture. Marlon Brando and James Dean portrayed the agony of outlaw youth in such pictures as *The Wild Ones*, and *Rebel Without a Cause*. Perhaps even more reflective of youthful dissatisfactions was the invention of rock-'n'-roll music, which was designed to cater to the needs of youth while screening out the adult audience. Borrowing from the subterranean "race music" of the blacks, it took youth culture themes and orchestrated them to a heavy beat. Elvis Presley, the king of rock 'n' roll, sang of loneliness ("Heartbreak Hotel"), oppression ("Jailhouse Rock"), and duplicity ("Houndog"). The themes of adult oppression, sexual frustration, isolation and loneliness, and postponed living were repeated throughout 1950s' rock-'n'-roll music.[9]

The youth of the 1950s lived in a context that on the one hand extolled youth as the ideal state of humanity, while on the other hand, resented the young for being youthful. Juvenile delinquency had become a serious problem. The 1960 White House Conference on Children had as its central focus the alienation and isolation of youth (Beck, 1973). The major issue was juvenile delinquency. The family was evidencing an inability to control its own young and the burden was falling ever harder on public authorities: teachers, counselors, social workers, and the police. Yet the adolescent "rebellion" was not a collective phenomenon, with the exception of the inner-city gangs.

Youth of the 1950s was characterized as "alienated." The young were living privatized, isolated, lonely existences. They were becoming members of the "lonely crowd" (Riesman, 1955), learning to be "cheerful robots" (Mills, 1951). Not only were they alienated from each other, but they suffered from self-estrangement. They seemed to be people without internal depth. The characterizations of such leading critics as Riesman (1955), Friedenberg (1959), Mills (1951), and Erikson (1950) indicate that something had gone wrong in the socialization of the young. The common element among the critics was that the young had lost their own sense of selfhood and a commitment to society. Kenniston decided to study the alienation of the young by selecting twelve "extremely alienated" men at Harvard and comparing them to "moderately alienated" and "unalienated" men, also at Harvard.

> Alienation . . . has two terms—the alienated individual, and the society from which he is alienated—and is by definition a social as well as a psychological problem. Paradoxically, the alienated themselves often throw us off the scent of the social factors which are involved in their alienation. Despite their sweeping criticisms of American Society, they see themselves as largely ahistorical figures, and consequently make it all too tempting to interpret their alienation as a private, individual, idiosyncratic response to their society. . . . When one alienated young man meets another, he is seldom able to believe that the other is "genuine" or "sincere" in his alienation; it rarely occurs to these youths that the problems they face, much less their response to these problems, might be common to many others. (Kenniston, 1960:177.)

Although the young were characterized as "adolescents," adolescence was no longer working. Kenniston's "uncommitted youth" were extreme characterizations of a whole generation. The "identity crisis" did not seem to resolve itself, but was perpetuated in the form of self-estrangement. Jules Henry (1963) in summarizing his study of high school youth, found that their lives seemed to be characterized by flight. The choices they made were second choices, designed to avoid confrontation with the realities of life. Thus, the "fun" orientation of the youth was not so much a joyful expression of selfhood, but a bulwark erected to screen out pain.

The youth of the 1950s were raised in a culture that substituted desires for needs. They were surplus people who were caught in the maelstrom of a consumer society which depended on the generation of desire to keep the economy going. They were also objects of consumption as bureaucracies were built around them to control their behavior and shape them into the next generation of consumers. With the intensification of the status struggle in the consumption of life-style, invidious distinctions separated them from each other. In comparing themselves with the cultural ideals, few could measure up. As they were manipulated, so they manipulated themselves and others, generating feelings of unreality, insecurity, isolation, and loneliness. This generation was taught to desire commodity items, status, respectability, and security. However, because they were continually competing with one another to sate their ever-encouraged appetites, their needs for love, caring, tenderness, community, commitment, spontaneity, and joy were untended. The commodification of sexual relationships interfered with love. The competition for status interfered with community.[10] The necessity to protect oneself from humiliation and status loss prevented caring, spontaneity and joy. The "adolescent" longing of the 1950s was the longing for the humanizing needs that the culture obfuscated. The only socially acceptable outlet for such necessities was sexually intense relationships. Yet, for adolescents, bourgeois mentality still reigned. "Going steady" was anathema to adults. Young women were supposed to tease but not give. Young men were to be manly and to be continually on the make. Sex was evaluated in terms of conquests which were turned into status points among peers. It was a zero-sum game, if a male student "made" a female student in order to gain status for his conquest, he would have to brag to his pals, leading to a concomitant decrease in status for the woman and opening her to continued exploitation by the men. This intense competition tended to poison the one possible outlet for humanizing tenderness. It was a barrier that had to be surmounted before the youth of the 1950s could get succorance and nurturance from one another.

The 1960s: Revolution and the Generation of a New Vision

The 1960s began as a continuation of the 1950s for youth with one exception: the civil rights movement had begun in the South and had attracted the interest and imagination of young leftists in the Northern elite schools. The vast majority of youth was left untouched by the civil rights movement, though their sympathies were with the emerging New Left. The civil rights movement sparked an awareness in the young, which, though not directly related to their own discontents, appealed to their sense of justice. The New Left ideology of the early 1960s was an attempt to right the injustices of America and ameliorate the contradiction between racial discrimination and segregation and the ideal of equality of opportunity. The freedom riders and voter registrars went into the South believing that the federal government would aid in the righting of the wrongs against the Southern black; but they were soon disillusioned when they found that despite the proclamations of Attorney General Robert Kennedy, the FBI was in sympathy with the white racist establishment and the federal government was looking the other way as they were threatened, beaten, and even killed by members of the local white racist establishment. John Kennedy was assassinated in November 1963; two months later four black girls were blown up in a black Baptist church in Birmingham; the church was a center for pro-civil rights activity. Medgar Evers had been killed in June by an assassin who shot him in the back during racial tension in Decatur, Mississippi. The Mississippi Freedom Summer voter registration drive resulted in the June 1964 murders of CORE workers James Chaney and Michael Schwerner and the summer volunteer, Andrew Goodman by local police officials. One veteran of the Mississippi Freedom Summer was Mario Savio, the leader of the Berkeley Free Speech Movement.

In September 1964, several campus organizations, including civil rights activist groups (Congress for Racial Equality [CORE] and the Student Non-Violent Co-ordinating Committee [SNCC]) attempted to distribute literature and collect donations on University of California property in Berkeley in violation of university regulations prohibiting political activity on campus. What followed was a four-month confrontation between the students and administration over the issue of freedom of speech. The Berkeley Free Speech Movement was the opening battle in a series of clashes between students and administrations around the country, with student demands, administrative resistance, violence, and confrontation escalating until May 1970, when four students were shot at Kent State University during a rally to protest the invasion of Cambodia by the Nixon Administration during the Vietnam War. Eight days later, two students at Jackson State University were killed. The student reaction was immediate. Over five hundred colleges and universities were shut down and as many as 4,350,000 students participated in demonstrations (Sale, 1973:636; Peterson and Biloursky, 1971). In between were the Columbia University rebellion in 1968, the Harvard strike in 1969, the San Fernando Valley State confrontation in 1965, the bank burning at the University of California at Santa Barbara in 1969, the burning of several ROTC buildings on various campuses, and literally thousands of demonstrations, confrontations, sit-ins, mill-ins, and building takeovers all across the nation. Berkeley was in continual turmoil throughout the period. The height of the conflict was the People's Park riot in 1969, in which James Rector was killed by Alameda County Sheriffs, and the National Guard was called in to occupy Berkeley.

The People's Park confrontation represents the most radical thrust of the movement. The conflict concerned property rights. The community had appropriated a vacant block owned by the University of California and turned it into a park. The University did not approve of their land being used for such countercultural activities as fucking, drug-tripping, seances, esoteric religious rites, drug sales, and general hanging out. Asserting their rights as owners, they attempted to bulldoze the park out of existence. Berkeley residents were alerted to the University's intentions and attempted to occupy the park, demanding that community needs took precedence over ownership. Many people refer to these events as the student movement. However, they were part of a much larger youth movement which began as liberal-reformist, but by 1967, to paraphrase Bob Dylan, there was revolution in the air.

At about the time of the Berkeley Free Speech Movement, young people were dropping out of their middle-class suburban homes and taking up residence in San Francisco just off the Panhandle section of Golden Gate Park. The new residents seemed to be an extension of the beat generation of the 1950s who revolted against bourgeois culture by rejecting work, cleanliness, punctuality, and straightness as virtues. However, the residents of this area, called Haight-Ashbury after the intersection at its heart, were younger, less intellectual, less elitist, and were users of different drugs. Instead of booze and marijuana, they began using marijuana and psychedelics. They lived together communally. New arrivals would stay in "crash pads." Sex was free and easy. The "scene" was held together by the Diggers, a voluntary group of "hippies" who scrounged money and food to feed the community a free meal daily. They also began a "Free Store" in which people donated what they didn't need and those who needed took what they wanted without money being exchanged. Haight-Ashbury in particular and hippies in general were living critiques of bourgeois culture and capitalist society. Believing in the post-scarcity notion that there's enough for everybody, hippies lived according to the maxim, "From each according to his inclination, to each according to his trip." By October 1967, when the "Death of Hippie" ceremony was performed in Haight-Ashbury, following the summer of love ("If you're going to San Francisco/Wear a flower in your hair"), every major urban center had a hippie neighborhood. Rural hippie communes were sprouting in northern California, New Mexico, and Vermont. The cultural revolution had begun.[11]

However, with the American involvement in the Vietnam War, the crackdown on drug use, hippie busting, selective service reclassifications, and an escalation of violence against the youthful protesters, the hippie love ethic went out the window in favor of "armed love" and "protecting our communities." The period between 1967 and 1969 witnessed the advent of the "freak-radical" who had adopted the life-style of the hippies and had become radicalized beyond the wildest dreams of the New Left of the early 1960s. The "freak-radical" critique of American society was *total*. The notion of politics extended from the government pursual of the Vietnam War to the minutiae of everyday existence. They rejected the consumer society (with the possible exception of stereo systems and rock albums) and made serious attempts to strip themselves of falsely implanted desires and learned to exist with the satisfaction of basic needs (Foss, 1972). Crosby, Stills, and Nash sang at Woodstock in 1969, "We've got to get back to the garden." Thus, freakified youth attempted to rid themselves of bourgeois hangups about sex, property relations, feelings and control. Within the freak community, attempts at desocialization and de-alienation were made by its members. Spontaneity and "going with the flow" were highly prized. New realms of self-hood were opened up and explored through the use of psyche-delic drugs, sex, and communal living. One of the most popular books during this period was Alan Watts's *The Book: On the Taboo Against Knowing Who You Are* (New York: Collier, 1967). It was only through revolt that youth could break the chains of alienation that characterized the 1950s.

The youth movement of the 1960s generated a subjectivist ideology which raised personal experience as the final arbiter of reality. Because of this, it never developed the coherence of a doctrine. Each formulator would emphasize different elements of the ideology, giving it a temporal quality. Thus, it could be subjected to quick changes depending on the collective evalua-tion of "where it's at" and "what's happening." Nevertheless, the movement of the 1960s did generate a "vision" which had five major characteristics (Foss and Larkin, 1976):

First, was the notion that the end of material scarcity made it non-sensical for the economy to continue accumulating for its own sake. It was now possible to allocate goods and labor on something other than the market mechanism. Thus, scarcity assumptions were mechanisms of the "capitalist-fascist-pig-establishment" which, in its hallucinated view of reality, continued repressive policies for the maintenance of its own dominance. Youth then attempted to intensify their own awareness of the repressiveness of the intrusion of the market mechanism in their own lives.

The second component was "love." Once the real material needs of the people are met, in the words of the Beatles, "All you need is love. Love is all you need." "Love" in the vision of the 1960s is a shorthand for elaborate and complex efforts to develop new forms, styles, and intensities of being which could only come to fruition in a social order yet to be constructed.

The third feature was the quest for higher states of consciousness. This quest began with the infusion of the drugs of consciousness expansion into youth culture by the hippies. However, drug use spawned "hippie mysticism," which focused on the non-rational elements of consciousness and generated the notion of "levels of consciousness" in which the higher levels were synonymous with "stoned." Freakified youth often tried to keep as high as possible for as long as possible because it was both pleasurable and perceived to be "more real" than straight consciousness. To be "stoned" was to be in touch with a reality that heightened subjective awareness of "vibrations" (called "vibes"), which were accepted as irrefutably real. Drug experiences often led to other sources of consciousness expansion, especially yoga. Many claimed that the problems with drugs were that they were an external source of a "high" and that, sooner or later, you had to come down. Meditation and various yogic exercises were employed in freak culture to induce higher states of consciousness. In the early 1970s, various meditative techniques and Christian gnosticism were proselytized to youth as methods of maintaining a continual high. ("Try Jesus, God's eternal trip!")

Fourth, was sexual liberation. Sexual freedom was upheld not only because of the possibilities of sheer pleasure, but because it was felt that the loss of sexual inhibitions was necessary for an oppositional stance against straight society.

Fifth was the rejection of hierarchical structure and organizational routine. Especially during the hippie phase, purposeful behavior was eschewed and avoided as individuals were involved in disentangling their "authentic" motivations from "inauthentic" experiences imposed upon them by a social order which made no apparent sense.

The youth revolution was both political and cultural, attacking the structure of dominance and the culture of alienation. It began with a small minority of students in elite universities and cascaded to high schools and dropouts. It was a movement of middle-class youth (though the parallel black movement tended to engage all strata of black culture). It was held together by a common culture of dissidence. It generated its own music (rock), art (op, pop, posters, head comix, etc.), language, drug habits, politics ("Do your own thing"), and interpersonal styles. However, as do all social movements, it had to come to an end.

The 1970s: Cultural Crisis and Declining Opportunities

Although there is a continuing debate over whether the youth culture dissidence declined as a result of oppression by dominant institutions or because of internal exhaustion and corruption, it certainly did not contract because of the easing of the contradictions that generated it. For those who saw the Vietnam War as the causal factor, we must point out that the youth movement (1960–70) preceded the war (1965–72) and the war antedated the movement. Even if the war might have been contiguous, its existence would not explain the cultural dissidence. For example, what does resistance to the Vietnam War have to do with communal living, psychedelic drug use, sexual liberation, self-exploration, or rebellion against work? Youth culture dissidence was *intensified* by the conduct of the war, and it was the youth movement that helped to undermine the war effort.

Once it was clear that the movement was fragmenting and dissidence was declining by late 1970, young revolutionaries were gripped by a sense of futility and despair. The attenuation of the movement made it obvious to the participants that the vision of an alternative society would not be possible to fulfill.[12] Caught between lives they had rejected as despicable and lives they would not be allowed to live, "post-movement groups" (Foss and Larkin, 1976) arose which claimed to keep the movement going under new means. These post-movement groups tended to add a bizarre element to youth culture, which had already invented some rather unconventional forms in the 1960s. Each of these groups took a fragment of 1960s' youth culture and used it to legitimate a highly authoritarian structure that regulated the minutiae of the everyday lives of its members. They were exclusive in that they made claims of a monopoly on Truth, which could only be experienced through some gnostic process (meditation, chanting, opening your heart to Jesus, etc.). Some took the form of authoritarian communes, such as the Manson Family, the Lyman Family in Boston, and Michael Metellica's "Spirit in Flesh" commune in the Berkshires. Others became terrorist organizations, such as the Weather Underground and the Symbionese Liberation Army. A rash of oriental sects flourished in the wake of the movement, namely the Hari Krishnas (International Society for Krishna Consciousness), the Divine Light Mission of the Teenage Perfect Master, Guru Maharaj Ji, and Nichiren Shoshu. Their more Christian-oriented counterparts were the various Jesus-Freak cults such as the Tony and Susan Alamo Foundation, the Children of God, and the Process Church of the Final Judgment, which like Scientology, predated the movement, but filled its ranks with ex-movement participants. Out of the ashes of SDS came several Marxist sectarian groups, such as the Revolutionary Union, Progressive Labor Party, and the National Caucus of Labor Committees (now the U.S. Labor Party). Each of these groups promised prospective members meaning in life and the assuaging of psychic pain. The youth of America had to make peace with what was formerly regarded as the enemy. The dominant institutions reasserted themselves; however, their legitimacy, which had been under attack in the 1960s, continued to decline, not only among youth, but in the larger society. They had, in Daniel Bell's terms, lost their transcendental qualities which are necessary to make participation meaningful (Bell, 1976). The behavioral conformity imposed upon the young was paralleled by a sense of absurdity and unreality.

Youth culture has returned to normalcy. The public consciousness has returned from collective resistance as the important social problem to juvenile delinquency. The war between the ages has taken a more selective turn. Stores in Miami have signs in the windows saying, "No more than three juveniles allowed at a time." Law enforcement officials are claiming that juvenile crime statistics are leapfrogging and are demanding a heavier hand in punishing delinquency. Meanwhile, the youth are ghettoized in schools that promise futures of underemployment as labor becomes degraded.[13] Those who want out immediately are thrown into a highly competitive labor market that puts a premium on experience, which is exactly what they don't have. For those who desire some sort of part-time employment, the job is lowly and underpaid. (Many students have had their bosses threaten firing and replacement when they slow down, reminding them that there will be somebody who will be more willing to take the job.)

In the field of sociology, both the more conservative functionalists such as Talcott Parsons (1959) and Burton Clark (1962) and the so-called radical Marxists such as Bowles and Gintis (1976) agree that the main function of education is to instill within the younger generation the qualities necessary for corporate bureaucracies (e.g., docility, deferred gratification, respect for hierarchy, the work ethic, etc.). In this, sociology has not moved from the original position of Emile Durkheim in 1903 (1956). Yet, if that *is* the case, then *why* would the most advantaged, privileged, best-achieving, and most promising of its products turn in vengeance upon the schools and other institutions of society and attempt to bring them down? If the system is "dysfunctioning," then why is it doing so? Bowles and Gintis's (1976) analysis of the relationship between schooling and capitalism ignore this question. *If* education forges the younger generation into the labor force of tomorrow, and *if* it reflects the interests of the ruling class, then *why* did those who had the most to benefit from conformity to the demands of the capitalist structure revolt? It is indeed interesting that Bowles and Gintis, who are obviously heavily influenced by 1960s' insurgencies do not answer the question.

Given the conditions of monopoly capitalism and its problem of surplus absorption, the socialization function of education has been eclipsed by the necessity for education to act as a surplus absorption device. The consequence of this is that education is primarily related to social *consumption* rather than to *production*. Large expenditures in education, like military expenditures, absorb economic surplus. The educational establishment employs white-collar workers who perform non-productive labor and form a significant segment of the consuming class in their private spheres of consumption. Students become the legitimation for their salaries. Thus, students must be *forced* to attend school, despite the declining rewards accrued from attendance. If they were not, millions of teachers, counselors, administrators, custodians, clerical workers, coaches, paraprofessionals, etc., would be out of work and the economy would be devastated! School, for the students, then, has become merely a form of *coerced consumption*. Yet as the problem of surplus absorption becomes more acute and the economy increasingly continues to be unable to use the total labor force, the necessity to keep students in school longer and longer compels them into choosing between dropping out prematurely and becoming a member of the marginally employed reserve labor army or pursuing further studies in a career that they may never be able to practice. (The more than 600 new PhDs in sociology granted in 1976 were vying for less than 150 academic positions.)

The fact is that students are forced to attend school, because of compulsory attendance laws, as in the case of most high school students, or there are no other viable alternatives, or non-attendance is an admission of failure in the status struggle, as in the case of most college students, contrary to the popular ideology that education is a privilege. This particular contradiction un-nerves students, since they tend to believe the popular ideology and have feelings of guilt because they don't really want to be there. They are caught in the double-bind of being coerced into a position which they believe is privileged. Their guilt emanates from the awareness that not everyone gets the opportunity for advanced schooling, while simultaneously feeling no personal commitment to it, because they are coerced. Since they are unaware of their own oppressive position, they manifest the psychological forms of self-estrangement, free-floating anxieties, meaninglessness, and drift. They blame themselves for not being motivated to "learn," castigate themselves for not being able to "get with it," and can't seem to get a grip on life.

The youth of the 1970s see themselves as caught in a bind. Education has become a meaningless exercise in necessity. As they pursue their futures, a new kind of scarcity sets in. It is not the scarcity of material resources, for they are relatively well off. It is the scarcity of being able to fulfill one's life through meaningful work. The paradox in which these students find themselves is that the harder they pursue their occupational goals, the most likely they are to be disappointed as opportunities dwindle. White-collar work in the last quarter of the twentieth century is following the same trend as blue-collar labor over the previous one hundred years. It is becoming subdivided into its basic elements and automated or routinized (Braverman, 1974).

The youth of the 1970s face an unique configuration of problems that make their position in society unprecedented. They live in a society in which all social institutions, including the schools they attend, have suffered loss of legitimacy and are increasingly incapable of commanding the allegiance of their members. The increased productivity of the economy, the degradation of white-collar labor, and the bureaucratization of work have seriously diminished the possibility of a youth of the 1970s to actualize themselves in a career that provides the intrinsic rewards of craftsmanship and involvement in the total work process. Perhaps this notion can best be summed up in an advertisement for *Psychology Today:* "Our parents lived to work. We work to live" (*The New York Times,* October 5, 1976). With the emergence of education as a mechanism of surplus absorption and coerced consumption, it can no longer fulfill the promises of good work with good pay that it once did. Motivation for school attendance is primarily negative and is not couched so much in terms of what rewards can be gained for continued effort, but what happens if one drops out.

The contradictions between the possibilities and the actualities of the 1960s still exist in exacerbated form, yet there is no social movement to combat or resist their encroachment on the lives of the youth of the 1970s. They must compete with their peers for increasingly scarce resources. Thus, youth culture has become split along social class, ethnic, and sexual lines. There are those who walk around campus with an air of authority and a sense of sureness. They are the ones who, because they have a supportive family, status, brains, talent, beauty, or a rare combination of such qualities, have been pointed out by the unseen finger of success. The rest attempt to be like them, or try to wage war against them, or drift aimlessly like most everyone else.

The most serious complaint among Utopia High School students is boredom. They are restless. Many complain of having nothing to do. They want to leave town, but have no idea of where to go. They are forced to compete with each other for grades, sexual attractiveness, hipness, and all the other minutiae that are involved in the status race. Since everyone else is struggling for the same, somehow scarcer rewards, friendship has a hollow quality to it. It is a gloss on a relationship in which vulnerabilities are hidden so they won't be capitalized on by others. The era of communes, tribes, affinity groups, and "doing your own thing" has been re-replaced by the "lonely crowd." Adults are viewed with ambiguity. On the one hand, they are necessary and *needed* since these young people are in a world that is extremely complex and confusing. Yet the adults themselves often have clay feet. They have no answers to the difficult questions. Besides, they are often too busy competing to be bothered by the complaints of the young, who must depend on their peers for most of the information they get. Not only are the adults unreliable, but they can be oppressing as well. They can become violent and can cause humiliation and pain. The most that these young people can expect from them is understanding, and that doesn't happen very often.

The youth of the 1970s does not have the open optimism of the youth of the 1950s, nor the defiance of the youth of the 1960s. They are attempting to be practical in an impractical world. In the 1950s, the meaning of life lay in the future: in finding love, a sexual outlet, getting a job, a house in the suburbs with a two-car garage, and combining a career with a family. In the 1960s, meaning in life was found in resisting the old "straight" society and constructing a new one. There is no such vision in the 1970s. Their optimism is a hoping-against-hope that things will some-how, nay, *must* get better. Meanwhile, the big task is getting through the day.

NOTES

1. How long this quiescence can be maintained is problematic, since there are limits as to how much loss of faith social institutions can weather before attempts at insurrection begin to take place. In 1978, a nation-wide taxpayers revolt was begun with the passage of Proposition 13 in California, where most social trends have begun. All over the country, taxpayers' groups are follow-ing the California example, which limits property taxation to one percent of the assessed valuation. If such a law were passed in Pleasant Valley's state, it would mean financial disaster to the school district, which has a tax rate of more than six percent (assuming that property is assessed at its market value).

   However, it is the cultural ramifications of the California example that are most interesting. The taxpayer's revolt was led by the political right, who were quoting the Declaration of Independence on the duty of citizens to abolish government when it becomes oppressive, and who were shouting, "Smash the state!" at their rallies. Even though the taxpayers revolt was led by the right, the sides were the same as in the confrontations of the 1960s: middle-class suburban whites against big government, labor unions and big business (all of which campaigned heavily against Proposition 13).

2. The term *monopoly capitalism* refers to the current phase of capitalist development in which the core of the economy is dominated by a few giant corporations which do not involve one another in price competition. Instead, prices are administered according to a pre-established calculus by the price-leader in the field, which is usually the corporation that has the greatest control of the market. Monopoly capitalism differs from competitive capital-ism in its internal dynamics: risk-taking is minimized, price-cutting is forbidden, and market shares are at least as important as profit ratio. The family owned corporation has been replaced by the large-scale global cor-poration (nearly all of Fortune's 500 largest American corporations are global in scope), which regulate the marketplace. Price competition is allowed only at the fringes of the corporate economy, or when expediency forces the issue,

as in the case of the influx of cheaper Japanese goods flooding the American markets, undercutting domestic companies. The response of several American corporations was to cut prices, which is anathema to them, so they invented the euphemism, "flexible pricing" (see *Business Week*, December 12, 1977).

3. Statistics from the U.S. Census (U.S. Department of Commerce, 1974:357, 713) bear this generalization out. In the manufacturing sector, the following indices were collected over the seventeen year period from 1955 to 1972:

	1955	1972	% Increase
Output index per worker (1967 = 100)	73.7	121.8	66
Salary per worker (1967 dollars)	94.4	123.5	31
Value added per worker per dollar in wages (1954–1972)	2.6	3.4	31 (27)

Thus, worker productivity increased 66 percent during the seventeen year period, while worker salaries only increased 31 percent. In 1955, for every dollar paid labor, $2.60 was extracted for management purposes. By 1972, management was able to extract $3.40 for every dollar paid out in wages. This index is independent of inflation, since it is a dollar to dollar ratio and though inflation would affect the value of the dollars, it would have no effect on the ratio. We can conclude, then, that the increased productivity of the individual worker is only partially returned to the worker and the rest is used for management purposes. If we correct value-added figure for the extra year, we can estimate that for the seventeen year period, the exploitation of labor power increased approximately 27 percent.

4. One of the major forces in the progress of capitalism has been the continual revolution of the means of production. The "Industrial Revolution" has been the handmaiden of increased profits through the mechanization of labor and the consequent increase in worker productivity. A major characteristic of capitalist development has been the movement from labor-intensive to capital-intensive enterprise. Notes Karl Marx (1967: ch. 25, sec. 2):

> . . . The growing extent of the means of production, as compared with the labour power incorporated with them, is an expression of the growing productiveness of labour. The increase of the latter appears, therefore, in the diminution of the mass of labour in proportion to the mass of means of production moved by it. . . .

The profits accrued from the exploitation of the worker's labor are reinvested in the means of production which alter the composition of capital. Using Marx's formula, $c + v + s = V$, where c represents investment in the means of production (constant capital), v is the investment of labor power (variable capital) and s is surplus value (or profit), and V is the value of the manufactured commodity, we find that as capital investment increases, the ratio of constant capital to variable capital increases. For example, prior to technological innovation, a capitalist might produce a commodity that has the following composition: $50c + 25v + 25s = 100V$. Following the revolution of the means of production, his capital will look more like this, keeping the amount of surplus value or profit constant: $70c + 5v + 25s = 100V$. Even though the rate of profit $(P = \frac{s}{c+v})$ is the same (33 1/3 percent), the exploitation of labor has dramatically increased. Prior to the technological innovation, the laborers were getting paid $1.00 for each dollar of profit made for the capitalist, thus generating a rate of surplus value at 100 percent (s/v = rate of surplus value). Following technological innovation, the rate jumped to 500 percent. Instead of 50 percent of the labor being unpaid, 80 percent of the labor of the worker is unpaid. Even with this, the laborer may experience an absolute increase in wages, due to the worker's increasing productivity, even though he or she is performing more unpaid labor in a working day.

5. Using the U.S. Department of Commerce census statistics, Phillips computed the index of economic surplus in the following way: he summed the sources of non-productive income and divided it by the gross national product for each year between 1929 and 1966. The indicators of economic surplus were headed under four major categories: property income, waste in the business process, government expenditures, and penetration of the productive process by the sales effort. The property income was computed by summing corporate profits after taxes, profit income of unincorporated enterprises, official depreciation estimates and subtracting from that total adjusted depreciation estimates. Business waste included the following expenditures: advertising, market research, expense accounts, maintenance of excessive numbers of sales outlets, and the salaries and bonuses of sales personnel. Penetration of the productive process by the sales effort includes the cost of model changes, superfluous product variation, and planned obsolescence. However, because of the difficulty in operationalizing the definitions in the last category, it was dropped from the final analysis, making the estimate of economic surplus conservative.

6. In 1977–78, the Carter administration has made a concerted effort to lower the unemployment rate. However, this has been very expensive, since it requires added investment of government into the non-productive labor force by increasing its payroll. Corporations are also doing their part to hold the unemployment rate down by failing to automate outmoded facilities. Instead, they merely raise the monopoly price for their goods, socializing the costs of waste employment. Both policies result in increased inflation.

7. "Taylorism" refers to the work of Frederic Taylor, who was a self-proclaimed "efficiency expert." He advocated breaking the labor process down to its atomic parts so that each worker would perform one simple act in an assembly-line supervised by management.

8. Cyra McFadden's book, *The Serial* (New York: Knopf, 1976) chronicles life in the center of the hip-competitive struggle as lived by the denizens of Mill Valley in Marin County outside San Francisco. The satire, derived from Ms. McFadden's personal experience as a resident of Mill Valley, concerns people who change sexual partners faster than they turn in their cars for new models; consume the newest fads in psychotherapies, consumer items, and "life-styles"; and speak a language McFadden calls "psychobabble." Perhaps a quote will give some insight into a few of the mechanisms of this hip-competitive struggle:

. . . Now that clothes were supposed to reflect the Inner You, getting dressed was always a problem. You couldn't just throw on clothes as if you were trying to keep warm. After some soul-searching, she decided on going Moroccan and put on her I.

Magnin herdsman's caftan and her rope-tied headband. The look wasn't complete, but Harvey [her husband] had been terrifically negative when she mentioned wanting to get her nose pierced, so she had to settle for her Beadazzled earrings instead. (P. 42.)

9. Some basic rock-'n'-roll music themes are: (1) sex ("Earth Angel," "Honey Love," "Be-Bop-a-Lu-La"), which seems to be the most pervasive; (2) adult oppression ("Wake Up Little Suzie," "Yakety-Yak"); (3) the postponed life ("Almost Grown," "Dream"); (4) infidelity ("Mabellene," "There Goes My Baby," "Sally Go 'Round the Roses"); (5) loneliness ("Heartbreak Hotel," "Tossin' and Turnin'"); and (6) fun ("Rock-and-Roll Music," "Long Tall Sally," "Let the Little Girl Dance").

10. Anthropologist Victor Turner (1969) has noted that societies alternate between states of structure (*societas*) and liminality (*communitas*) where structure dissolves and makes way for spontaneity. In primitive cultures, communitas is experienced in liminal states such as rites of passage. However, in Western Society, with its bureaucratic-rational structure, communitas is only experienced as a widespread phenomenon within the context of a social movement. As a matter of fact, bureaucracy is erected as a bulwark against communitas. Thus, fifties' youth, although kept in a liminal state for longer periods of time, were prevented from the experience of communitas because of the restrictions placed upon their behavior by the demands of rationalized structures with the ideological supports of bourgeois culture.

11. The youth movement of the 1960s has not only spawned its own literature, but has also generated a rather large literature about it by academics. Many movement "heavies" have written their own books about their experiences. Jerry Rubin (1970) attempted to exhort the young into revolutionary fervor in his book *Do It!* Emmett Grogan in *Ringolevio* (1972) uses fiction and a pseudonym to cover an account of his life, first as a street-wise Brooklynite and later as one of the San Francisco Diggers. He claims that Abbie Hoffman stole his ideas that were the core of Hoffman's writings in *Revolution for the Hell of It* (1968) and *Woodstock Nation* (1969). Hoffman attempted to codify what he was doing in the form of freak anarchism. More than any other movement participant, he was able to grapple with what they were for and what they were against and he attempted to develop strategies by which straight society could be undermined. In addition to revolutionary guides and how to do it books, the movement sponsored a whole arena of mystical literature. Alan Watts's books on Zen Buddhism were gobbled up by freak culture adherents. Carlos Castaneda's visits with a Yaqui Indian shaman became the basis for three countercultural favorites: *The Teachings of Don Juan* (1968), *A Separate Reality* (1970), and *Journey to Ixtlan* (1972). Miraculous literature of other cultures also was consumed by youthful dissidents: *I Ching: The Book of Changes* (Princeton: The Princeton University Press, 1967), noted as the oldest book in the world, full of Confucian and pre-Confucian wisdom used for divinations; *The Tibetan Book of the Dead*, the *Ramayana* and *Baghavad-Gita* from Hindu literature; and the writings of such mystics as Gurdjieff and his student, Ouspensky.

Academics have added to the extensive literature on the youth movement. In addition to the myriad of articles in professional and popular journals, several books have been published about it. Most notable are: Richard Flacks's *Youth and Social Change*, a thoughtful Marxian analysis of youth as the vanguard of social change; Theodore Roszak's *The Making of a Counterculture*, an ideological defense of 1960s' subjectivism; Charles Reich's *The Greening of America*, which managed to proclaim that the revolution was coming just as it was ending. (It also claimed that America would be "greened" by a new consciousness that would change our social institutions for the better.) Lewis Yablonsky's *The Hippie Trip* documents his attempt to subject hippie culture to standard sociological analysis; and Daniel Foss's *Freak Culture*, is probably the best attempt at analyzing the cause of youthful dissidence and also the best analysis of the 1960s' subjectivist ideology.

12. This is brought home by Daniel Yankelovich (1972) in a student survey. Fifteen percent agreed with the statement, "I find the prospect of accepting a conventional way of life in the society as it now exists as intolerable." An additional 18 percent agreed with the statement, "It's not going to be easy for me to accept the conventional job-marriage-children and home-of-your-own kind of life, but I don't see any other alternative." Fully one-third of the student population who were queried in 1971 perceived difficulty in readjusting to the resurgence of dominant institutions. Because of the wording of the question, it may underrepresent the dissatisfaction students have with accommodating to conventional life. Forty-nine percent agreed with the question, "I anticipate no great difficulty in accepting the kind of life the society has to offer—a good job, marriage, children, living in a pleasant community, and becoming part of the community." The item is strongly biased for a positive response by assuming society is offering everyone "a *good* job," and "a *pleasant* community." If that weren't enough, the item begins with "I anticipate no great difficulty . . ." Those who registered dissatisfactions, then, registered *strong* dissatisfactions. Only 17 percent of the sample agreed with the one other statement: "I would like just about the same kind of life for myself as my parents have." Since it was students who were sampled, not youth in general, it must be realized that these are the people who are heading for conventional careers. One could reasonably predict greater dissatisfaction from those who have either dropped out or have been excluded from higher education.

13. Harry Braverman, in his brilliant analysis of the degradation of labor by monopoly capital, makes this very point:

> . . . The continuing extension of mass education for the nonprofessional categories of labor increasingly lost its connection with occupational requirements. At the same time, its place in the ecomonic structure became ever more firmly guaranteed by functions which have little or nothing to do with either job training or any other strictly educational needs. The postponement of school-leaving to an average age of eighteen has become indispensable for keeping unemployment within reasonable bounds. In the interest of working parents (the two-parent-job-holding family having become ever more common during this period), and in the interest of social stability and the orderly management of an increasingly rootless urban population, the schools have developed into immense teen-sitting organizations, their functions having less and less to do with imparting to the young those things that society thinks they must learn. In this situation the content of education deteriorated as its

duration lengthened. The knowledge imparted in the course of an elementary education was more or less expanded to fill the prevalent twelve-year educational sojourn, and in a great many cases school systems have difficulty in instilling in twelve years the basic skills of literacy and numbers that, several generations ago, occupied eight. This in turn gave a greater impetus to employers to demand of job applicants a high school diploma, as a guarantee—not always valid—of getting workers who can read.

We cannot neglect the direct economic impact of the enlarged school system. Not only does the postponement of the school-leaving age limit the growth of recognized unemployment, but it also furnishes employment for a considerable mass of teachers, administrators, construction and service workers, etc. Moreover, education has become an immensely profitable area of capital accumulation for the construction industry, for suppliers of all sorts, and for a host of subsidiary enterprises. For all these reasons—which have nothing to do with either education or occupational training—it is difficult to imagine United States society without its immense "educational" structure, and in fact, as has been seen in recent years, the closing of even a single segment of the schools for a period of weeks is enough to create a social crisis in the city in which this happens.(Braverman, 1974:439-40.)

3

JOCKS, GRINDS, FREAKS, GREASERS, BOBOS, RAH-RAHS, HARD GUYS, NERDS AND OTHERS:
The Social Structure of Utopia High

> Get born, keep warm
> Short pants, romance, learn to dance
> Get dressed get blessed
> Try to be a success
> Please her, please him, buy gifts
> Don't steal, don't lie
> Twenty years of schoolin'
> And they put you on the day shift
> Look out kid, they keep it all hid
> Better jump down a manhole
> Light yourself a candle, don't wear sandals
> Try to avoid the scandals
> Don't wanna be a bum
> You better chew gum
> The pump don't work
> 'Cause the vandals took the handles.
> *Bob Dylan*, "Subterranean Homesick Blues," 1965

The social structure of Utopia High is extremely complex, involving such dimensions as race, ethnicity, sex, social-class background, aspirations, and historical relations to earlier phases of youth culture. The students are organized both formally and informally into a number of hierarchies resulting in a pluralistic elite structure. Within the school, there were four distinct subcultures and a rather large undifferentiated majoritarian mass. It is to this set of structures and their consequences for students that we shall now turn.

ELITES IN UTOPIA

There are three "leading crowds" at Utopia High: the jock/rah-rahs, the politicos, and the intellectuals. Each crowd operates somewhat independently of the others. Although there are special cases of overlapping constituencies. The jock/rah-rah crowd operates as a social elite and its members are pointed in the direction of what Clark and Trow called "the collegiate subculture" consisting of fraternities, sororities, sports, parties, drinking, and campus fun (Clark, 1962: ch. 6). At the high school level, this excludes campus fraternities and sororities but, nevertheless, encompasses the ethic of sociality of the "collegiates" that inhabit most college campuses.

At Utopia High, the jock/rah-rah crowd is referred to in these terms because the ideal type male is the athletic star and the ideal female is the cheerleader. It consists primarily of athletes and their admirers and female students involved in more traditional roles of gaining success through the achievements of their boyfriends. This crowd dates, it is the core of the "school spirit," and it provides the most willing workers for such activities as homecoming and the prom. At one time it held cultural and political dominance on the high school scene (see Gordon, 1957; and Coleman, 1961). The paroxysms and "freakification" of youth culture in the sixties undercut their dominance as *the* leading crowd and diminished their percentage of the student population as well as their unchallenged dominance as *the* elite.

Even the term applied to them by their peers implies that they may well be an anachronism and may be viewed as a holdover from earlier eras. No longer the purveyors of youth cultural innovation, they are the conservers of a tradition.

The jock/rah-rah crowd is populated from the ranks of upper middle-class youth primarily of Protestant background. Their parents are middle- and upper-level executives of large corporations and successful entrepreneurs. Those who are bright enough will follow their fathers' footsteps into the Ivy League schools. Those who are not will be attending schools where the academic requirements are not as rigorous but where thriving collegiate subculture still exists (e.g., Penn State, Southern California). The jock/rah-rah crowd used to be politically dominant in the school. However, when youth became politically radicalized in the sixties, political leadership was wrested from the jock/rah-rahs by the more insurgent elements of youth who could not tolerate their toadying for the administration. The insurgent students attempted, both at the college and high school levels, to use student government to represent the demands of the students rather than to provide a convenient cover for administration interests. This change is reflected in the elite structure of Utopia High.

The politically active students share a common heritage that originates from the student movement of the 1960s. Although this crowd does not have a label like the jock/rah-rah crowd, they are, nevertheless, a distinct group who are easily identifiable. Providing the political leadership of the school, they hold the student offices and are prominent in the committees that operate the student government. Because they hearken back to the politics of the 1960s, which popularized "freak-anarchism" and were hostile to all hierarchy, they are very sensitive about their anomalous position as a student elite. In addition, the freedoms which were won in the struggle in the 1960s are increasingly under fire from adult authorities, and they find themselves in the unenviable position of attempting to suppress the activities of their own peers for fear that their hard-earned privileges will be revoked.

BECKY. Well, you see, I've been doing some, sort of, studying, myself. Little bit in a sub-committee of [student] council.

LARKIN. Tell me about it.

B. The interesting thing we've been noting, that, um, sixties wanted freedom, a certain kind of freedom of expression and all that, also . . .

L. They also wanted an end to hierarchy.

B. I don't know. I'm not sure the way you look at it. I don't know whether I see it that way. But now, people have abused this freedom . . . [and] we, *we* want to put restrictions on our peers to stop vandalism.

I mean, so we are now again trying to restrict the freedom that was won, because the conscientious people are aware of how some people abuse the freedom that they have gained. And, so we are starting the cycle again. *We* are *repressing* our peers. It's an incredible thing to me. (Recorded March 29, 1976.)

There are two reasons for the trepidation of the political elite. Other, more dissident students make them painfully aware that they are an elite. Consequently, the student council is continually plagued with the problem of its elite status and the issue is repeatedly raised in their deliberations. One student told the investigator that the student council spends half its meeting debating whether or not it is elitist. The problem is not limited to the student council. The editorial staff of the student newspaper has also been accused of being a self-congratulatory elite in-group. The elite status of the politicos does not fit well with their freak-anarchism origins of late-1960s. (Notice Becky's attempt to limit the 1960s' demands for freedom to include only expression and her aversion to the addition of hierarchical dominance as part of the insurgencies of the 1960s.) Their discomfort is intensified by the criticisms from non-elites. Members of the "freak" subculture (the inheritors of the "counterculture" of the 1960s) are always accusing them of being elites and suspect them of being toadies for the administration.

The second factor that undercuts the legitimacy of the politicos is that Jews are overrepresented among them. The conspicuousness of Jewish leadership in school politics leads to a certain paranoia among the Jewish students and has generated a vicious whispering campaign among the non-Jews in the school. The following was elicited from two student leaders:

> **JANE.** "The Jews actually run the place." People have actually said that. . . . In December, there was a thing going around. A girl came up to me and said, "Do you know that, that, there is a thing going on . . ."
>
> **BECKY.** I got that, too.
>
> **J.** ". . . that the people running the school are all Jews, and that no one else is allowed?"
>
> **B.** It's so strange, because we get elected.
>
> **J.** Yea. (Recorded March 31, 1976.)

While Jews are overrepresented in leadership positions vis-a-vis their percentage of the student body, it is hardly a Jewish cabal. For example, the student body president is black, and white Protestants and Catholics are represented in student body offices and on student council.

The third elite crowd, which overlaps somewhat with the politicos, is the intellectuals. The presence of an identifiable crowd of intellectuals that are an elite can be attributed to two factors: the presence of a large Jewish minority and the academic emphasis of the school. Indeed, it is rare to find an intellectual crowd in high schools, much less one that is accorded an elite status. Nowhere in the sociological literature has such a group been found in high schools. At Utopia High, I found students who were reading Thomas Mann, T. S. Eliot, and Karl Marx for their own edification. Several students told the author of their desire to study music, mathematics, philosophy, anthropology, literature, and sociology. One student was planning to live in Paris after graduation to study the flute, another had decided not to go to college upon graduation from high school, but rather, concentrate on writing her poetry. One student confided that she wanted to be a Nobel Prize winner! None of these students was the stigmatized "weirdo" who might have been described as the "egghead" of the 1950s, but all were integrated into the student subculture system of the school. They were respected by their peers: the term closest to an epithet used that might deride serious scholarship was "grind." Yet, that term was not specifically applied to the intellectuals, but to any student who compulsively attended classes.

The tripartite elite structure tended to represent the three major functions of the high school: (1) social activities, fun, and sports, (2) governance and citizenship, and (3) intellectual development. Each elite provided a link between the student body and some adult constituency. The jock/rah-rah elite tied the students to the larger community by providing an identity through sports and to the faculty in their non-academic functions. The politico elite linked the students into the administrative structure through its own governance procedures, participation in administrative committees, and to the larger community through the organization of political demonstrations. The politicos also represented the student body to the Board of Education and, through the student newspaper, reported on their deliberations. The intellectuals tied the student body to the faculty in their academic functions. They were role models exemplifying the pursuit of knowledge. While each elite did provide a bridge, such a characterization would oversimplify the situation. Within the student body exists tremendous antagonisms and differences of interest. With the exception of the intellectuals, whose authority is only exemplary, the legitimacy of the jock/rah-rahs and the politicos was quite tenuous among their peers, as we will see later.

Because the intellectual and jock/rah-rah crowds were based on subcultural affinity rather than formal positions, it was extremely difficult to estimate the size of their membership.[1] The matter was complicated by the fact that none of these groups was static and there was a frequent turnover of members. However, the core of each of these groups consisted of from twenty to fifty persons. Because of the diversity of its activities, the jock/rah-rah crowd was the most difficult to estimate. The best guess of the size of the jock/rah-rah crowd is that it was closer to fifty. The intellectuals had a core of approximately twenty-five persons, while the politicos numbered between thirty and forty.[2]

THE FREAKS

At Utopia High, there is an identifiable subculture who call themselves "freaks" in the tradition of the late 1960s. The core of the freaks numbers approximately 30, but the subculture commands the allegiance of around 200 students primarily from upper middle-class backgrounds. The freaks see themselves as the legacy of the counterculture of the late 1960s and pride themselves on their drug use and free and easy ways with sex. The politicos draw their *political* heritage from the dissidence of the 1960s; whereas, the freaks are the *cultural* descendents. As the politicos transformed the radical anarchism of the 1960s into liberal-reformism of the 1970s, the freaks have inverted the psychedelic exploration and sexual revolutions of the sixties into competitive struggles for social status among their peers. One disillusioned freak grumbled:

> **TOM.** I think that what ought to be studied is how youth of the seventies and how the youth of every time is just like the adults, only on a smaller scale.
>
> **LARKIN.** You really think so?
>
> **T.** Yea, really do. Bums me out. Because all my life I always spent saying how I'm not going to grow up to be like mommy and daddy—I still don't think I am—but I see that everyone around me is growing up that way. . . .
> There are a lot of kids who talk about freedom and equality and they talk about . . . it's cool if you get high, you know. You know, if somebody comes over, "He's cool, he gets stoned, he's cool." What does that have to do with whether [he is] being cool or not? . . .
>
> **L.** Well, what do you want to do? . . .
> **T.** I want to be *honest!* . . . That's what I want to be. I want to be honest.
> **L.** In other words, what you are saying is that the young people have just as many pretensions as the old folks, and though the words change, the line of bullshit is the same.
>
> **T.** I think so, pretty much. And I think that all the cliques and all the ways of thinking are all pretty much all set before you're out of high school.

L. And it's pretty tough to break through all that. . . . That's a pretty heavy statement.

T. I think it's true. (Recorded March 23, 1976.)

The freaks, then, tend to carry over the hedonic subjectivism from the sixties ("if it feels good, do it"), but it has been inverted into a form of social striving. Thus among the freaks, sexual and drug macho are important in the achievement of peer status. The male freaks mimic the old standard of bragging about conquests. (Sex will be discussed in detail in chapter 4.) Unlike the politicos, who are closely aligned with the normative structure of the school (which, as we have already mentioned, is permissive), the freaks are antagonistic to it. The most important modes of dissidence among them are smoking marijuana on campus and cutting classes. During my first day of observations, I stumbled onto about thirty freaks lounging on the playing field behind the main school building, enjoying the warm sun. Upon finding that I was in no way associated with school authorities, they passed out marijuana joints and someone went to the local market and bought two six-packs of beer. They frolicked on the grass, smoked pot, drank beer, and two or three couples commenced "making out" until the gym teacher, the vice-principal, and Mr. Seraph came out to see what was going on. I was called over and asked if I was drinking, and the students were told to pick up the empty bottles. Following the incident, the students, much chastened, admitted to me that they had been showing off and that it was rare for them to be drinking on campus.

The freaks tend to be ambivalent toward school. They are anti-authoritarian, but also realize that they are privileged to be in a school that is so even-handed and permissive. Although their disaffection is not destructive, they represent a clear threat to the politicos since their proclivity to miss classes and smoke pot on campus invites retribution from the community and pressure on the administration to crack down on their behavior. Both groups have their legacy from the sixties, but they are in conflict over cultural differences. The politicos emphasize responsibility and moderation, while the freaks are prone to excess and hedonism.

The politicos reprimand the freaks for their apathy, lack of participation, and threat to the freedoms they are trying so hard to protect. The freaks, on the other hand, see the politicos as "grinds" and "structure-freaks" who are more concerned with their elite status than serving the students. The conflict between the freaks and politicos is one of the most important cleavages within the student body, since their antagonism prevents the formation of a united student front against adult encroachments on their autonomy.

CASTE AND CLASS: THE LOWER REACHES OF THE STUDENT SOCIAL SYSTEM

At the bottom of the student social system exist two often mutually antagonistic groups: the blacks and the "greasers." Since the blacks operate almost entirely as a separate social system, we will consider the greaser subculture first.

A Tribute to the Fifties: The Greasers

All the subcultures and interest groups on campus occupy specific territories, with the exception of the politicos, who, because they are so busy with classes and committees, do not seem to have any well-demarcated place. On warm days, the freaks will hang out on the lawn behind the gymnasium. Another favorite hangout of theirs is the lounge of one of the houses in the school. Blacks can be easily located on the back stairs, the jocks are usually in the gym or on the basketball courts, and the greasers are found in the parking lot behind the auto shop. Impressed by how it was dominated by the greaser element, I dubbed this area "greaser's alley."

The greasers, like the jock/rah-rah crowd, have their roots in the youth culture of the 1950s. As a matter of fact, they are a romanticization of the black-leather-jacketed juvenile delinquents made popular in the public mind in such 1950s' genre movies as *Blackboard Jungle*, *The Wild Ones*, and *Rebel Without a Cause*. With the resurgence of fifties' nostalgia in

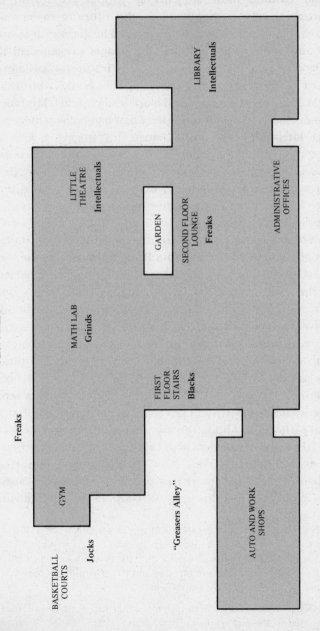

**Location of Subcultures and Interest Groups
Utopia High School: Spring 1976**

PLAY FIELDS

Freaks

LIBRARY
Intellectuals

LITTLE
THEATRE
Intellectuals

GARDEN

SECOND FLOOR
LOUNGE
Freaks

ADMINISTRATIVE
OFFICES

MATH LAB
Grinds

FIRST
FLOOR
STAIRS
Blacks

GYM

"Greasers Alley"

AUTO AND WORK
SHOPS

BASKETBALL
COURTS

Jocks

popular culture, those students at Utopia High who are characterologically sympathetic to the fifties' greasers have imitated them in dress and mannerisms. The greasers at Utopia High also seem to be imitating the images presented in the television show "Happy Days," which features a saccharine "greaser" as its most popular character, "The Fonz," who dresses in tight levis, white tee shirt, and black leather jacket. His hair is long—ducktail style—and a ringlet of hair hangs down the center of his forehead. "The Fonz" snaps his fingers a lot, has mannerisms that approximate the dirty-boogie, and is, of course, always running a comb through his hair. In the show, he is shown always as an individual, never as part of a gang, and, though he has a tough exterior, the producers are wont to show that underneath exists a heart of gold. "Happy Days" was a spinoff of the academy-award-winning movie *American Graffiti*, a film about adolescence in Santa Rosa, California in the early 1960s. (One must be cautioned that fifties' culture extended well into the 1960s, especially at the high school level.) Both *American Graffiti* and "Happy Days" underemphasize the negative aspects of the youth experience of the 1950s, such as gang violence, personal intimidation, invidious competition, exploitation, alienation, and loneliness that were central to fifties' youth culture. By sugar-coating the 1950s, they glorify the past that never was. Because of this distortion, and the greasers' tepid adherence to it, they tend to be viewed by the rest of the student body as caricatures. Though greasers like to call themselves "hard guys," the rest of the student body calls them "greasers" and, even more disparagingly, "bobos." One "hard guy" at Utopia High who had lived the first fourteen years of his life on New York's Upper West Side, had this to say of Utopia's greaser element:

TONY. You talk about greasers and you talk about all that stuff, I used to live in the city for fourteen years, and . . . I would like to send some of these kids down to the city to see what it's really like. . . . They go in there one day and they [would] get their ass kicked. . . . There's no comparison . . .

LARKIN. What you're saying, then, is that this is small potatoes compared to the city, right?

T. Well, they're just some people tryin' to be what they're not.

L. And what is that? What are they trying to be?

T. People that they're not! They jus', you know, goin' around like they're tough, but they don't know what it's like to be in a place where you really have to be tough. . . .

L. In other words, what you are saying is that there's no beef behind the swagger?

T. True—all talk, no action . . . (Recorded March 31, 1976.)

The leather-jacketed greasers at Utopia High, then, are much less fearsome than the "hard guys" of the 1950s. When pushed to a confrontation, they are likely to deflect or even back down from it. The leader of the greasers playing dice in the hallway quoted in the first chapter told me that he and his pals were "the hardest guys in the school." Yet when a teacher asked him to be quiet, he and his buddies acted as if the teacher were a cop and mawkishly pretended that they were being threatened by a superior force. In another incident that occurred on the greasers' own turf, a black female student came up to two or three male greasers and about the same number of their female followers and found them sitting on the fenders of her car:

BLACK FEMALE STUDENT. Get off my car! I said, "Get off my car!" Shit! I didn't park it there for you to sit on! (*Unintelligible*) Get off my car!

MALE GREASER. You're not supposed to be parked here anyways.

B.F.S. I said, "Get the hell off my damn car!" I ain't parked this car for *nobody* to sit on. I'll park it where I want to park it, understand? (*Greasers mumble to themselves*) If you got some shit to say, say it to me ! (*Unintelligible*) If you don't like it, *too bad!* If I find a dent . . . I'm comin' after all your asses. (Recorded March 31, 1976.)

The male greasers were rendered speechless by this outburst, and the women were reduced to embarrassed giggles. Yet, they all moved off the car. About five minutes later, the black student returned with two female friends, got in the car, protesting that nobody could tell her where to park, and drove off.

The fascinating aspect of this confrontation is the fact that the greasers resorted to defending themselves in terms of the legitimate rule structure. The parking lot was for automobiles awaiting repair in the auto shop and not for student parking. The black student was illegally parked and was able to intimidate the greasers even though there was no doubt that she was in the wrong. If such an incident has occurred at a predominantly lower-class school, a racial riot might have ensued. (A similar incident sparked racial conflict at a neighboring school the previous year.) The greasers did not take baseball bats and bash out the windows of her car, nor did they even respond verbally to her obviously provocative remarks while she was present. After she left, one male greaser, who must have weighed 250 pounds and was over six feet tall, said, "Dumb nigger bitch," and one of the greaser women said, slightly awe-struck, "That's what you call 'Black Power.'"

The greasers do not seem to engage in much violence against their peers; however, they are a source of conflict within the school. It is common knowledge that most of the vandalism within the school is attributable to the greasers. The politicos view them as the greatest threat to the permissive atmosphere because they "abuse their freedom." The student leadership complained about them coming to dances and movies sponsored by student government and hanging out and milling around without really participating in the organized activity, but rather, using the event as a place to congregate, get drunk, smoke marijuana and cigarettes, and make a general nuisance of themselves. Because of this element, the student leaders complained, the sponsors would have to hire security police and have the event heavily chaperoned. In addition, it is the greasers who come to school drunk. Many of them use both marijuana and booze before they stumble onto campus. My observations seem to confirm popular sentiment: it was only in greaser's alley behind the shops that drunken students were observed.

In addition, the greasers and some of the freaks are prone to have trouble with the local police. According to the chief juvenile officer, the police department in Pleasant Valley spends ninety percent of its time on juvenile crime. The most common juvenile problems are drug abuse and vandalism (including petty theft). The freaks continually complain about being harassed by the local police for possession of marijuana, but it is the greasers who constitute the prime target of police activity, since they not only tend to be drug abusers, but also participate in acts of vandalism. As a matter of fact, one greaser confided to me that the center of his life was his conflicts with the police:

Two students are hanging out in the dreaded first-floor men's bathroom

LARKIN. Have any of you had an experience that really [was significant] . . . ?

STUDENT 1. Yea, a few. Here's a weird experience for you. Okay, it's just an experience. It was me and a bunch of my friends—thirteen of us. We're walking down ——— Road and we split up. Two of us took a short cut, me and another kid. And we met a drunk lady. So we yelled for our friends to come and the lady, she came out of the house, and she was yelling, "Looking for a fight, man?" and "Shut up, or I'll cut your throats." Anyways, so all my friends came and we start bustin' on her and she yells, "Touch me and you're dead!" So one of my friends hits her on the back of her head. (*The greaser listening to the story laughs*) Now, she started going nuts and the cops came and took us away. We jumped out of the car and ran when we [the police car] stopped. . . . [I] get in chases with the cops. A lot of chases. Every night, (*corrects himself*) every weekend we get in chases with the cops in summer and spring. They'll do anything to us when they catch us.

L. What kinds of things do they do to you?

S. 1. They handcuffed us a few times, one took a swing at us, swung back, you know. We don't take no shit.

STUDENT 2. Oh, yeah. Over the winter, we had fights with other towns. People from———[a nearby town]came and looked for fights. (Recorded May 19, 1976.)

The behavior of the greasers is viewed with alarm by the politicos, but the freaks seem to have a certain kind of sympathy for them, owing to their shared disaffection for authority and hierarchy. One freak told me that he could understand why the greasers vandalized the buildings, and that there were times when he felt the impulse to tear something apart. However, this is not to imply blanket endorsement of the nefarious activities of the greasers. Although they did not feel vulnerable to attack by greasers themselves, the freaks had witnessed greasers harassing and threatening ninth graders. They were shocked and disconcerted that they would pick on the younger and smaller kids in school and tended to think of them as bullies.

The greasers are predominantly from working-class backgrounds. There is no evidence that their families have suffered more divorces than those of the upper middle-class students; however, they do tend to live in single-parent households more frequently than their more affluent peers. In every case of single-parent households, the youth lives with his or her mother. The male students tend to be primarily interested in cars or motorcycles. Those with whom I talked were planning to work in a local automobile assembly plant, and like Eli Chinoy's automobile workers, shared the dream of owning their own shop or gas station (Chinoy, 1955). The female students who hang out with the greasers comtemplate graduation from high school with no firm plans—perhaps they will go to junior college, or take a job—but marriage is the ultimate goal. Though these women prior to the sexual revolution would have been described as "tramps," "sluts," or "skags" because of their open sexuality, such is not the case. The latter two words have been dropped from the adolescent vocabulary, and the term "tramp" is used for female students who cheat on their steadies.

The Blacks: Separate and Unequal

There are approximately seventy black students at Utopia High. Almost all of them live in a small ghetto in one of the townships that Utopia High serves. They, along with the greasers, form the academic lumpenproletariat of the school. All, with the exception of a few middle-class blacks, are to be found in the lowest two of the five program tracks of the school. For the most part, they are tolerated and ignored by the white students. The greasers, on the other hand, tend to regard them with suspicion and contempt, apparently sensing them as more of a threat to their relative status than the others. Although student attitudes toward the blacks range from liberal to redneck, most racism is displayed in sublimated form. The term "nigger" is bandied about by Utopia High students quite freely when they are with their peers and out of earshot of blacks. The behavior of the majority of blacks is looked down upon by the whites. The following unsolicited remarks were made by students who identified themselves as "freaks":

MALE STUDENT. For the most part, right now we are at the point where we have the ideas, you know, that we are going to revolve upon for practically the rest of our lives. You know, the way we think and how we look at things. You know, we *know* how we are going to be. I know how I look at people. Like I don't just, you know, say about a person, you know, look at the way they look, you know, they're definitely not my type. I find out how a person is first before I make any judgment on him. I guess I prejudge people to an extent.

FEMALE STUDENT. Everybody does, you can't avoid it.

M.S. But, I mean like, . . . I can truthfully say that all but ten black kids in this school are jerk-offs.

F.S. (*Breaks in*) And that's why we think the blacks at this school are so mean.

M.S. And I can say that without feeling guilty about it because it's true, you know. They hang out on the stairs, you know . . .

F.S. (*Interrupts*) It's not because they're black, but because that's the way they are.

M.S. Yeah. It's not that they are black people, it's . . .

F.S. There isn't that many. . . . There are also white kids that goof around who are just as obnoxious as they are.

LARKIN. What do you mean by obnoxious?

F.S. I don't know they just sorta stand there.

M.S. (*Breaking in*) Between lunches there's fifteen minutes between two lunches and they hang on the stairs down to the cafeteria and if you are walking through there by yourself, they try to trip you and push you and stuff. They hassle you—they're a bunch of jerks.

F.S. They say the upstairs door is locked [when it isn't]. (*Laughs*)

M.S. That's class!

F.S. We do the same thing. We gotta admit people go through the stairway where we hang out, they must think we're the biggest jerk-offs. (Recorded March 22, 1976.)

The female student, in the course of conversation realizing that they were engaging in the same behavior as the blacks, added some redeeming value to their patently racist observations. Yet, implicit in the minds of the white students is the notion that negatively sanctioned behavior is *black* behavior and whites will, on occasion, stoop to acting like blacks. Perhaps the most blatant example of such thinking came from a male student, who, in a surge of egalitarianism suggested that not all "niggers" are blacks:

MALE STUDENT 1. By this time, you are at the point where you have more freedom to think for yourself, but you have come down with the ideas everyone else has given to you, you know. Through grammar school, you know. Like, it's basically how . . . the way I think now. I mean, . . . [that's] how I'm going to think for the rest of my life. You know, the way I look at people, and how I think about them. Whether I say, "Oh, he's black, he's a nigger." I find out what kind of person he is first.

MALE STUDENT 2. Even white people are niggers. I know a lot of white people who act like niggers. Like look at ———. ——— is a nigger.

FEMALE STUDENT. He is not! Drop dead.

M.S. 2. The kid's a nigger.

M.S. 1. I thought he was white.

F.S. I thought he was white, too.

MALE STUDENT 3. He's not using nigger in that sense of the word.

M.S. 2. That kid, ———, is a *nigger*. (Recorded March 24, 1976.)

The official line is that the school is integrated and there is intermingling between the races. Such coexistence is determined by several hard and fast rules. First, there is almost no interracial dating, though there is no spoken rule against it. When asked, several students could only think of one case of interracial dating. Second, almost all interracial friendships are between middle-class blacks and their white friends. The working-class blacks do not seem to have many white friends themselves. The exception to this rule is that one or two of the black male students have adopted the "greaser" mode and hang around the parking lot behind the auto shop. Third, tokenism is allowed. To reaffirm the liberal image of the school, several blacks are displayed in prominent positions. The single most important example is the student body president, a middle-class young black man. Other points of visibility are in the traditionally black endeavors, namely the football, basketball, baseball, and track teams.

Racial relations at Utopia High are characterized as good by both blacks and whites. However, such evaluations of racial relationships are relative rather than absolute, since a neighboring school recently had a full-blown race riot. There are several factors that allow for peaceable relations between blacks and whites at Utopia: First, the small number of blacks in the school does not threaten the dominance of whites. Thus, blacks can participate freely in all political and cultural activities of the school without creating fear of a black takeover. Second, none of the blacks attending Utopia High can really be characterized as lower-class, since the ghetto in the township is at least two steps above the poverty-stricken ghetto in the large city near Pleasant Valley. This makes for a certain congruency of social-class background that alleviates tension. Thus, whites don't taunt blacks, nor do blacks intimidate whites or extort them for lunch money. Third, there are enough middle-class blacks in school to provide exemplars for both white and black students and to mediate between the races. Fourth, because the administration operates on the principles of democratic participation and lenient rule enforcement, pressures do not build up over repressiveness that often become vented in interracial conflict. Fifth, much of the student leadership is provided by Jews, who themselves have a history of oppression and tend to be somewhat sympathetic to the problems of the blacks. For example, the black student body president could never have been elected without considerable white support, the vanguard of which came from the Jews who are the single most important student group in the governance structure. Finally, the blacks themselves are quite willing to overlook the racism of their peers. The following segment of an interview with several black students near the stairs where they hang out, illustrates this:

LARKIN. Do you find that white students are prejudiced . . . ?

MALE STUDENT 1. Well, a *few* are. Some are.

MALE STUDENT 2. Not all of 'em.

M.S. 1. Not all of 'em. What you do is just look up on that wall over there. . . . It says stuff like "Niggers are not good," and "Blacks are slaves," and mess like that. But, you see, it doesn't phase us, you know. We just let it go ahead, 'cause it's *nothing*. (Recorded May 3, 1976.)

There is some tension between the races at Utopia High; however, it is managed by mutual restraint as evidenced by these black students. There also is restraint on the part of whites even in the face of provocation, as in the parking lot incident between the black female student and the "greasers."

THE PROCESS OF SUBCULTURAL DEVELOPMENT

One aspect of youth culture is its tendency to generate rapid subculture development and equally rapid decline. For example, in the 1960s, youth culture evolved through four successive phases with each succeeding phase shorter than the previous one. (For a detailed explanation of the youth culture of the 1960s, see Daniel Foss and Ralph Larkin [1976].) In 1960, the "New Left" phase developed along with the civil rights movement lasting five years. It was superceded by the hippie phase which lasted from 1965 until 1967, when the "freak-radical" phase (1967–1969) emerged as psychedelic posters came down and those of Che and Mao went up, "love" was replaced with "armed love," acid rock gave way to hard rock, and be-ins were replaced by confrontations. On the heels of the "freak-radical" phase came the "Wood-stock-Aquarian" phase which lasted from mid-1969 to early 1970. Hard rock was replaced by folk rock, vegetarianism and communal living came into vogue, and the cultural ideal of "together" (consolidation of the self in a posture of revolt) was replaced by "mellow" (calm luxuriating in simple joys).

It was noted above that each of the subcultures at Utopia High has ties to prior phases of youth culture development, even though cultural inversions have taken place to cope with the reality of the 1970s. At the time of the research, the freak subculture is in the process of expanding, while the politicos are stabilized. Both the greasers and the freaks are growing as a result of the increasing disaffection of youth from the larger society and the demands of hierarchy. The freaks are expressing middle-class modes of disaffection (skipping classes, marijuana use, and verbal abuse of those in positions of authority) while the greasers manifest working-class modes (violations of rules because they exist, interpersonal violence, cultural retrogression, vandalism, and physical confrontation with authorities).

Even though there is no evidence that the jock/rah-rah crowd is increasing in numbers, its power has increased over the past year, since it embodied the aspirations of a growing number of adults in the community. As a result of the budget crisis at the beginning of the year, the sports teams were forced to exist on smaller budgets. The policy of reducing investment in interscholastic sports generated heated opposition in the community. A watch-dog group has formed that has been pressuring the high school principal and the Board of Education into expending a greater percentage of the budget on sports teams. There is considerable discontent in the community over the win-loss record of the football team, which has traditionally been poor. In the midst of this regression to the ethos of the 1950s, the jock/rah-rah crowd is the beneficiary of community pressure for greater investment in their activities by the school district.

The student subcultures apparently expand through mitosis. The basic building block of the subculture is the clique. It ranges in size from three to eight members. Once it expands beyond its ability to maintain easy face-to-face relationships among its members, it will split. The splitting process is not conflictual, but based on personal affinity, accessibility of peers, and common interests. As cliques expand and split, members of the crowd still maintain contact, but it is less personalized. As the process of growth occurs, subculturalization takes place. The group gets together at larger events such as concerts, parties, and dances which have general appeal and reinforce subcultural cohesion. Sarah, a member of the freak subculture, related the following:

SARAH. Our group started in the beginning of the year.

LARKIN. This is the group of people I met out in the back?

S. Yeah, uh-huh. And it has grown and split. And each of those groups has grown and split. So we're now quadruple the size, but in more individual groups. We've sort of narrowed ourselves down. It's like choosing—you start out with a big bunch of things and selecting, and then getting all you select together and refining it even more, so you can really be with the people you really want to be with.

L. Does the original group have any common interests? Does the whole group which has quadrupled get together, or is it relatively fragmented into a clique structure?

S. Well, it's not really a clique structure. It's not nearly as bad as junior high was. [In] junior high the groups were so tight, you couldn't even go past without feeling nervous. When you see a group of kids [in junior high] in the hall, you try to go the other way. Not because they would harm you in any way—you just felt, "This is their group. I shouldn't be walking by them."

L. You felt a boundary.

S. Yeah, you definitely felt strong boundaries; really strong boundaries. But here it's much looser. I mean twelfth graders mix in with eleventh and tenth graders, which was never done in junior high. Ninth, eighth, and seventh graders were absolutely divided.

I think it's a lot better here. It's not so tight that you feel uncomfortable when you go into somebody else's group if you know someone there. You know, there are floaters—people who go around to just any particular group they feel like that particular day. And, you just go in and you start talking and it doesn't matter. Nobody really cares. I think that's really good. It's quite an improvement over junior high.

Thus, within the subculture there is an acceptance of members from other cliques, so long as that person's behavior conforms to subcultural expectations. Although it is an improvement over the cliquishness that was characteristic of Sarah's junior high school experience, it has its drawbacks as well. Behavioral expectations are not articulated in the form of a code, but they nevertheless have a powerful impact on the behavior of its members. For not only does the subculture provide a ready-made group of friends and acquaintances, it also establishes barriers to authentic communication among members. Because the subcultural expectations are unarticulated while the demand for conformity is extremely strong, relationships are characterized by David Riesman's (1955) "other-directedness." This is true even among the freaks, who draw their legacy from the freaks of the 1960s, who attempted to revolt against inauthenticity and hypocrisy in personal relationships. Yet Sarah, a sage critic of the behavior of herself and her peers, admitted the following in reference to what she and her peers do:

SARAH. You talk, but you talk superficially—you know, about dumb things like, um, "Oh, I really got high last Friday night," or something like that.

LARKIN. So the conversation tends to dwell on what? Externals?

S. Yeah. Very external, superficial things that don't really matter.

L. You go to movies and talk about movies and stuff like that?

S. Right. Yeah. Or, or how you are doing in school . . . or about some teacher you have.

L. You intrigue me, because what I think I hear you saying is that in most cases, students around here tend to hide themselves from each other through superficiality. . . . [T]here's this kind of external you. It's a facade and it's cool . . . and it does the right things and listens to the right music and all that. And then there's this inside of you which has feelings and emotions and—

S. Different tastes, even. (*Completing my thought*) I mean that if I told anybody that I *love* Gilbert and Sullivan. I think it's really great music. But it's just not said. Or that I like a certain piece of classical music. It isn't said. And you *do* have to put up a big front especially here at [Utopia], 'cause you have—you feel you have a new chance to start out fresh. And if you didn't have any friends before, as I never did until the eighth grade and ninth grade—'till I started smoking [marijuana] and I started fixing myself up. Because I used to be unbearable . . . I used to correct kids' grammar and things like that. *Awful* things. But you do have to put up a big front to change yourself. You do have to change yourself if you want friends. Because, no matter what anybody says, peer pressure is there, *and you have to follow it to survive.* [Emphasis mine.] . . . It's not a very idealistic thing, like you should be, you are supposed to be yourself, you're supposed to be an individual. There are few people who can dare do that. And you have to start way at the beginning to be an individual. You can't suddenly decide to be an individual.

I Mean, the kids around here, who wear long flowy weird kinds of clothes who are extremely intellectual or something like that and don't think about anything else—they've been doing it for so long, you don't even notice. But when somebody suddenly starts coming apart [from the group], you know, being his own self, being what he wants to do, they suffer. They suffer a lot. Because peer pressure is one of the biggest things that influences—

L. Coming apart? . . .

S. Coming apart from the group. From your peers. Becoming what you want to be.

But it just can't be done. There's no practical way to do that and still have friends, unless you make a very small elite group. So it's difficult to make friends. You have to put up a front all the time. After awhile you sort of get into the swing of it and you just don't notice it any more and your real you starts to disappear. It's kinda scary sometimes. I took classical piano lessons for ten years. . . . And lately I haven't gotten near it to practice at all. [I still take lessons, but] I'm not as interested, and now, um, I've put up that facade that, that front to everyone, because I want to show people, "Hey, look at me. I'm cool, you know. I smoke pot. I'm one of the okay people."

L. Mm-hmm. So smokin' dope and drinking and going to parties becomes part of a struggle for acceptance.

S. Yeah. You have to *do* certain things, you have to give up a lot of individuality if you want to be with a group. . . . A group is singular. It's not really that much composed of separate people. Different bodies, but pretty much the same mind. (Recorded April 26, 1976.)

Sarah's admission that she was lonely and without friends until the eighth grade was surprising since she seemed so well integrated into the freak subculture. In addition, her admission that her behavior among her peers was merely a front was equally as disturbing. It was obvious that she had learned her lessons well, since she was observed in the midst of the group, cheerily talking with friends who obviously liked her and seemed concerned about her. Yet, her claim that a front was necessary for survival laid bare the underpinnings of her experience. The peer group enforces demands for conformity. Those who find themselves in conflict with those demands suffer. Before the reader assumes that this is an isolated case, we might recall the male student who wanted to be honest and despaired at the fact that he saw all his associates immerse themselves in the same hypocrisies as their parents. (See pp. 74–75.)

The adolescent peer group not only reflects the larger society (and, to some extent, caricatures it), but is also the crucible in which the psyche of the young is tempered. It shapes the experience of these young people and generates a *geist*, or cultural theme. The *geist* of the 1970s is that of external conformity and internal isolation.

THE SILENT MAJORITY

Most of the students attending Utopia High are not intellectuals, politicos, jock/rah-rahs, greasers, freaks or blacks. At first, they appear as an undifferentiated mass, which comprises the bulk of the student body. They are middle-class, come to school in the morning, attend classes, return home in the evening, do their homework (most of the time), watch a little television or go out with a small group of steady friends (called cliques), date, attend dances, work on automobiles (for the male students), look forward to summer when the beaches are warm, and so on. Yet, this group can be further differentiated. Many of them are involved in various interest groups on campus. Small clusters of students ranging from three or four to ten or twelve members can be found hanging around places like the gym, ceramics lab, each of the shops, library, printing lab, mathematics lab, and the audio-visual center. During the commons periods, before and after school, these students will gravitate to their favorite place to work on a project they are in the middle of or just shoot the bull with like-minded friends.

None of these groups is large enough to be considered a subculture, especially since none of them generates a mythos beyond their own membership. In addition, none of these interest groups has direct implications for personal identity, even though such interests may be pointing in the direction of a future career. Students do not label themselves on the basis of such interest groups, and, frequently, such interest groups may pander to subcultural proclivities. For example, several freaks hang around the art department and work on macrame. They think of themselves as "freaks," not artists.

Perhaps the most well-formed and easily identifiable of these interest groups is the math lab cluster. It includes about ten or twelve students (mostly males) who hang out in the math lab where the school computer is located. They combine work with pleasure, writing up programs for their computer programming course, solving math homework problems, playing computer games, and working as lab aides. The school had apparently received a federal grant to build the math lab and install the computer. There was money left over, so they hired some of the students who are math whizzes to help a teacher staff the lab and watch the computer. The pay was minimal—$1.50 per hour, well below the minimum wage of $2.30. However, when the budget crisis resulted in a reduction to $ .50 per hour, the lab aides developed a case of acute irresponsibility, resulting in a small scandal and their firing en masse. The lab assistants were accused of mislaying programs, running their programs before they would serve others, and programming the computer to use obscene language.

Of course, affinities transcend the boundaries of the school. Some of the Jewish students are members of church-sponsored youth groups. The local Lutheran Church sponsors a youth program that includes regularly scheduled dances "religiously" attended by Jews and Catholics as well as Protestants. The dances rank along with football games in their ability to draw both black and white students from the high school. In addition, there is the obligatory hamburger joint that is the local hangout. Although it is frequented by various groups of students, it is a favorite with the greasers. It is allegedly one of the best places around to meet a member of the opposite sex for sexual purposes. When the weather is good, the "reservation," a nearby forest preserved in its natural state, quickly becomes populated by young people from miles around, including Utopia High students.

Thus, the social system of Utopia High students is highly subculturized and fragmented. In the wake of the movement of the 1960s, social class, ethnicity, and youth cultural heritage have emerged as barriers to cohesion among the young people at Utopia High. The politicos complain of the apathy of the masses, the freaks complain of the elitism of the politicos, the blacks complain of the prejudice of the whites, the jock/rah-rahs complain about lack of school spirit, and the greasers, whose complaints tend to be articulated through action rather than words, fight the class struggle against their more affluent peers. Meanwhile, the majority of students go through the motions of everyday existence untouched by a subculture. Many complain about not being able to get it together and they fondly remember a student strike in junior high school that spontaneously took place and that made everyone feel *together;* and they remember how, for a few short hours, the teachers and administration were rendered impotent; and how, all of a sudden, all the barriers were transcended and they all felt the bond of brother- and sisterhood.

NOTES

1. Subcultural affinity is manifested by sharing a vocabulary, participating in activities together, hangingout as a group, and choosing friends primarily from within the group. This was certainly true of the jock/rah-rahs and the "freaks." However, the politicos, with a few exceptions, tended to know each

other on a more formal basis, with most relationships being based on working together. Thus, they tended to be more of a work group than a subculture, often picking friends and lovers from outside the politicos.

2. The politicos were the easiest to estimate, since they occupied formal positions in the student power structure. The estimate includes the student body officers, class officers, house officers, participants in various student body and governance committees, and the editorial staff of the newspaper and yearbook. The jock/rah-rah crowd is most problematical since not all participants in sports activities are members of the jock/rah-rah crowd. Thus, the core of the crowd was estimated by looking at the size of the letterman's club, cheerleaders, pep squad, and those students who hung around the gym. The intellectual crowd was estimated in two ways: Roz, an intellectual, was asked about the size of the intellectual crowd. This estimate was corroborated by two teachers who were asked. In addition, all estimates were verified by several students who read the manuscript.

4

PAEAN TO DIONYSUS: SEX AND DRUGS

One pill makes you larger
And one pill makes you small.
And the ones that mother gives you
Don't do anything at all.
Go ask Alice
When she's ten feet tall.

And if you go chasing rabbits
And you know you're going to fall,
Tell 'em a hookah smoking caterpillar
Has given you the call.
Call Alice
When she was just small.

When men on the chessboard
Get up and tell you where to go.
And you've just had some kind of mushroom
And your mind is moving low.
Go ask Alice
I think she'll know.

When logic and proportion
Have fallen sloppy dead,
And the White Knight is talking backwards
And the Red Queen's lost her head

Remember what the dormouse said:
"Feed your head.
Feed your head.
Feed you head."

The Jefferson Airplane, "White Rabbit," 1967

I kissed you once, will I kiss you again?
Be certain with sex and you'll always have friends,
Your glands wanna freak, your hands wanna speak,
And your mind slips away at the peak.

Todd Rundgren, "Number 1 Lowest
Common Denominator," 1973

THE SEXUAL AND CONSCIOUSNESS REVOLUTIONS

The dissident youth culture of the 1960s spawned the sexual[1] and the consciousness revolutions. To address ourselves to the youth of the seventies without consideration of the roles of sex and drugs in their lives would be a grievous omission. For not only are they important in the lives of most of the students at Utopia High, they are the be-all and end-all of existence for a significant minority. Like their elders, the attitudes and behavior of most students in the realms of sex and drug use are extremely complex and varied, while at the same time highly circumscribed and ritualized. On the face of it, these attitudes and behaviors seem to be a mass of contradictions and confusion. The reason for such a state of affairs can be found in the contradictions between public ideology and private practice concerning the issues of drugs and sex in the larger society and the fact that the youth of America were the ones to provide the vanguards for the sexual and consciousness revolutions.

With the decline of dissidence in the 1970s, sexual permissiveness and drug pushing has been incorporated into commodity advertising. Meanwhile, we have witnessed the simultaneous resurrection of the conditions of material scarcity among young people. Corporate executives, high government officials, and juvenile authorities are attempting to control the behavior of the young through increased surveillance and exhortations to reinstate heavy-handed disciplinary measures. Thus, for most students at Utopia High, drugs and sex are both desired and feared and are the sources of ecstasy and despair, not to mention trouble. Although youth culture is protected by its insularity and isolation from adults, sexual and drug behaviors are the ones most often surveilled by local authorities and parents. Once laid bare, they can be the source of intense conflict and pain.

Since sex and drug indulgences are almost totally confined to the peer group (only a small minority of students will drink, smoke marijuana, or speak frankly of their sexual experiences with their parents), parents and school authorities tend to ignore, overlook, and tacitly avoid awareness of the sexual and drug habits of the young. For the most part, there is a conspiracy of silence about drugs and sex. Yet, every so often, a drug bust, pregnancy, venereal disease, or an intrusion into the world of the young by the parent, by accident or by design, will provoke a confrontation which usually leaves the younger and weaker participant less happy and serves as a reminder that he or she does not have freedom, but privilege.

One aspect of the youth revolt of the 1960s was the attempt to remove the last vestiges of bourgeois constraints on sexual behavior. Freakified youth of the 1960s, claiming that straight society was prudish about sex and fearful of the impulses of the body, set about liberating their own sexuality from those restrictions. Along with drugs (liberation of the mind), the full exploration of the erogenous zones was seen as a method of freeing oneself from the constraints of the dessicated sexuality of the adult world, where gray flannel suits and sublimation were coupled with the free-flowing anxieties of the sexually repressed housewife. Many adults pooh-poohed the sexual revolution of the sixties and young people's claim to have rediscovered sex by pointing out that they were the inventors of sex in the back seat of cars; however, they were not prepared for the varieties of sexual exploration that occurred. The 1960s featured new directions in public nudity and sex, group sex beyond the confines of the sexist "gang-bang" in which males line up to have sex with a single woman, increased toleration of homosexuality, and exploration of sex while under the influence of mind-expanding drugs. In the latter case, LSD, mescaline, and marijuana were extremely popular in generating intense sexual experiences. In addition, there was DMT, commonly called the "love drug," which increased the subjective awareness of feelings of romantic love while making orgasm next to impossible; amylnitrite, the heart stimulant which lasts a minute or two and which intensifies the feelings of the lovers exponentially when taken slightly prior to orgasm (subsequently used with great frequency in the homosexual subculture of the 1970s); and in the early 1970s, sopors or Quaaludes, which also intensify sexual feelings.

Concomitant with the exploration of sexuality beyond the

confines of dominant notions of "normality" was the emergence of feminism. In part a rejection of sexism by the New Left, it continued the sexual revolution on the political plane. On the one hand, feminists attempted to throw off the dominance of males in their lives as they strove for self-determination. On the other, they attempted to forge a new social order based on the vision of "sisterhood." For some, this meant radical lesbianism ("How can you sleep with the enemy?"), while for others it meant entering into sexual attachments with men on equal footing.

However, once the dissidence had subsided, the sexual revolution became codified into a sexual competitive struggle, which had been extended to include both younger and older people and has intensified through the increase in circulation of sexual commodities during the early 1970s. Advertising had always used sex as a device to sell commodities; however, it now propagandized sex itself. No longer was marriage akin to sexual monopoly and withdrawal from the sexual marketplace, but rather, it was a way-stage before reentry into the marketplace as nearly 40 percent of all marriages ended in divorce. The marriage decision (and the decision to have children) was postponed as people returned repeatedly to the sexual marketplace to reestablish their sexual value. Perhaps the new ideology can best be expressed in an ad for *Cosmopolitan* magazine in *The New York Times*, September 29, 1976:

> Sometimes when I've been in love—three times at age 26—and things have been a little rough, I say no more of *that* . . . I'll just stay friends with a man . . . a cool and collected loving *friend*. Hah! I have about as much chance of keeping that resolve as I do of staying on a permanent diet, getting all my Christmas cards addressed by Halloween and not *breathing* for a couple of days. I'm about to plunge *again* and I'm hopeful (he's terrific!) but not totally confident. My favorite magazine says *plunge* . . . life isn't *supposed* to be safe—only memorable! I love that magazine. I guess you could say I'm That COSMOPOLITAN Girl.

Is the Cosmo "Girl" a swinging single, gay divorcee, or merry widow? The use of such a pitch to sell magazines to women in the 1950s would have been incomprehensible. Any attempt to do so would have been scandalous to the point of evoking widespread outcry.

These cultural shifts are not without their effects on the students at Utopia High. Sex and drugs are an accepted part of their lives—if not necessary to them. Sexual attitudes, especially concerning feminine behavior, have radically changed since the 1960s. Feminism has had its impact as young women challenge the assumptions by males of their "natural" docility and sub-servience. For a significant minority of students, sex has been incorporated into "meaningful relationships" which are per-sonally intense, but are not necessarily directed toward marriage.

LOVE AND MARRIAGE

Central to the popular ideology of the 1950s was that Mr. and Miss Right would find each other, get married, settle down, buy a house, and raise a family. Sexual relations among adolescents were directed toward marriage. Young women were the gate-keepers of the marital path. Oftentimes, sexual intercourse fol-lowed pledges of maritial vows, and, in many cases, trapped couples into marriages that might not have occurred except for the fact that they had engaged in intercourse which sanctified the relationship and committed them inexorably to the marriage bed. For most young people in the fifties, sexual congress implied lifelong commitments unless a male had intercourse with a prostitute or with a peer who was free with her sexual favors and was consequently classified as a "tramp," "slut," "nympho-maniac," "whore," "easy lay," or otherwise stigmatized for her sexual behavior. In those days, males made distinctions between "nice" girls who were eligible for marriage and "good" girls who could be exploited sexually, but were not marriageable because of their lack of virginity, which was a prime criterion for marital eligibility among young women. Thus, most premarital sexual intercourse occurred between couples who planned to get mar-ried. When such liaisons broke up, the young woman suffered much more than the young man, since she had given him her most prized possession. Once she reentered the sexual market-place, she would have to become extremely circumspect in her relations with other young men. Since she had already lost her prime value, she could be stigmatized as a non-virgin which would lead to her devaluation and exploitation by males who perceived her as a sexual object whom they could plunder at will. Pregnancy was another concern that made sex in the 1950s a delicate affair. Many females were kept in ignorance about their bodies, and contraception was primarily a masculine respon-sibility. The birth control pill (which provided impetus to the sexual revolution of the 1960s) was not available in the 1950s, nor were alternative safe methods, such as the diaphragm, available to unmarried women. Condoms were the most available contra-ceptive devices around; yet, the purchaser was required to ask the local pharmacist for them—a prospect which generated such anxiety that adolescents would travel to places where their iden-tity was not known to buy them.

The 1970s present youth with a much different situation. Sexual and contraceptive information is much more readily available. With over one million divorces per year, the doubling of the divorce rate since 1964, and the extension of youthful dependence well beyond high school graduation, marriage does not assume the immediacy that it once did. I did not encounter a single student who planned to get married upon graduation from Utopia High School. When queried about marriage, most stu-dents stated that they would like to get married—eventually. Sarah put it this way:

LARKIN. Do you feel any sense of betrayal [by a boyfriend who dropped her for another girl]?

SARAH. For the other girl?

L. Yes.

S. I think that's a lot of bullshit, because we're not married. I mean, we're just kids. . . . It's dumb when girls act like they're jealous and very protective. Save that for when you're an old hag and nag at your husband. I don't know. I don't think a lot of girls feel that way though. I do. A lot of girls are really protective and I think that's really dumb. It's really stupid—they're trying to act a lot older than they really are. (Recorded April 26, 1976.)

There is still possessiveness in the sexual relations among Utopia High students, but it is apparently not due to the necessity for young women to protect themselves from revelations about their virginity or lack of it. Surprisingly, virginity has ceased to be an important issue among students at Utopia High. Rather than affecting the reputation of women in terms of their ability to snare a husband, it seems to be an item of curiosity more than anything else. I asked a group of students about attitudes toward virginity:

LARKIN. Tell me, among your peers, what is the greater fear—to be a virgin or be pregnant?

PAUL. Be pregnant.

JANE. Be pregnant. Yes.

P. Yes, definitely.

L. But, is virginity a negative thing these days?

P. In a peer situation it is. In a personal situation, like, in my own personal group of friends I know one or two people who are virgins—males—who are really unhappy about that for their own self-image. But as far as the group goes, there's no visible pressure to be experienced that I see.

L. How about . . . the women. Is there pressure for you to get rid of your virginity as fast as possible, maintain it, or is it a deep dark secret, or what?

BECKY. To the extent that it's not even talked about that much, really. I mean where I hang around—like you say, it depends on the group. In some groups you would really be an outcast, you know.

J. I think people want to know whether you are or you aren't. But I don't think that it's like a social pressure that you have to . . .

GARY. That all depends on where you are. Like the group that you say always talks about sex, they say, "I'm thinking about taking out this girl, but can I get her?" That's like the main priority. [They say,] "Someone else did [take her out] and she doesn't give, we don't want her." You'd be surprised . . . (Recorded March 29, 1976.)

Thus, the sexual revolution seems to have reversed the pressure on young women. In the 1950s, they were caught in the position of withholding sex in the face of masculine demands. If they succumbed to the demand without protecting their marketability, they were relegated to the trash heap (e.g., "trashy women"). In the seventies, they are expected to accede to masculine demands or else they *lose* value in the sexual marketplace. Virginity for women at Utopia High is a mark of excessive prudery or evidence of low market value. For men it is simply an indication of poor marketability. Notice that in the contradictory statement of Paul, he both admits and denies that there is peer pressure to become sexually experienced. Yet he is very much aware that lack of sexual experience on the part of male students is cause for loss of self-esteem. At Utopia High, inherent in the status struggle is the quest for sexual competence. Such evaluations are more insidious than overt, thus accounting for the confusions. Paul states that there is no *visible* peer pressure, but nevertheless observes the consequences among his friends who do not measure up to the norm. Students at Utopia High generally agree that virginity is not a valuable asset to a person in terms of sexual attractiveness. I asked a female student whether people would hide the fact that they were a virgin. She responded with, "There's nobody to hide it from." Virginity, then, has ceased to be an important issue in the marriage market, with the possible exception that it may be looked upon as evidence of sexual unattractiveness.

Yet, there is a basic confusion about sex among Utopia High students. Sexual behavior is so private that there is very little sharing of information. Those students who "always talk of sex" seem to do so only in the most ambiguous of terms. One's own sexual experiences are the province of personal existence and are not usually shared with others. Thus the sexual lives of peers are shrouded in mystery and each individual is pretty much left to his or her own devices to learn sexual behavior and to deduce what others are doing. Although it is obvious that sexual information is shared, the very sharing is as intimate as the act itself. When sexual behavior becomes public knowledge, it is almost always in terms of labels, e.g., so-and-so is suspected of being a homo-sexual,———is an easy lay,———is a "night hog" (promiscuous), and so forth.

THE BIRDS AND THE BEES

When Utopia High students attempt to reflect upon the way they learned about sex, they become somewhat perplexed. It seems that a good portion of it is absorbed subliminally. To quote one student, "It's almost like osmosis. You can't remember when someone sat down and told you specifically what and all, but you just know." Although the peer group is probably the most relied-upon source for sexual information, parents, school, and the mass media, including pornography, are also important sources. Pornography is often used as visual aids to the peer group, much like the "pillow books" (graphic illustrations of couples in sexual congress in myriads of positions) which the Japanese used to instruct the young in sexual practices. It is clear that most Pleasant Valley parents tend to avoid discussing sex with their children, but there are many who do, especially with their daughters. Oftentimes, parents are the sources of practical advice: talking about what to expect upon menstruation, informing them about contraceptive devices. Parents may admonish their children to "be careful," but it is rare that parents in Pleasant Valley will overtly attempt to suppress the sexual life of their children. However, when it does occur, this suppression can be quite brutal. We will discuss such parental behavior below (see p. 107). Sometimes attempts by parents to instruct their children on sexual behavior can border on the ludicrous. One male student told me the following:

> I have a friend whose father really embarrassed the hell out of him. He took him to a drugstore and he said, screaming at the top of his voice, "Here's a rubber!" He's buying it for him in the middle of

this store and everybody's looking at him and he's trying to hide his face. (Recorded March 31, 1976.)

The school helps to fill in the gaps in the sexual education of the students in the health course. The students claim that most of the sex education material is pretty well known by the time the school gets around to presenting it, yet they sometimes find out something new.

Sexual knowledge is obtained through the process of "learning by doing." Most sexual experimentation occurs at parties. Introduction to sex usually begins in the junior high school years. Because sex and parties in Pleasant Valley are so highly intertwined, the party structure must be outlined. They are held at the homes of young people when the parents leave for an evening or a weekend. Usually nobody knows about a party until a few hours before the event. When a person finds out that the parents are going to be out of the house, he or she will begin calling friends and inviting them over. A telephone tree quickly develops as friends call other friends. On any given weekend, there may be several parties on Friday and Saturday nights. Many students will hop from one party to the next. It is quite common to have a certain amount of flow between parties. The average party includes about 35 persons. It becomes common knowledge to members of the particular subculture (freaks, greasers, jock/rah-rahs, but not necessarily the politicos). Teenagers arrive at the party house bringing liquor and pot; they set up a record player, turn on the television, sit around and talk, dance, and couples will go off into the bedrooms for trysts.

Sexual behavior among the youth in Pleasant Valley is highly stereotyped and follows a definite pattern, varying only with increased age and intimacy among couples. A very small minority said they had been involved in group sex. Although some sex did occur in the back seats of cars, several students told the author that it did not occur very often. There are at least two reasons for this: first, it is much easier to get caught in a car, especially since the police know the lovers' lanes in the area and surveil them with great dispatch and alacrity; and second, the party structure provides a much more comfortable atmosphere and greater provisions for privacy. Because of the relative inexperience in sexual behavior, the young people begin their sexual explorations following the prescriptions of a well-organized system. Sarah revealed the system to me (because of the delicacy of the situation the interview is presented in its entirety, complete with repeated phrases):

LARKIN. Well, how did this [petting] occur? Was it with boyfriends or was it at parties or . . .

SARAH. Yeah, with boyfriends. (*Pauses*) At parties. (*Giggles*)

L. It usually took place at parties?

S. What?

L. Your petting usually took place at parties?

S. Yeah.

L. I hate to be intimate, but, jeez, I gotta know.

S. That's all right.

L. Well, what would you do sexually with each other?

S. Umm. I don't know how to explain that. I know a kind of a—I should explain, like there's a system.

L. A system?

S. No. Not exactly a system. It's called, I don't know, like I don't know if it was in the fifties or the sixties or what. But right now it's like first base, second base, third base, and so on.

L. Oh, okay. That's interesting. Okay, so there is an informal sort of—now "home" is sexual intercourse, right?

S. What?

L. Home.

S. Yeah.

L. Now okay. So in other words people have this informal system that has been set up. In other words, when you get to first base, second base, third base *with her*, it's usually male-oriented, right?

S. Uhhhhh.

L. Or is it?

S. Yeah. It is.

L. Okay, so tell me about these bases.

S. Well, first base is just making out. Second base is petting and third base is petting below the waist.

L. Let me ask you something. Is this what guys do to girls or are girls actively involved in sex? Does this take the form of masturbating a guy or giving him head.

S. Sometimes. Not usually.

L. Not usually, so it's something a guy does to a girl?

S. Yeah.

(Recorded April 26, 1976.)

The "baseball sex" system, then, allows the sexual novices a framework on which they can rely so that they can approach a new situation that is highly charged with anxiety with a certain notion of how to proceed. In addition, it prescribes the sex roles with its implicit assumption of active males and passive females. Also implicit in the baseball system is the time-honored notion that the male is the "batter" and tries to "score," while the girl is cast in the role of "umpire," controlling how far he gets. In that sense, things haven't changed much. The decision to have sexual intercourse is still the burden of the female while there is increased pressure for her to submit to the demands of the male. Since this is the case, it is also usually up to the woman to take care of contraception. Sarah, unbeknownst to her parents, has a diaphragm. She had lost her virginity at fifteen and a half years, two months prior to the interview. Although her case was unusual in that she was seduced by a man twice her age while on vacation, she had a rather common experience faced by women her age; her period was late, she panicked and ran to a gynecologist for a test, which was negative, and immediately had herself fitted for a diaphragm. If she had been pregnant and her parents had found out, her world would have caved in since her parents are strict and her father has beaten her on several occasions. The week or two she spent in absolute dread sobered her to the necessity of taking contraception into her own hands. Sarah's experience is not unique. In talking with Utopia High students about sex, young women continually voiced concern over the increased consequences of sex for themselves. Said one, "It [sex] is different with a guy. They just pick themselves up and leave. . . . I know a lot of guys who just pick themselves up from their girl friends and take off. You know, they got the girl pregnant and they *left*." (Recorded April 26, 1976.)

SEXISM AND THE SEXUAL-COMPETITIVE STRUGGLE

We have already alluded to the sexual marketplace and the intensification of the sexual competitive struggle. The basic relationship between males and females has not really changed over time, even though attitudes have relaxed and sexual intercourse is more or less accepted behavior for high school students these days. Yet in the marketplace, the women are still the supply and the men still demand. Increased permissiveness has put more pressure on women to increase supply and has lessened sanctions for doing so. Thus, there is some credence to the claim of some feminists that the sexual revolution was a male conspiracy to satisfy their desires without much consideration for the needs of the women (see Rowbotham, 1973; and Mitchell, 1971). Prior to the sixties, if a man got a woman pregnant, pressure could be brought upon him to assume responsibility for the situation, even to the point of marrying the woman. With such strictures, it was incumbent upon the male to assume responsibility for contraception. Thus, in the fifties and early sixties, males would often carry condoms around with them in the hopes that they would someday use them. However, the new contraceptive devices and those old ones that are more easily available today have one characteristic in common: they all require the woman to assume responsibility. With the advent of abortion on demand, the pressure on women is even heavier, due to the fact that society assumes that it is her fault if she gets pregnant, and, if she does, the decision to abort is hers. The consequences of pregnancy are not so life-shattering as they once were, but the responsibility still falls most heavily on the shoulders of the women.

Another disadvantage felt by the young women at Utopia High is the fact that they enter the sexual marketplace as individuals and compete against each other for the attention of young men. Males have the advantage of mutual protection as a group that is lacking among the women. In addition, the normative strictures on a female are much stronger than those on males. The women are still expected to take on a passive role in the selection process. Any woman who violates that rule is subject to sanctions from both sexes:

SARAH. When a girl likes a guy, she doesn't want to come on too strong, 'cause the guy's gonna think, "Wait a minute. Get away." . . . So she's not going to do anything at all to hurt it. She may flirt, but nothing direct! And, um, it's pretty touchy. You have to be very careful how you go about it if there's a guy you really like.

LARKIN. What is likely to happen to a girl if she's, say, too forward?

S. Well, she'll be considered by other girls as slutty, and by guys— outwardly they'll say, "Oh she's a real—" they'll say, "Get away, What are you doing?" You know. "Attacking me." Inside, I think, a guy would say, "I'd like to get her in bed, because she'll do it without any problems, without having to go through any bullshit to get her." . . . Outwardly that's what they're *supposed* to say. They're supposed to agree that she is too forward and shouldn't act the way she does and she's very loose and it's disgraceful. But inside—well, boys *and* girls, girls inside would sorta wish they could and get away with it, but they know they can't. They know they can't. (Recorded April 26, 1976.)

Another example of the male domination of the sexual market-place is the fact that such terms as "slut," "two-timer," and "tramp" are used primarily to label women for their behavior. Yet, men are not sanctioned for the identical acts. With the exception of the term "night hog" which refers to anyone whose primary sexual outlet is one-night stands, the only thing that males can be sanctioned for is homosexuality or asexuality. When it comes to the women, though, anything goes. So the double standard, in altered form, remains intact. As Sarah noted in reference to "cheating": "If a girl goes with another guy, the word gets around much faster than if a guy does, because the guys will

protect the guy. But the girls don't. They're kind of sneaky."
(Recorded April 26, 1976.)

Thus, the major effect of the sexual revolution on students at
Utopia High School has been the increased circulation of sexual
commodities. The situation has improved for women in *absolute*
terms vis-a-vis the 1950s, but their relative situation with men is
unchanged. The *fundamental* relationships of the sexual marketplace have not changed, and sexual relationships between male
and female at Utopia High are still male initiated and male
dominated.

However, this situation does not seem to be the case among the
intellectuals and the politicos, who are elites. In the interviews,
these students indicated they were much more likely to carry on
sexual relations beyond the confines of the high school campus
and include them within the context of a "meaningful relationship." The following is a discussion with two politicos:

> **BECKY.** . . . Now people are more serious. I think people are
> more serious to get to know the person.
>
> **LARKIN.** Meaningful relationships.
>
> **B.** Yeah.
>
> **GARY.** I think there are great extremes. I think we have just the
> opposite. You have that, and you have people who just don't care.
> (Recorded March 29, 1976.)

Among these two groups, then, sex is more likely to be tied to a
sense of personal intimacy and mutual exchange. The apparent
reason for less sexism among these two groups is the fact that the
women are focused on careers rather than on the opposite sex,
which is not the case with the other elite group, the jock/rah-
rahs. This group still maintains the football hero/cheerleader
syndrome and the prom queen mentality that was chronicled in
Gordon (1957) and Coleman (1961). Since the material well-being
of intellectual and politico women is not perceived to be dependent on the earning power of their future husbands and sexual
involvement, if anything, may hamper their career goals, they
come to the sexual marketplace with much greater leverage and

can demand equality of participation. Consequently, many go out with older men or relegate sex to the periphery of their lives.

SEX AND MEANING

Sexual relations in the 1950s were dominated by the romantic myth. Apart from sexual exploitation, in which males hired prostitutes or went with "easy women," sex was closely tied with love and marriage. Because sex had consequences for the future, high school romances were tremendously important to couples. When couples began going steady, the question of marriage always had to be considered as they became more seriously involved. The playing out of the romantic myth and the perceived consequences of the relationships tended to give them meaning. They were *serious*. Marriage was a possibility. Many young marrieds became disillusioned later; however, they believed the myth as adolescents and it gave direction and purpose to their lives. Perhaps this myth can best be seen in a famous rock-'n'-roll song popular in 1958:

> To know, know, know him
> Is to love, love, love him.
> Just to see him smile
> Makes my life worthwhile.*

In addition, sex had meaning since it was suppressed by adults. Rock 'n' roll was a response to the suppression of teenage sexuality. It effectively screened out adult listeners who were offended by the music and the catering to the tastes of the teenager. The music of such rock-'n'-roll stars as Chuck Berry, Elvis Presley, the Coasters, Bill Haley and the Comets, the Platters, all spoke to the repressed sexual desires of the young. The gyrating hips of Elvis Presley that were anathema to adults were a testament to their yearnings. Tin Pan Alley was superceded by the hard-driving heavy beat of rock-'n'-roll music,

---

which spoke of the suppression of the young. Chuck Berry's song "Almost Grown" is archetypal of rock-'n'-roll themes, emphasizing the wish on the part of the young to be left alone from prying adult eyes. The song ends with the protagonist getting married, settling down, ending with the line, "Anyway, I'm almost grown." In the same genre of adolescent protest songs are "Yakety-yak" by the Coasters and "Get a Job" sung by the Silhouettes, both litanies of carping by adults.

In the sixties, sexuality was incorporated into a posture of opposition to straight society. Thus, involving oneself in sex became an act of liberation. Jerry Rubin ends his apocryphal book, *Do It!* (1970:256), with a parody of Karl Marx's famous aphorism about unalienated life, ". . . to hunt in the morning, fish in the afternoon, rear cattle in the evening, criticize after dinner . . ." (Marx and Engels, 1970:53) that reads: "People will farm in the morning, make music in the afternoon and fuck wherever and whenever they want to."

The seventies, however, is characterized by no sexual mythology. Participation in sex is no longer oppositional and it certainly has been stripped of its consequences for marriage. For example:

LARKIN. You mentioned awhile back that what happens here [at Utopia High] does not affect your future. Are you talking about relationships you have with people here [that] tend to be inconsequential?

SARAH. Right. They just begin, they end, and you don't think about it any more. *And it's just like trying a new food.* . . . I don't think it affects your later life. I mean, [when] you choose a person you want to be with for the rest of your life, you're not going to think back and say, "Oh, I remember that person." You may remember some of them. But they don't—I don't think they have any effect on you unless it's a very special person. (Recorded April 26, 1976, emphasis mine.)

Even though sexual relations may be fraught with intense feelings, Sarah's perception is essentially correct. Most Utopia High School students are going to college. It is the rare person who, at this time of his or her life, is looking for a marital partner.[2] The inconsequentiality and interchangeability of friends and sexual partners that is structured into the life of the Utopia High student creates a situation in which meaning is drained from the relationships among peers. When trying new lovers becomes akin to tasting new food, the commodification of personal relationships has reached its apex. Perhaps the most alienated form of sex was expressed by a male student when I asked him what was the most significant experience he had had in the past year:

> **MALE STUDENT.** The most significant thing that happened to me was, um, I got laid. That was one.
>
> **LARKIN.** First time?
>
> **M. S.** No. No. But it was significant because it was the only thing I had to do this summer. (Recorded May 19, 1976.)

The use of the term *meaningful relationship* seems to indicate that most relationships are not. Despite the proliferation of sex, intimacy is a rare thing indeed. Observing young people making out on the lawns of the school and in cars in the parking lot and listening to students placidly talking of sex, lead me to the tentative conclusion that in the context of alienated relationships, sexual and social competition, and subcultural demands for conformity, sex among Utopia High students seems to be a joyless affair, for the most part, pretty much divested of meaning, intimacy, and caring. For most students, it seems to be little more than ritualistically sating a biological urge, akin to scratching an itch. This underlying sense of absurdity and despair becomes apparent as Sarah speaks of her feelings for her ex-steady who dumped her to take up with another woman:

> **SARAH.** . . . I met Fred, the boy I was going out with. I really like him a lot. He's the only boy I've ever gone out with who ever *bothered* to *talk* to me first and find out what I like and what my views are on things, my level of intelligence by talking to me and so on. I think that's really nice.
>
> **LARKIN.** Apparently that's a relatively unusual experience for you.

S. Yeah. Guys—I don't know, they're not grown up enough to do something like that. I don't know whether "grown-up" is the right word.

L. Well, [focus on] what seems to happen, rather than make judgments about whether they're grown up or not. What seems to happen in most relationships with boys?

S. Well, a girl goes out with a boy because he's good looking, or because he's nice—fun to be around. Whatever. You don't usually delve into the person's personality that much. Not by personality—I mean views and opinions. They just don't talk about that. (Recorded April 26, 1976.)

The sad irony of Sarah's life is that the one person to whom she could talk, express herself, and reveal her vulnerabilities dropped her when her father grounded her for two weeks. At the time of the interview, Sarah was nursing hopes that he would return, since the girl he was now with was not particularly likable, but had a car.

The attitudes of Utopia High students toward sex create a puzzle. Their sex lives seem to be a jumble of contradictions: they are blasé, yet curious; they talk about sex a great deal, but little is said; sex is open, yet hidden; and they are experienced, yet ignorant. One thing for sure, sex has become a convention among Utopia High students. One can enjoy it, withdraw from it, or participate in it meaninglessly; but all are expected to participate.

DRUGS AND THE CONSCIOUSNESS REVOLUTION

One of the central aspects of the youth revolt of the 1960s was its generation of subjectivist ideology. Sixties subjectivism emphasized a reality system that was based on highly personal, mythic, ecstatic experiences of the actor. It was adopted by dissident youth as an opposition ideology to "straight" conceptions of "objective" realty. Daniel Foss (1972:152) notes.

. . . the youth consistently and, to some extent, consciously experiences organized society as incompatible with, or in contradiction to, what he is aware of as his most authentic and "natural" impulses and inclinations; his youth culture validates his discontents and assists in refining and focusing them. As this consciousness develops, organized society comes to be felt as a clever conspiracy for humiliating, smothering, castrating, manipulating, and possibly even killing him. The more his subjectivity is intensified, the more he feels confronted by a monolithic array of the forces of death intent on the suppression of sex, love, life, beauty, freedom, insight, untapped psychic powers, being, depth, peace, joy, music, novelty, sensory experience—everything summed up or implied by the word "groovy."

The subjectivism of the sixties was fortified by the drug experience of freakified youth, especially through the ingestion of psychedelics such as LSD, mescaline, and psylocybin. Drug experiences helped to give currency to the notion of "levels of consciousness." The psychedelics were the keys to the doors of higher levels of perception which were navigated by dissident youth. Pot quickly became the staple of youth culture during the latter half of the 1960s. Although the effects of it were much less dramatic than the psychedelics, its main psychological effect was to increase the user's subjective awareness. Within youth culture itself, pot and psychedelics were viewed as drugs of "consciousness expansion" while speed was feared because it "turned your brain into swiss cheese." (Gracie Slick of the Jefferson Airplane who sang the drug advocate song, "White Rabbit," recorded radio spots proclaiming to youth "Speed Kills.") And downers, alcohol, and heroin were viewed as drugs of "consciousness constriction," even though plenty of freaks drank "Red Mountain" wine while they smoked pot.

As the movement subsided in the early seventies, there was an abrupt change in the drug use patterns of youth. Psychedelic use declined precipitously, even though the research that was being reported found it to be physically less harmful than aspirin (Weil, 1973). Many ex-freaks became victims of the "downer syndrome," as they switched to drugs that would obliterate consciousness such as sopors (Quaaludes), alcohol, and heroin.

In the wake of the movement of the sixties, the consciousness revolution has been assimilated into the mainstream of American society. Freak subjectivism has been incorporated into modern advertising which often associates consumer products with orgastic pleasure. For example, Newport cigarettes proclaim, "If smoking isn't a pleasure, why bother?" even though cigarette smokers are addicts. Astrology has had renewed currency among the middle classes to the point of serious university research on its validity.[3] However, the most visible legacy of the extension of subjectivism into modern life is the rapid development of the "happiness industry," which combines contemporary psychotherapy with Eastern mysticism. With the proliferation of Transcendental Meditation (TM), Werner Erhard's *est* program, Arica, Silva Mind Control, and the human potential "movement," subjective consciousness has become a new commodity on the market to be sold by corporations (as in the cases of TM, *est*, Arica, and Silva Mind Control) and by individual entrepreneurs (e.g., the human potential "movement").

By the mid-seventies, youth culture had returned to normalcy. Psychedelics were still in use; however, they had lost their myth-generating power and were confined to a small minority of explorers. However, pot continued its popularity to the point where only a small minority of youth could claim that they had never tried it. The downer syndrome of the early 1970s continued in muted form, with alcohol as the most important drug of consciousness obliteration.[4]

DRUGS AT UTOPIA HIGH

The infusion of marijuana into the drug habits of high school students has created massive headaches for administrators and parents. First, it is infinitely easier to conceal than liquor, which comes in bottles and cans that are bulky, cumbersome and take a great deal of effort to hide. A student can stay high throughout the school day on three joints of marijuana. They can easily be concealed in cigarette packs, pockets, notebooks, briefcases, and lockers. Thus, the school administration cannot enforce anti-drug laws without seriously infringing the rights of the students.

Second, the visible effects of marijuana are much subtler than those of alcohol. Unless a user makes it obvious that he or she is high, it is almost impossible to tell from the student's external appearance or from his or her classroom behavior. It would be relatively easy for a teacher to identify a drunk student. However, pot smoking could lead either to inattentiveness *or* to increased concentration in the material, depending on the proclivities of the individual student. About the only visible sign of marijuana use is the reddening of the whites of the eyes. Yet this can be caused by many other factors (such as lack of sleep, swimming, or air pollution) and is not easily perceptible unless one is looking for it. Thus, the official policy of the school is to try to discourage its use, gingerly hoping that they won't have to confront a student on the subject. An administration prior to Mr. Seraph's tenure reportedly generated serious trouble when the local police force planted an undercover agent on campus in an attempt to suppress drug use and sales. However, when the agent "came out of the cold" and named names, everyone started screaming "entrapment," and there was evidence to indicate that the undercover agent himself was the source of many of the illegal drugs on campus. Since then, the administration has attempted to treat the drug problem through drug education, overlooking minor infractions, counseling individuals who seem to be using drugs in self-destructive ways, and crossing their fingers that something doesn't happen to arouse public sentiment that would require them to use strong enforcement measures.

Drugs, along with vandalism, is probably the most polarizing issue in Pleasant Valley. Even though there is relatively little drug abuse among the students at Utopia High, it can be the source of a tremendous amount of fear, hostility, and paranoia among both young people and adults. Drugs, more than anything else, is the source of greatest conflict between parents and children, young and old, even though there is, according to several students, a significant minority of adults in the community who are pot smokers themselves. The evidence seems to suggest that the drug problem in Pleasant Valley, with the inclusion of marijuana, is probably less serious than teenage

drunkenness in the 1950s. A major fear of parents in the 1950s was that their children would combine alcohol with reckless driving. They had good reason for their fear, since automobile accidents were at that time (and still are) the prime cause of death for teenagers. Paradoxically, the most important concern of the parents in Pleasant Valley seems to be the use of marijuana, even though alcohol abuse is increasing in prevalence and is much more dangerous. This concern is reflected in the drug enforcement policies of the local police who are quite vigilant and rigorous in their enforcement of drug laws.

There is no issue on which there is more mutual suspicion between youth and adults than drugs. Student after student told of parents ransacking their drawers in search of marijuana, examinations by parents for bloodshot eyes, adolescent demands for privacy being interpreted as excuses for drug use, and on the occasions that parents did find evidence of pot, the most dire of consequences:

> **LARKIN.** How did your family react to [getting busted]?
>
> **TOM.** I went to court. They said, well, "He's no good. We don't want him." You know. Then I got into a fight with my father in court, and that's the reason why I went away. [Tom was sent to a residential drug rehabilitation program.]
>
> **L.** A physical fight, or was it yelling?
>
> **T.** It would have been [a physical fight] if I could have gotten close to him. I would have killed him. I really would have. He goes, "I don't want the scum." I just jumped up out of the chair. I was ready to fuckin' rip him apart. I was ready to kill him. (Recorded April 13, 1976.)

Another student told of being reported to the police by his parents when they found marijuana in his drawer. Still another student told his story:

> **LARKIN.** What is the most significant thing to happen to you this year? . . .
>
> **DUANE.** I would say the most significant thing [was] I got into some very deep trouble a ways back and it's been giving me troub—

it's just a hassle. A friend of mine called me and complained about some pot I sold him.

L. Was he complaining about getting burned? . . .

D. He was complaining because it wasn't worth what he said it was worth and he said I shouldn't sell the stuff because—and my father was listening on the phone. My father was on the extension.

L. Unknown to you?

D. Of course. . . .

L. So what did your father do?

D. Quite a bit. He jus—it's just that once I get home I stay home.

L. You're grounded?

D. And I haven't seen money for awhile. And he goes through my pants, frisks my room . . . (Recorded May 26, 1976.)

Paranoia about drugs seems to poison the lines of communication between parents and their children more than anything else, according to the students I interviewed. Because of the difficulty of detection, and the exaggerated fears concerning the effects of marijuana, parents become easily suspicious of their children. Those parents who maintain vigilance falsely accuse their children as being under the influence of drugs when they are merely feeling good. Likewise, because of feared consequences of detection, students become skilled at "maintaining" or hiding the effects of the drug while in the presence of their parents. This practice is a source of a certain type of gallows humor on the part of the young which reveals the contempt they feel for their parents who despite their suspicions can be easily fooled.

SARAH. Parents are really dumb.

LARKIN. In what way?

S. I was so drunk [at a party she was having]. It was incredible. I had gotten really drunk. My mother didn't notice a thing. I sat there and talked to her and she didn't notice. I almost burst out laughing in her face. And I can come into the house after school completely stoned [on pot] out of my mind and just act normal—have a straight face and act kind of angry or so, and she won't say anything. If I come in in a good mood, she'll accuse me of being high or if I am eating candy she'll say "It's that craving for sweets. You know it's one of the symptoms." It's ridiculous! (Recorded April 26, 1976.)

One can understand the desire of parents to protect their children from danger. However, the public propaganda concerning the use of marijuana has, in many cases, strained the relationships between parents and their teenage children. As a matter of fact, the major criterion for youth's evaluations of their parents revolves around their ability to understand and tolerate the sexual and drug indulgences of their children. Many students have told the author, "My parents are cool. They let me smoke." or "My parents trust me. They're really great." Those students who had parents who were concerned, yet open-minded, were considered by the others to be extremely lucky.

"NORMAL" AND "DEVIANT" PATTERNS OF DRUG USE

At Utopia High, there is a more or less assumed pattern of acceptable drug use. Even those students who use no drugs whatever tend to agree and tolerate "normal" use, which covers cigarettes, alcohol, and, of course, pot. Probably twenty to thirty percent of the students at Utopia High are habitual cigarette smokers. Although the legal age for purchasing cigarettes is eighteen, the school makes no attempt to enforce regulations against minors who smoke illegally. However, there are "No Smoking" regulations inside the building, with the exception of one designated area for student smoking in inclement weather. Students heed the regulations fairly carefully with the exceptions of the bathrooms, which continually smell of stale smoke. It is not uncommon for non-smoking students to consider cigarette smoking the most abusive drug habit among their peers. They complain more about the pollution of the air at peer gatherings than they will of drinking or marijuana smoking. Women, especially, complain of having to wash the cigarette smoke out of their hair and airing out their clothes after attending a party.

For most people, pot smoking and alcohol consumption is strictly associated with weekends and vacations. It is at the parties that alcohol (usually beer) and pot are consumed. Occasionally, they will be consumed after school or on weekday evenings. However, this is the exception rather than the rule. There is a minority of perhaps thirty to fifty students who habitually smoke pot on campus and attend classes stoned. On festive occasions, students will break out pot and begin passing it around to smoke. This is especially true of the "freaks." For example, when I began interviewing the freaks on the lawn of the playing field, they began passing around joints and it turned into a celebration of a pretty spring day and of the fact that there was a sociologist who was busy recording their voices for posterity. While there are few students who drink before they enter school, and even fewer who come to school drunk, they seem to comprise a smaller fraction of the student population than those who smoke pot. Yet, according to the local juvenile officer, teenage alcoholism in the area is on the rise. But it seems that the drinking of alcohol on campus is confined to the greasers and perhaps to a few unidentified individuals who kept their drinking to themselves. When the freaks brought liquor on campus in their celebration, it was more an act of bravado and showing off to the researcher rather than any ongoing pattern.

Several students told me that pill-popping (the taking of "uppers" and "downers," i.e., amphetamines and barbiturates) was popular in 1974, but that it had declined. There are probably two reasons for this. First, the production and distribution of these drugs were sharply curtailed when the government discovered the major drug manufacturers making many times the amounts of such drugs than were being prescribed by doctors. Supposedly for foreign distribution, the bills of lading were sent to Mexican border towns while the drugs were shipped to underground distributors within the states. Second, the currency of pill-popping had declined as a youth culture activity following widespread dissemination of the pills' deleterious effects.

Psychedelic use at Utopia High is apparently confined to a small minority of persons from the freak and intellectual subcultures. Nobody knew of anyone who was getting stoned on psychedelics on a regular basis. Those who were using them were dabbling in the psychedelic experience. The use of psychedelics is not particularly common. Their rather stable and restricted use has little to do with either their price ($1.00 a tab) or their availability. The reasons for their lack of popularity are more because they are inappropriate for this phase of youth culture than for whatever legal or health hazard they might incur. This is not a time for the generation of new visions, the proclaiming of new realities, or the exploration of new kinds of consciousness. It is a time for holding onto what is there, struggling against the erosion of gains, and getting through another day.

CONCLUSION: THE ROUTINIZATION
OF PLEASURE

The young people at Utopia High are neither tortured nor ecstatic. Although many feel the sense of loss as expressed in a kind of pervasive feeling that something is missing but nobody knows exactly what, they do not have a sense of tragedy. They do engage in pleasureful activities—both sex and drugs are sources of pleasure. Yet it is the rare student who feels joyful. Drugs and sex, for the most part, have lost their oppositional content and their visionary capabilities and have been incorporated into the regulated lives of these students. Pleasure comes easily to them, but joy does not. Underlying the consumption of pleasure is a sense of malaise. This uneasiness is not to be mistaken for guilt, for there is little guilt expressed about sexual and drug indulgences. It seems to be tied to the feeling that sex and drugs are *inconsequential* except for the fact that they can become the source of trouble. Even then, the trouble that is caused has no moral consequences, since the problems can be managed by parents: one can get an abortion, be sent to a drug-rehabilitation program, or get punished. Yet the punishment is merely an indication that the world in which Utopia High School students live is merely arbitrary, since, for the most part, the acts they get punished for are essentially harmless.

With sex and drugs incorporated into the routine of daily existence, life assumes the texture of white bread and the mountains and the valleys of life have become hills and dales. The young of Pleasant Valley are being forged into the next generation of cogs in the corporate structure. They have learned to consume with pleasure, manage their emotions, and keep their eyes on the light at the end of the tunnel. They have learned to cope with the realities of existence with a fair amount of sophistication. Yet they have a hard time connecting means with ends. The lives they lead seem to be characterized by perseveration, rather than progress. This "senseless sense of senselessness" assumes a central feature in their views of the world. The major problem that young people at Utopia High must face is not drugs nor sex, but the lack of meaning in their lives. To this we will now turn.

NOTES

1. I fully realize that a revolution in sexual ideology and practice occurred in the 1920s. Its main features were: (1) the popularization of the writings of Freud and the Freudians, such as Reich (most Freudians believed that sexual repressiveness was, at least in part, responsible for neurosis), (2) feminism in the form of the demand for equal political participation and liberalization of restrictions on women's public behavior, and (3) general liberalization of sexual mores and parental restrictions on sexual behavior. Of course, the Roaring Twenties, like the Turbulent Sixties, was a time in which the level of surplus was rising rapidly, undermining the constraints of bourgeois culture. While the twenties made sex acceptable as an activity, it was to be restricted to the marital bed. With the exception of certain avant gardes, premarital relations were sinful. The sexual revolution of the 1960s was qualitatively different and built on the successes gained during the 1920s.

2. While writing this book, I came across one of the students I had interviewed the previous spring. He was on campus and was in a foul mood. He was trying to get into a university, but did not have the necessary grade point average. He was unemployed. But most upsetting of all, his steady had gone away to college, and, upon returning home for Christmas vacation, she told him that he did not fit into her new life-style and that she wanted to end their romantic involvement. He felt betrayed and told me that she had relegated him to the trash heap. All of a sudden he was not good enough for her. He looked at me plaintively and said, "I would have married her."

3. In the American Sociological Association meetings held in New York City, August 1976, a paper was presented by Francis Butler of Allegheny College entitled, "Solar System into Social System: A Symbolic Analysis of Astrology." The paper was an attempt to construct an astrological cosmology into which Talcott Parson's four-function paradigm of the social system could be integrated. The author proposed that the twelve houses of the zodiac could be seen as functional equivalents to Parsons's conception of adaptation, goal attainment, integration, and latency functions of the social system.

4. In the middle and late 1970s, there has been a rise in the use of PCP by young people. PCP was originally produced as a livestock tranquilizer. Called "angel dust" on the street, it desublimates the user, thus, allowing him or her to express repressed feelings. Police maintain that "angel dust" users are prone to be violent while under its influence. PCP not only anesthetizes the rational brain, but apparently does irreparable damage to the cerebral cortex. Although there is controversy among experts as to how much permanent damage is done to the brain, there is evidence that persons who continually use it lose the capacity to perform abstract cognitive functions and linguistic competence declines.

5

THE POLITICS OF
MEANINGLESSNESS

It was gravity which pulled us down and
  destiny which broke us apart.
You tamed the lion in my cage, but it
  wasn't enough to change my heart.
Now everything's a little upside down;
As a matter of fact the wheels have stopped.
What's good is bad, what's bad is good;
You'll find out when you reach the top
  you're on the bottom.
I noticed at the ceremony your corrupt
  ways had fin'lly made you blind.
I can't remember your face any more;
Your mouth is changed, your eyes don't look
  into mine.
The priest wore black on the seventh day
  and sat stonefaced while the building
  burned.
I waited for you on the running boards
  near the cypress tree while the
  springtime turned to autumn.

Idiot wind, blowing like a circle around
  my skull,
From the Grand Coulee Dam to the Capitol.
Idiot wind, blowing ev'ry time you move
  your teeth.
You're an idiot, babe; it's a wonder that
  you still know how to breathe.

Bob Dylan, "Idiot Wind," 1975

When adults discuss youth of the 1970s, it seems inevitable that someone will state, usually with a great deal of assurance and support, that youth culture has returned to the era of the 1950s. Such generalizations tend to be made with a certain amount of relief and self-satisfaction, as if such superficial comparisons negate the intense generational conflict of the 1960s. Of course, there are parallels to the 1950s: the privitization of youth interests, ritualization of drug use, resurgence of alcohol abuse, and, most of all, the disappearance of collective disobedience. Yet the youth of the 1970s is *fundamentally different* from 1950s' youth, which was caught up in sex, dating, cars, fun, rock 'n' roll, football, and drive-in movies. They were activity-oriented. They were not particularly introspective. That was left to the intellectuals or the misfits. With a blithe optimism, 1950s' youth could charge full force into the future showing little concern for the reasons they were doing so. Even as they entered college and came to grips with "ultimate questions," 1950s' youth did not seem to be seriously affected by such issues as whether or not God existed. There were goals and means to achieve them. One merely applied the recipe. If the procedure didn't make sense, one didn't ask too many questions and one tolerated absurdity for the purposes of achieving the goal.

For the young, the 1960s wiped away the naive assurance that one could become employed in an occupation that would afford both a comfortable living and add to the social good. The evils that were attacked by youth in the 1960s still exist (with the exception of the Vietnam War) in exacerbated form. With no movement to articulate discontent, the contradiction is experienced as a cultural crisis, which, at the individual level, encompasses the problem of making meaning out of one's life. Utopia High students have inherited the introspectiveness that emerged from the 1960s' revolution, when youth began to explore aspects of selfhood they never dreamed existed prior to movement involvement. Once the individual ego was liberated from the contraints of bureaucratic-rationality, the consciousness revolution escalated as freakified youth made concerted efforts to explode the barriers of the bourgeois ego[1] through the use of drugs, sex, radical therapies, mysticism, and by consciously living insecurely and communally.

Introspection has been absorbed by the youth of the 1970s. They are *serious* about themselves: they are concerned about what kind of people they are and will be. They are suspicious of social labels. They struggle against overwhelming odds to be themselves: authentic, real persons. Yet the larger society works against such authenticity, since it would upset existing social relationships. The young are forced to play the game and put on false fronts. The problem becomes fiendishly difficult for them, because many have already slipped into their personas without really being aware of the fact that they are inauthentic. This constitutes one of the most serious problems for these young people. The assault on the self was described by Jennie, a very bright senior:

> **JENNY.** . . . I always have my mind, you know. Now, I don't know if that's a consolation. Sometimes it is and sometimes it's not. But I *do* have my mind. My mind is always mine. *No one* has control of my mind. . . . The worst thing is when you give over your mind and say, "Here, take it, do with it what you want."
>
> **LARKIN.** There were a whole lot of people in the early 1970s who did just that. They wanted nothing better to do than to give up their minds.
>
> **J.** Well, it's close. I am struggling in my life right now to really hold onto myself. See, 'cause I'm fighting hard against values, things that school and society—really, like measures of your worth in terms of achievement and things. I mean, I am really—I've been pulled into that to a certain extent, you know. I travel in certain circles up there where people are very much aware of the old college scene, you know. I am just struggling very hard. (Recorded March 29, 1976.)

Jenny sees society and its agent, the school, as mechanisms which sort people into various statuses which have impact for ego valuations. She is fighting the ego gratifications offered her by society for her high level of achievement. To her, the acceptance of such rewards reduces her ability to develop an autonomous mind ("My mind is always mine"). She has to be constantly on guard against temptations of the bourgeois ego, which asserts its superiority through the performance principle, and of becoming colonized by bourgeois institutions. Jenny is fighting against the colonization of her own mind.

Jenny is rare, but not singular among her peers for her ability to articulate the inherent contradiction she experiences between herself as a self-aware individual and the social forces against which she must contend to maintain her own individuality. For most of her peers, such a conflict is not so much thinkable, but feelable. To explore the psychodynamics of the "student in the street," we must examine the *emotional* tenor of their complaints.

BOREDOM

Boredom is the universal element that transcends all social divisions at Utopia High. Throughout the study, the theme of boredom recurred. For the active students, engrossing themselves in projects and events provided a bulwark against it. For the more passive, it has become a way of life. Boredom hung over Utopia like a thick fog. It was something everyone had to cope with: a fact of life even for those who chose to avoid it. Several students led frenetic lives in which they ran from one activity to the next so they would not succumb to boredom. However, most gave in to it.

Boredom was manifested at Utopia High in the following ways: hanging out, the "nothing-to-do syndrome," disdainful views of Pleasant Valley, cynicism, despair, cruising, fantasies of leaving the area, and restlessness. As mentioned earlier, because of its policy of liberalism and indulgence, the school was a site for much hanging out. Many students ditched classes and hung out on the premises. They stood or sat around in groups of four or five and passed the time of day talking about inconsequential topics or "goofing off." When asked what their lives were like, they unanimously stated that they were boring. On the first attempt to interview a group of students, the following occurred:

LARKIN. . . . I'm a sociologist.

STUDENT. Well, what do you want us to say?

L. Well, I don't have anything for you to say, I am interested in what your lives are like. Really.

S. Boring!

OTHERS. That's right! All the way. [They all start talking at once and the tape becomes unintelligible.] (Recorded March 22, 1976.)

In another instance, some students were hanging around in "greaser's alley." We were talking with the tape recorder on. The subject was baby sitting rates ($1.25 per hour), when all of a sudden a female student said, "I'm a sophomore. We lead humdrum lives." Another said, "It's boring," and still another said, "There's nothing to do around here." Nearly a half hour later in the same interview, some males decided to have the last word on the subject:

LARKIN. I seem to get the same story from everybody, that this place [Pleasant Valley] is boring, that people really have nothing to do.

STUDENT. It's not boring, it's dead. This town is dead. There's nothin' to do. (Recorded March 31, 1976.)

A great many students harbor fantasies or desires to excape the deadening non-existence offered to them in Pleasant Valley. One young man, who was raised in an urban environment retreats to the city every weekend. A young woman was awaiting the summer so she could escape the unidimensionality of Pleasant Valley to become a camp counselor. Still another saw his visit to his sister's farm in New Hampshire a blessed escape from suburban miasma. Only a small minority of students saw their home town as one in which they would wish to settle themselves. Most felt restless. Since the study was conducted in the spring, many were looking forward to the summer, when they would head for the shore or the mountains. Many students felt like captives of their environment and told me of their desire to "bust out." Yet, they continued to play the waiting game.

Now that the boredom and its manifestations have been described, we must ask of what is it indicative? For Utopia High School students, *boredom is the result of the repression of the impulse to rebel.* They are dissatisfied with their lives. Yet there is no movement to give that dissatisfaction a collective articulation. Acts of defiance or "busting out" are meaningless and accomplish nothing but a ripple in the existing order and they play into the hands of the forces of oppression. For example, some students threw a coke machine down a stairwell, creating a furor in the school for a day or two. The perpetrators of the act were suspended (or at least, the alleged perpetrators—those who said they were in the know claimed the wrong ones were punished). Most of the students were upset by it, since it could be used for legitimating increased surveillance of the students by the administration. The day after the incident, teachers were pressed into patrolling the halls, a task they detested and the students disliked. A show of force was made, and things returned to normalcy. Yet the increasing vandalism works against the interests of not only the vandals themselves, but also the majority of students, since community leaders use such incidents to justify their claim that the young should be more closely supervised. Collective dissidence is no longer a viable tactic in asserting student interests. When the Student Rights Committee attempted to shut down the school and march on the board of education in protest over budgetary cutbacks, their efforts turned into a miserable failure. Student politics are no longer considered seriously by students or adults. Students are not usually consulted on school board policy which concerns them. When they are, it is usually after the decision has been made and a token presentation is allowed on behalf of the students.

When the dissidence of the 1960s subsided, the alternatives for lives to be lived outside conventional institutions declined. Also, conventional careers tend to have declining intrinsic value and merely offer the promise of an income satisfactory enough to buy consumer items to compensate for the loss of meaningful work.

Who or what is to be revolted against? What are the tactics? These are basic questions that must be answered in the context of a social movement. In its absence, youth in the 1970s are forced to make individual adaptations. Defiance does not generate collective sentiment against authority structures. It, therefore, becomes an exercise in egoism and serves to complicate life with needless aggravation. Yet, the desire to "bust out" smoulders in the recesses of the consciousness of these young people.

These students see themselves processed, manipulated, allocated, and even oppressed, despite the "humanistic" orientation of the school administration. They dutifully proceed through the routine of school, knowing pretty much that it will prepare them for the routine of work, fearing that meaningless routine may be the dominant rhythm of their lives:

BECKY. [Complaining about student apathy.] Take any kid in our history class. Just a regular kid. Pick any of them. They're not involved in any school government, they really have no hobbies— no hobbies dealing with the school, and they're not involved in athletics. They just exist. I don't know how they can make it through the day.

ANDY. I fit into that category. I have two free periods at the end of the day in which I usually just sit around. . . .

B. Do you ever get the urge to break something?

A. Every once in awhile.

PAUL. I do too. All the time. Let it out.

LARKIN. What is it that has to be let out?

P. I don't know.

A. He means school the whole day. *(To Paul)* Any hard-working day, what do you do?

P. When you do a whole lot of work, you need to get away from it.

L. So is it the routine that drives you batty, or is it a feeling that what you are doing doesn't have much purpose?

A. I think it's the routine, that, like . . .

GARY. I don't agree with that. I can totally fall asleep in a class where I think all we're getting is just busywork and everything. And in past years that's been in all cases. But this year, if there is anything I think I can get anything out of, which is rare, but does happen, you know, I really get involved. But the majority of the stuff you get now is just a bunch of busywork. (Recorded March 23, 1976.)

On several occasions, students compared Utopia High to a prison. I was inclined to regard such statements with a high degree of suspicion; when I pointed out to the students that they were a privileged lot, they agreed. Yet upon analysis, the prison analogy may supply more than what meets the eye. These students are not imprisoned by the school officials, nor by the community residents themselves. They are imprisoned by the lack of alternatives to what they are doing. What else could they be doing? Life in the street is mean and brutal. Full-time decent jobs for high school dropouts are extremely rare. The students are the recipients of a social policy of containment. They are being "contained" in schools until such time as they can assume adult roles. In the schools, administrations are attempting to contain potentially antisocial behavior by limiting it in such a way as to make it controllable by administrative means. An example is the smoking regulations at Utopia High:

STUDENT 1. You know, this school is really mixed up. . . . Seraph [the principal] is more concerned about administration than he is about us. [We're only allowed to smoke] on the basketball courts. In the winter they want us to go outside. They won't even let us on the stairs. We gotta go out to the blacktop.

STUDENT 2. Last year, they had smokin' in the cafeteria. The year before that, they had it in the boys' bathrooms.

S. 1. So now we smoke in the stairways, and they say, "This is no good." And he comes around and says, "You can't smoke here. We're working on a . . ."

OTHERS. (*Interrupting*) They've been working on a plan for twenty years!

S. 2. (*Continuing*) ". . . a smoking lounge."

STUDENT 3. Centuries.

STUDENT 4. They went to ——— House, but they couldn't because it cost too much to get it redone. They have to get new chairs . . .

STUDENT 5. What for?

S. 4. Because they catch on fire. There will be no curtains, no chairs.

STUDENT 6. There's a teacher's lounge.

S. 1. And we have the blacktop. (Recorded March 22, 1976.)

The students bridle at being the instruments of administrative decision making. Yet, all they can do is complain. Student initiatives are doomed before they start if they do not have any faculty or administrative support. Petitions flow freely around campus; however, most students view them as a waste of time. They sign them, hoping that maybe they will do some good.

STUDENT POLITICS:
AN EXERCISE IN ABSURDITY

In the 1960s, Bob Dylan counseled youth, "Don't follow leaders, Watch the parking meters." Students at Utopia High seem to have pretty much taken his advice to heart. Few students aspire to leadership posts and those who do are distrusted by the rest. Recruitment for student leadership is extremely difficult. Those who do fill the posts are continually frustrated by the fact that they receive no support from the student body and when called upon to lead, there are usually very few persons willing to follow. Becky, a house president, made the following statement:

> I have the trouble where if I could find the leader, I could have the people [to move politically]. I can't find the leaders. No one wants to lead anything! What can you do? That's . . . the problem. (Recorded March 29, 1976.)

Of course, student government has traditionally been the pawn of the administration and has been impotent to exercise any autonomy. However, in the past it served important social functions, such as providing high visibility for popular students and rewarding them by offering them prestige within the formal organization of the school. Thus, the student body president usually was one of the most popular students in school and school elections were, for the most part, an expression of social liking rather than political platforms, policies and preferences. During the 1960s, school elections took on a more politicized cast and student issues became integrated into campaigns. In the 1970s, the political activism has waned and student politics has become pretty much a rear-guard operation. Student apathy is rampant. Few vote in the elections. Political office no longer has the social significance that it once had. To be elected to student body office no longer connotes great popularity or even the respect of the student body. Student politicians are viewed with the same suspicions as their adult counterparts. Student leaders at Utopia High generally agree that theirs is a thankless task. Most students don't really care about student council or the various committees that participate in the governance procedures. Participation in student governance is a disheartening process, especially since it is done, for the most part, out of lofty intentions. Student politicians want to work for the betterment of student conditions. They work hard at trying to promote student interests. Yet they are faced with their own powerlessness in a world dominated by adult interests and they are additionally frustrated by the suspicion and apathy of those whom they are supposed to lead:

LARKIN. How do students, in general, feel about student politics?

BECKY. They don't care.

PAUL. The ones who are not involved are disinterested.

L. You've got a lot of boredom.

P. Yea. People couldn't really care less. A lot of apathy. And the people who *are* involved are not as cynical but are also not willing to exert energy, as far as getting anything done.

L. So you've got a lot of apathy.

P. Yea, yea. There are—they *sound* more like they care, but it's not very well demonstrated. (Recorded March 31, 1976.)

There is some indication that the student leadership is cynical. A few participate for the purposes of padding their college applications in the hopes that an activist façade will increase the probabilities of acceptance. They know that in matters of policy, the students are the last to find out. Also, they are aware of the fact that despite their attempts to move the student body into political action, the students are immovable objects and they are anything but an irresistable force.

This formalized student leadership has all the disadvantages of formality, but few of the advantages of formal legitimation. Student council meetings are characterized by wrangling over procedure and debates as to whether it is an elitist body. One student leader mockingly characterized student council as debating, "Should we vote on this today? Should we vote on voting?"   •

Student government finds itself fighting a rear-guard battle. They are trying to maintain the gains that were wrested from the administration through the activism of the 1960s; namely, input in decision-making processes that affect the student population, student participation in curriculum development, continuation of commons periods instead of study halls, and continuation of the informality of the school atmosphere. The budget crunch has begun to erode some of these gains. First, teacher time has been rationed more strictly, cutting into the student-initiated individual study programs. Teachers no longer have the time to guide independent research into areas of individual interest. Second, the community has been influenced strongly by the culturally reactionary "back-to-basics" trend, with the election of conservatives to the school board who want to see the curriculum offerings cut and greater emphasis put on the mechanics of basic skills. Such an approach diminished the students' power to influence curriculum construction. Third, with the increase in vandalism in the school and community, there is mounting pressure upon the administration to "crack down" on the students and re-institute oppressive techniques of student regulation.[2]

The student political apparatus has been powerless to do much about these onslaughts to its already fragile power. It first protested the budget cuts. Some activist students formed a group

called the "Student Rights Committee" and attempted to lead a
march on the Board of Education during class time. It was
estimated that about 300 students began the march. However, by
the time the marchers reached the Board of Education, only about
50 students were left. The rest used the opportunity to ditch
school for the day. Once at the Board of Education offices, a
delegation of students attempted to negotiate with school district
administrators. According to the student newspaper, the administrators were more concerned about the fact that the students had
walked out of their classes than the issues raised by the budget
crisis. The students complained that the budget cuts were ill-
conceived and tended to cut deeply into the educational program
while leaving the administration unscathed. (The actual cuts in
the program reported in chapter 1 tend to bear out this complaint.) The administration and students worked out a series of
recommendations which included: (1) a student representative on
the committee to reorganize the school district, (2) the high
school principal's consultation with students in formulating the
high school budget, (3) an assembly where students would be able
to draft questions in advance to be asked of the district superintendent, (4) the formation of a student budget advisory committee, and (5) a program priority list to be submitted by students.
All students who participated in the walkout were then given one
to four hours detention. Although the walkout occurred in
November 1975, the only action that had been taken on the
recommendations as of May 1976 was that the district superintendent held two question-and-answer periods with student
leaders. For all the disadvantages and the ineffectuality of the
student council, it made a concerted effort to politically educate
the students about the effects of the budget crisis on the educational program.

The year 1975–76 saw a new addition to the curriculum of
Utopia High School. There was a new experimental course that
was to be taught through the sponsorship of federal funds. Its
title: The Science of Creative Intelligence, also known as Transcendental Meditation, based on the teachings of the Maharishi
Mahesh Yogi. The course was an immediate success among the

students: approximately 40 signed up for the 25 spaces. However, it was not long before certain members of the community heard what was happening and launched a campaign against it. By February, the controversy had reached such a pitch that a national campaign against the use of TM in the schools had been generated. *Time Magazine's* religion section featured the controversy in its March 1, 1976 issue. Detractors from the community claimed that TM was thinly disguised Hinduism and, therefore, the school was teaching a religious doctrine and practice. The school officials claimed that there was no doctrine and only the techniques of meditation were being taught. However, in order for each of the students to be given a mantra to chant as a part of the meditation process, he or she was required to attend an initiation ceremony in which a token of love (flowers, fruit, etc.) was given to the Guru in return for the mantra. The ceremony itself was called a *puja*, which is the Hindi word for "worship." *Time* noted:

> TMers insist that all this is much ado about nearly nothing. Robert Kory, who runs the [state] project for TM, explains that the mantras are just "meaningless" sounds, that the *puja* simply reminds the teacher of the highest ideals of his profession, and that the deities [Brahma, Vishnu, and Siva] it invokes are only "the forces of nature." (*Time*, March 1, 1976, p. 183.)

Ironically, the forces of opposition, which included many local clergy, were the same people who several years earlier led a drive to institute non-sectarian prayers into the school curriculum. For the local disputants, the issue revolved around the problem of whose ox was getting gored. If the Christians weren't going to get their prayers, the Hindus weren't going to be allowed to infiltrate. This was not lost on the students, who seemed to be in favor of the TM course. The problem was resolved by prohibiting meditation in the classroom, which effectively gutted the course to the point where half the students officially dropped it, since there was nothing to do when they attended class. Of those who were left, attendance dropped so that the average class was attended by five to eight students. Meanwhile, the case went to the state Supreme Court which ruled against TM.

The Transcendental Meditation fiasco had its cultural impact upon the students. It was originally greeted as an important innovation in the curriculum, complete with front page write-up in the school newspaper. Yet the TM program was found to be structured according to the requisites of the TM bureaucracy and had not been adapted for high school instruction. The high school program had obviously been a ploy by the TM people to increase their potential following. Yet it was presented to the students as a high school course. The school newspaper quotes one of the disillusioned TM students:

> Chris . . . , junior, is one of the students who dropped the course. She said, "It wasn't doing much good for me." Chris thought that the course was supposed to last about 33 days, but it seemed it was being dragged out for an entire year. She added that TM "just got silly after awhile and didn't make any sense." (April 30, 1976.)

The students found themselves caught in a crossfire between adult factions. Again, their opinions didn't matter. A constitutional question had to be settled and that was *adult* business; the students were assumed to be dupes of cynical TM manipulators and they were given no part in the decision. They had the choice of attending a gutted program or dropping the course altogether. The students were well aware that debates among themselves as to whether or not TM was a religion were of no consequence. Therefore, the Transcendental Meditation course became a joke around campus.

The student leadership is caught in the position of mediating between student and adult constituencies. They are in a position to assess the intentions of the adults who determine the conditions of their lives. They can see an adult crack-down coming before the rest of the students. In their attempt to preserve student privileges in the face of increased pressures by adult authorities to reduce them, they find themselves attempting to repress the behavior of their peers in order to preserve privileges, as noted by Becky in chapter 3 (p. 71). Thus, the co-optation of the student leadership by adult authorities also generates a certain feeling of unreality. Even though the student politicians feel themselves as fighters for the student causes, their very characterology often gives them greater affinity with the adults. For example, it is the student leadership that declares that there is irresponsibility all around them. The following observations were made by Paul, a house president.

> I think the problem [of students not taking responsibility] that you are talking about, Dave [Editor of the student newspaper], is all part of a big trend toward irresponsibility, I guess. What you said about not being able to find leaders, I find to be true about student council. People do not want to take responsibility for things. And that applies to many levels. It applies to trying to get a straight answer out of our principal. It's virtually impossible because he will not take a stand. He will not take responsibility for something he has said. He gives us these roundabout answers. And that's true on the level of the Board of Education and the superintendant of schools and anywhere you go. They keep passing the buck around to each other, and throughout the whole thing no one will state—no one will commit themselves to one opinion and follow through on it. (Recorded March 29, 1976.)

Since student leaders are the ones who shoulder responsibilities, work hard, attend meetings, and try to make informed judgments as to what course to follow, they tend to view their less responsible, drifting, apathetic peers with disdain. Because of this, they are much more vulnerable to the acceptance of adult definitions of the situation, and by implication become agents of adult will.

THIS SENSELESS SENSE OF SENSELESSNESS

The convoluted relationships between adults and students, the students' sense of powerlessness, and the general lack of direction that the lives of students take on are important in generating the *geist* of Utopia High. Incidents such as the Coke machine episode, the great walkout, and the Transcendental Meditation fiasco seem to punctuate the meaninglessness of it all. The students float through their lives, sometimes in a fog, sometimes in a pot-induced stupor. The complexities of everyday life often seem to engulf them, forcing a retreat into a defiant present-orientation.

LARKIN. If you wanted to tell the world something, what would you tell it? . . .

STUDENT 1. "Don't worry about what somebody else is gonna say, just do what you want to."

STUDENT 2. My Philosophy: "Live today, because tomorrow may never come." That's my philosophy. (*Laughs*)

STUDENT 3. That's something like mine. My philosophy is, "Live today. Live today."

S. 1. You know what they do to you in school? All your counselors, all they ever tell you is do good in school because you have to go to college, if you want to get into a good college. Everything is centered around college. You should do what you want to do, because you will never be this age again. Just enjoy life. (Recorded March 22, 1976.)

Of course, one knows that to get to a good college, one needs good grades from a good high school such as Utopia. A good college means a good job, which means a good income, a good house in a good community (like Pleasant Valley), good cars, and so forth. Utopia High School students are beneficiaries of the so-called good life that is the result of their parents jumping through these same hoops. They sense that something important is missing. School authorities are telling them to postpone their lives and they are not convinced. Work certainly doesn't hold much for these students. They are aware that some day they will have to get out in the "real world" and make a living. However, most hope that they can do it with a minimum of effort.

Many students feel that they are hemmed in. Their lives are not their own to lead. Yet there is no apparent reason for the constraints. School seems to exist because it is there. High school is preparation for college which is preparation for graduate school which is preparation for . . . and so on ad infinitum.

LARKIN. Tell me about an experience that you really felt "hemmed in," or that feeling that you felt. [This was in response to her complaint that she had a feeling, a "pathos" that was very difficult to explain.]

JENNY. Are you asking why, um . . .

L. Yeah, a concrete experience.

J. You see, it's very hard because I'm not really . . . A lot of it gets turned into a mental experience and then I . . . *(Pause)* Well, I just always feel hemmed in. Because I'm never . . . you know, I— I'm always hemmed in.

L. What would you be doing if you didn't have to go to school?

J. Well, if I didn't have to go to school, I'd probably be working on my art. And studying philosophy and theology. Would I be doing anything else? I would do the things I'm not doing now, basically. (Recorded March 29, 1976.)

Thus, Jenny is oppressed by the requirements that constrict her life. She feels the constrictions all the time. If liberated from them she would aspire to be a scholar-artist. The oppressive necessities of school get in the way of her own authentic education. Those things which give her life meaning; such as art, philosophy, and theology, are obfuscated by high school graduation requirements.

Bureaucratic regulation is a continual sore point for the students. They complain of surveillance by the school computer through the attendance procedures. Programing, counseling, and record keeping are sources of discontent. Even liberalization of regulations can be the source of a "Catch-22" situation. One student remarked:

If you are eighteen, you are supposed to have all the rights of an adult. But, still, to write your own [absence excuse] notes, you have to bring a note from your parents, so you can write your own notes. . . . When I went to see those [unintelligible] and things, you know, they asked me if I was eighteen, I said, "Yeah." They said, "you have to bring a note from your parents." *(Laughs)* (Recorded April 26, 1976.)

Although the students are highly sensitized to their own manipulation and the lack of control they have over their lives, they are disheartened by their own reactions (or more likely, their lack of reactions) to their situation. They see themselves as apathetic, yet sense that their own apathy works to the benefit of the adults who control their lives:

ROZ. . . . It's just that not so many people are willing to fight back, anymore. It's just like . . .

MARY. Give up!

R. Yeah.

JAN. Yeah. Even about the budget—

JED. End of the line, man. You gotta get off. (*Everyone chuckles*)

JAN. (*Continuing*) Yeah, it's even about the budget.

R. Well, there is nothing we can do about it. We can't—we're not responsible for what happens. So we just sit back and wait. And that's just what they want, too. They don't want to have to deal with any kids running around. (Recorded April 26, 1976.)

Not only are the actions of the adults the source of sense-lessness, but many times the behavior of peers are sources of absurdity. The toadying of the student leadership and the elitism of the newspaper staff are looked upon as ridiculous and stupid by the freaks. Vandalism, while understood and sympathized with by a substantial number of students who do not vandalize, is viewed as insane by the more adult-oriented students. Several students responded to the throwing of the Coke machine down the stairs in the following manner:

GARY. Some guys threw a vending machine down the stairs. It took a large chunk out of the . . .

BRENDA. That's sick! That is sick!

JENNIE. I think that is the most ruthless act of vandalism I have ever heard of. It is so meaningless, I couldn't believe it.

G. Especially if there was somebody underneath there. It would have killed them.

B. Did you see what they did to the stairs? I think that's sick!

LARKIN. One of the things you mentioned was that it was a meaningless act.

J. Senseless. (Recorded April 14, 1976.)

The "senseless sense of senselessness" is pervasive. It seems to engulf the student as a totality and can be seen in practically everything he or she does. The hopes of the 1960s are dead and there is nothing to take their place. The students are frustrated by their lives, yet see no alternative. The following is illustrative of their assessment of the situation:

LARKIN. What is the most frustrating experience you have ever had in this school?

JED. Going. (*Everyone laughs*) Gettin' up in the morning.

ROZ. Probably trying to . . .

JAN. Get up early.

R. Yeah, that too. I have a lot of hassles about that. But probably trying to bring changes. Trying to organize people. [Roz was one of the leaders of the great walkout.] Like I'm a homeroom representative. So I go to my homeroom and I try to talk to people. They don't care what's going on, and I can identify with that.

JED. You know, it's the first thing in the morning and you're still sitting there asleep. I know I am. I never listen to anything anybody says. Terrible.

R. And it gets pretty defeating after awhile, just trying to say that something's wrong with school. And I can't even fully identify it, but I know that in my ideal educational system, it would not be at all like this. At all. And trying to change it and being just totally frustrated because there's not the money, there's not the interest or the excitement or the energy or anything, except for the people who agree with me and talk about it.

LARKIN. Why do you think that apathy seems to be the mode of the day?

R. Because there's nothing to look up to. You see the government. After Watergate, who could have faith in anything? And then you see that the economy is falling apart and there is hardly any jobs any more and teachers are getting fired in our own school.

JAN. Even in the sixties, the people who were active in it—

R. Look at who is running for president this year. Who can we identify with? Jimmy Carter—I don't see anything in him.

JAN. Or even like the kids in the 1960s, like they're going to law school now, or they're going to med school. They've all lost something. Like my brother was pretty radical and he's going to law school in September. He says he's going to bring about changes that way, but it strikes me because I really looked up to him. [It

seems] like he's giving in, maybe to economic factors. I don't know.
I'm so idealistic. (Recorded April 26, 1976.)

In short, these students have managed to generate a critique of
everyday life ranging from getting up in the morning to trust in
government. They find everyday existence difficult to tolerate.
Roz has made strenuous efforts to change the system, but her
efforts have been in vain. Her ideal education system exists in her
head with no possibility of actualization. Jed has difficulty
making it through the day. Nobody sees the situation getting
better. As a matter of fact, that which they do have seems to be
eroding away. Opportunities are declining. The youth of the
1960s who were responsible for generating a vision of an alternative society are busy selling out and settling down to professional careers. Jan says sixties activists have lost something—
and they have: their idealism, their vision of a society in which
material necessity would not be a coercive force; they have lost
their hopes of a social order based on love. Roz, Jan, Jed, and
Mary are not really aware of the vision of the 1960s, but they are
aware that life as it is lived at Utopia High School in Pleasant
Valley is depressing. They are marking time until they can get
out.

THE GREAT REFUSAL

Now we are prepared to examine one of the most glaring para-
doxes of life at Utopia High. Students claim they are bored and
there is nothing to do. Yet extra-curricular activities are withering
away because of lack of student participation. Student leaders are
often found begging other students for participation in club or
committee events. Gordon (1957), in his study of Wabash High in
the 1950s found that the extra-curricular activities (called the
semi-curriculum by him) were a device used by the school to
maintain the allegiance of the students and co-opt them into
school participation through appeals to their interests. It is clear
that in the 1970s at Utopia High, the students are not being co-
opted in this manner.

Over the past several years, but especially in 1976, there has been a precipitous decline in student participation in school-related clubs. It was estimated that in the past school year, one-third of the student clubs had stopped functioning because of declining enrollments. Gary, the editor of the school yearbook, described the situation:

> **GARY.** Well, all I know is our activities editor went to supposedly all the clubs that existed and it seems that none of them exist any more. No one cares or—
>
> **JENNY.** They've become obsolete.
>
> **G.** Yeah, they just didn't exist this year.
>
> **LARKIN.** Would you say there were half as many clubs that exist this year than last year?
>
> **G.** Yeah. (Recorded March 29, 1976.)

In a discussion with the activities' editor who was in charge of soliciting all the clubs for yearbook pictures, I attempted to verify the fact that the club structure had undergone rapid decline:

> **LARKIN.** It was mentioned to me that there are half as many clubs this year as there were last year. Is that correct?
>
> **ACTIVITIES' EDITOR.** Yeah, well, it's not quite half, maybe two-thirds.
>
> **L.** What clubs have gone by the wayside?
>
> **A. E.** The tutorial committee. That's not a club, but it's . . . a committee that took students during their free time and other students and they would help them in, like, say one student, let's say I was having trouble with math and May was good in math, then she would help me in it. We'd take my commons and her commons [periods] and, you know, get me up to the rest of my class.
>
> **L.** Do you know why that went down the tubes?
>
> **A. E.** It sort of went down when we started having commons periods, because no one wanted to give up their commons. The reason being that during formal study hall students didn't mind giving up their formal studies to be helped in a subject. Once they had commons periods, kids didn't want to give up their free time. So it wasn't that they couldn't find kids to tutor, they couldn't find kids who wanted to be tutored.

L. Oh. Because the commons time is used for hanging out?

A. E. Yeah. Pretty much. . . . I have just found in my involvement as the activities' editor with the students . . . and the
teachers . . . that there is a huge amount of—and Gary will back
me up on this—of just, I can't think of a word—apathy? They just
don't care. I would send out three notices and a teacher wouldn't
answer. And then I would call them up and they would say, "Okay,
come take a picture of the club. I'll call a meeting." I'd get there
with a photographer and there would be one kid there.

GARY. Some clubs just exist for the fact of having a yearbook
picture and are supposedly in the yearbook. But otherwise, they
have no function. They don't do anything.

A. E. They've never done anything. . . . I have just noticed,
because I have looked through last year's yearbook and the year
before to get some idea of how to put my section together. Just a
noticeably marked decrease in the number of people who are
involved in things like that around this school.

G. Even in the clubs that do exist, there are like half the amount of
people in them.

A. E. We used to have clubs in which you had to have three pictures
to get them in. And this year they fit in one. . . .

G. Well, we practically—we were just going to put in a picture of
empty chairs and say, "This is a typical—"

A. E. "Utopia Activities Committee," we were going to call it. I
thought it was a good idea. This was after [the] speed reading [club]
didn't show up for the fourth time in a row. . . .

L. Are there any clubs that are as successful as those in the past?

A. E. There's a couple. The prom committee. Things that are, oh I
don't know, they have something to *do*, not just they meet. . . .
The prom committee is only one year. You know it's forty girls
planning a dinner. And, you know, they devote a whole year to it.
So it's perpetuated because every year there's a new class president
and there are new people who want to plan a prom. (Recorded April
14, 1976.)

The prom committee, the Black Students' Union (BSU), the
skiing and cycling clubs were all cited by the editor as being
successful clubs. The BSU caters, of course, to the black students,
most of whom are outside the cultural mainstream of Utopia

High. It has been a stable group over the past several years. The cycling and skiing clubs both sponsor activities beyond school participation. The prom committee, which has the sole task of planning the senior prom at the end of the year, is not as successful as the editors of the yearbook think. I found the prom committee hard at work a week and a half before the prom was to be held. Three students were working on prom bids. One was the senior class president and the other two were her close friends and most dedicated workers. Although sixty-eight young women showed up for the first meeting of the prom committee, the number of people actually working had dwindled to about twenty, half the estimate of that of the yearbook editor. The sale of prom bids (tickets) was going slowly. The prom committee workers feared that they might have to cancel the prom due to lack of interest. The prom was held, although only 135 of the 175 bids were sold.

Why has club structure fallen apart? Why is the prom, once the highlight of the social calendar, no longer an important event. Why do students cut classes at ever-increasing rates? We might term this phenomenon "the Great Refusal." When given the alternative of voluntary participation in school activities without coercion, students would rather not participate. The Great Refusal is the negation of the liberal assumption: If students are given greater freedom to choose within a formal structure, they will be thankful for the opportunity to select from administratively determined alternatives. This underestimates the alienation of students and misinterprets the predominant student view of schooling. Most students view school as *inherently* coercive. Therefore, any participation in school activities is participation in one's own oppression. Students would rather hang out and tolerate the boredom and meaninglessness of their own existence than participate in an activity presented in the context of an authority structure. Students tend to view schooling as *unpaid labor*. Therefore, their response to it is to minimize their commitment as much as possible and to try to get away with as little work as possible, given the constraints of grades.

An example of this phenomenon is the substitution of commons periods for study halls. In study halls, students were compelled to use the time for academic purposes under the supervision of teachers. The commons periods removed the compulsory study requirement and allowed the students to structure their commons period activities as they saw fit. Although most students were much happier about not being forced into study halls, the presence of commons periods has raised a new question that reflects the alienation of students from the structure of schooling. Equating schooling with class attendance, students are questioning the necessity of remaining on campus when they do not have a class. It is seen as a waste of time, because that time could possibly be used for working at a job and earning money. The relaxation of coercive means does not necessarily co-opt the student population into believing that things are better than they were in the past, but, rather, helps to convince them that all the time spent in school is not necessary. This argument was presented to me in the following conversation:

LARKIN. Are you in a commons period right now?

LOUISE. Yeah. It's one of the things I don't like, 'cause all you can do is walk around and talk to people. You don't feel like doing your homework all the time. I have at least two free periods.

LARKIN. So what do you do during those free periods?

LOUISE. I either go to the library and do my homework or read a magazine. Or I walk around—I usually walk around or go out to eat.

VINNIE. You weren't supposed to say that. [Indicating that it is illegal to leave campus during school hours.]

LOUISE. I know.

LARKIN. What would you do during your commons periods if you had unlimited resources? I mean, what would you really want to do during your commons periods? Would you want to eliminate them or what?

LOUISE. I think they should be eliminated.

V. I don't.

LOUISE. (*To Vinnie*) Because school isn't the place to come and play.

LARKIN.   You'd just as soon come in here, get your work done and go home?

LOUISE. I mean, split session. I'd come in [at] eight o'clock and leave at twelve. That's enough time. That's about as much time as I spend in class anyway.

LARKIN. So you feel that you are confined to school longer than is necessary.

LOUISE. Yes. It's like they are baby sittin'. (Recorded May 2, 1976.)

Thus, school is viewed by Louise in terms of its instrumental function only. It is a place to attend classes and do schoolwork. Beyond that, there is no reason to hang around. One's time can be used to one's own purposes better if one were not legally required to be in school. This view is a popular one held on campus. Louise, although alienated from school, is the president of one of the school's more successful clubs, the Black Students' Union, and received a scholarship from Duke University. Similar views were held by members of the "freak" and "greaser" subcultures.

THE COLLAPSE OF COMMUNITY

The instrumentalization of the high school has had important consequences for its function as a community institution. Schools, along with churches, have been the major enforcers of the community moral order. With the decline of the legitimacy of schools and the increasing reluctance of school officials to enforce repressive sanctions, the moral order of the school has declined. Even at the high school, the *en loco parentis* function has diminished. Teachers no longer see themselves as the enforcers of community norms, but rather attempt to limit students' behavior for purely instrumental reasons (e.g., controlling disruptive behavior in the class when it interferes with the instructional process), as occurred in the first chapter, when a student with a cigarette asked a teacher for a light. In the 1950s, every high school seemed to have its teacher, who, at school dances, would walk around the floor with a ruler to make sure that couples were not dancing too close together. Underage smoking was grounds for suspension. The regulation of student behavior was arbitrary and rigorously enforced. The students of those times were able to tolerate much greater repression than the students of the 1970s.

The teachers do not see themselves as representatives of the community moral order, especially since they are unhappy with the way the school district has been treating them lately. They are nearly as alienated as the students. They see their jobs primarily in their capacity to impart knowledge to students within the confines of the classroom. Supervision of students outside the classrooms is onerous labor. The high school has become a complex bureaucracy with competing constituencies and departments. This functional specialization of bureaucracy leads to a fractioning of responsibilities and jurisdictions in combination with an underlying alienation. Responsibilities have become formalized in contract negotiations, and jurisdictional control is compulsory. Teachers do not want to patrol halls, and non-classroom duties are included in negotiations with the school board.

With the loss of the communitarian aspects of the educational process comes the notion that school is just a job—nothing more, nothing less. As a matter of fact, it seems inconceivable that students at one time heavily involved themselves in schooling beyond the mere attending of classes and that teachers involved themselves beyond the mere teaching of classes:

> **JED.** . . . I remember [looking at] the yearbook [for the year] my father graduated from here. I couldn't believe some of the clubs, you know, some people got so into it, you know, when he went to school. The Red Cross Club was standing there with their uniforms on with their little boxes with the red crosses on them. (*Laughter*) I couldn't believe it.
>
> **JAN.** That's just like another thing that goes along with apathy. Everyone like wants to get out of school as soon as possible.
>
> **ROZ.** Yeah, *it's like a job.*
>
> **JAN.** The teachers, too.

R. Nine to three. And then, maybe there's a little bit of homework. Sticking around after school is just not done. After three o'clock the halls are empty, it seems to me. (Recorded April 26, 1976, emphasis mine.)

The school, then, has lost its ability to capture the allegiance of its participants. It no longer has any transcendent legitimation. Although the leadership and power of the educational institution is in the hands of adults, they no longer use their status *as adults* to command authority over students. Their formal roles as teachers and administrators are the basis for their authority. But they are very hesitant to use their positions as adults to sanction student behaviors. This is, in part, due to the residue of the youth movement. These young people are still suspicious of anyone over thirty and regard adults, by virtue of their status as adults, as oppressors. If a teacher attempts to sanction a student's personal behavior, he is likely to find himself questioned as to the basis of his authority. Such incidents are likely to encourage the wrath of parents, who also perceive the teachers as instrumental specialists who have no moral authority over the students beyond the rules for maintaining an orderly school.

Students have been freed from the constraints of continual adult surveillance and oppressiveness, and their private behavior is their own. Teachers and administrators no longer "hassle" Utopia High School students over such private behaviors as hair length, dress codes, facial hair, or jeans for women. Drug use is overlooked, so long as it doesn't overtly affect the instructional program. Smoking is allowed, and the norm of reasonableness reigns. However, the problem is that this liberalization has occurred in a climate of alienation and estrangement. Rules are left unenforced not so much because of overriding concerns for the rights and privileges of students, but because it *requires extra work.* Instead of a group of autonomous individuals working toward common goals, the school has become divested of its communal spirit and has become a hollow shell where teachers and students put in time. Existence at Utopia High School has become dreary and devoid of life.

THE REFUGE OF THE SELF

The general decline in the legitimacy of all social institutions has led to radical individualism. Students at Utopia High find that the one thing they can believe in is the self. With the fragmentation of the movement of the 1960s, John Lennon sang, after declaiming the emerging deities (e.g., mantra, Buddha, Jesus, etc.), "I believe in me/Yoko and me,/And that is reality." This certainly seems to be the case among Utopia High students. Sarah (in chapter 4) found meaning in an otherwise capricious world in her love affair with Fred. The freaks found meaning only in adhering to a radically present-oriented subjectivism. They also found it in activities in which they could be their authentic selves:

STUDENT 1. We have a good time, man. We don't fuck anybody else over. You know?

STUDENT 2. That's what—we're just doing—

S. 1. We do our thing. We do our thing.

STUDENT 3. [Being] ourselves. "Suit yourself."

S. 1. I mean, we get high and have ourselves a good time. We don't go around destroying things, and in getting high we don't fuck other people over, like we don't make it harder for other people to live, you know.

S. 2. Yeah, we're not bothering—

S. 1. We are looked down upon because of the name that pot's been given. But, like, if you ask me, I think we're better off than most people around. Like, I mean, we all have our problems and everything, but we know where it's at more than a lot of other people do. You know, we're not like plastic people, you know? We're ourselves. So smoking pot and drinking beer and partying and having a good time is being ourselves. (Recorded March 22, 1976.)

The freaks find authenticity in non-coerced activities, such as partying, drinking, and smoking pot. In this respect, they are similar to the greasers who see themselves as authentic on the weekends. Perhaps the most articulate statement on the subject was made by Jennie:

LARKIN. What makes sense these days?

JENNIE. I make sense.

L. You make sense.

J. Yeah.

L. I mean, is there anything outside of you that makes sense?

J. What do you mean?

L. You were saying that things have a sense of senselessness to them. I was just wondering what is it in your life that gives meaning and purpose to it.

J. Some people I know. My own mind. . . . Myself. What I was born with.

L. What were you born with?

J. My personality. The genes to have the personality that I do.

L. What "genes"?

J. I believe that everybody is born with something that makes them take impulses a certain way. . . .

L. What I am trying to get from you is what makes your life meaningful, because I have been talking to a whole lot of people around here and they don't seem to be able to attach much meaning and purpose to their lives.

J. The people that I know. The things I do with my life. If I write a poem. I write poetry. If I write a poem, I think that gives meaning to my life. If I love a person, that gives me meaning. That's enough. (Recorded April 13, 1976.)

What is fascinating about Jennie is that she does not seek meaning from school or career, but in such personal experiences as writing poetry and loving another person. By implication, then, the time she spends getting an education, preparing for a career is not central to her sense of selfhood or meaning. Contrarily, as she indicated (see p. 128), schooling is an actual threat.

Thus, the self seems to be the mooring of last resort for Jennie and the others. Consciousness is the one thing they can call their own. It is the one thing they can work on that is perceived to be totally their own construction. Why does Jennie attribute the self, which is so obviously a social construction, to genetics? It is my hypothesis that Jennie, like so many of her peers, sees society as *only* external, factitious, and imposed. The internalized self exists in *opposition* and in *contradiction* to the social order. Therefore, according to her own internal logic, the self is the opposite of social: emergent, spontaneous, *self-created*, intuitive. To her, it is a residue of that which is egalitarian, loving, and universal. It is the expression of this vulnerable aspect of herself that gives her life meaning. Society is seen as the enemy of the internalized truth. It is a set of alien structures.

AN OPTIMISTIC FEAR OF THE FUTURE

As the students turn inward for meaning and purpose rather than looking for them in a predominantly arbitrary and meaningless institutional life, it is indeed surprising that they view the future with optimism. Although their optimism is guarded and often stems from the belief that "things have got to get better," the students are, nevertheless, optimistic. However, the optimism of Utopia High students is tinged with fear. They realize that sooner or later, they will have to work for a living. They hope that good jobs will be available. Many look forward to settling down to conventional existences, raising a family, and living a stable life. But such plans tend to be thought of as occurring "someday." Most Utopia High students see the process of settling down as a manifestation of a vague and distant future.

For the students from working-class backgrounds, the future is somewhat more immediate. Upon graduation, they plan to get a job or go to technical school to learn a trade. It is through this training that they hope one day they will open up their own businesses. This desire adheres closely to the great American dream. In discussing the future with several working-class students, the following conversation transpired:

LARKIN. What do you see yourselves doing in, say, ten years?

MARGE. Working.

L. Working? Do you plan to get married?

ROGER. [In response to the prior question.] Owning my own shop.

M. Oh, yeah, I want to have my own kids.

R. (*To Marge*) You want to work for somebody all your life? . . .

M. What else? What else am I going to do?

R. Open up your own place.

M. So? I'm still workin'.

JOE. . . . I'm startin' a business selling TVs. I do all right now. I make money.

L. You are actually in business now?

J. Well, not quite. I don't have a license for it yet. (Recorded April 13, 1976.)

For the college-bound students, the future takes on a more nebulous character and they are much less sure what direction their lives will take. However, they tend to be quite optimistic about the possibilities. Jed, who is not college-bound, shares the uncertainties voiced by those who are going to college:

LARKIN. What do you see as the most important issues, problems, or concerns you have?

JED. Getting out of school. (*Laughs*) What are you going to do for the rest of your life.

L. Do you have any answers?

J. Well, I have some things I want to do—that I think I want to do, but I don't know if I want to do them. I'm not sure, you know? (Recorded April 26, 1976.)

Many students were unsure of what direction their lives were going to take beyond high school, but they were not overly concerned. They figured that they would find something to do and that the future would take care of itself. When asked how they viewed their future, a group of students (some college-bound, some not) responded:

JAN. With optimism.

JED. Optimism, definitely.

LARKIN. Do you think things are going to improve?

ROZ. I figure by next year, there's going to be enough unemployed people and dissatisfied people in this country, that if something big doesn't happen it will be amazing. That's what I think. I think that there is no way that it can keep getting [worse] without people fighting it. (Recorded April 26, 1976.)

When asked what they saw themselves doing in ten years, they were very unsure of themselves, but figured that, for the most part, life would present them with the opportunities to provide themselves with what they wanted:

LARKIN. What do you see yourselves doing in ten or fifteen years?

ROZ. Not much. (*Laughs*)

JED. Work. That's what I think about.

L. Do you think about having a family, getting married?

J. Oh, no. It's going to be hard enough supporting yourself.

CHUCK. Yeah. There's a lot before that.

L. You're going to put that off for quite awhile?

J. Yeah. We'll put that aside for now.

L. (*Indicating Mary*) How about you? Do you see yourself as getting married right away, putting it off, or never—

MARY. I don't know, really. . . . I know I'm not going to be a secretary taking steno fifteen years from now.

L. What are the alternatives?

M. I can get married—be married and have a family.

L. Does that appeal to you?

M. Eventually. I don't know. . . .

L. How about the rest of you?

R. I guess I've always been taught, directly or indirectly, that if I want to do something, I can do it. And so I kind of—I don't want to be one thing. You know, you ask people, "What are you?" "I'm a lawyer." or "I'm a—a—." I don't want to do that. I don't want to be a professional. I think I want to—I don't know. I want to live on a farm. I want to live in the city and take shitty jobs and do other things on the side. I want to travel. I want to start a school. I want to start an artists' thing. I don't know. I just kind of assume that the whole world is open to me and I can just get and take from it what I want. I don't think I am going to continue in the life-style of my parents. (Recorded April 26, 1976.)

Roz sees the very loss of legitimacy and the decline of institutional functioning as a source of optimism. She is much more intellectually sophisticated than her counterparts. Her analysis is reminiscent of the 1960s:

LARKIN. What concerns me is that if education doesn't work, politics don't work, if religion doesn't work, if the family doesn't work, which is, I think, true for most people, what does?

ROZ. People do.

L. Yeah, but people have to band together in some sort of ways, in some sort of collective effort. Oh, yes, and work certainly does not work.

JAN. That's what makes it scary.

R. That's what this country is, you know. I think that is one of the most frightening things. No, wait. It's *not* the most frightening thing. There are a thousand other things that are threatening. But, like, that puts a lot more responsibility on me, which I want. But I am scared of the—there's no system that I can put in the data and the answer will come out of what I should do. Like there's no system of religion, there's no—I don't believe in the American system of values, as I see them. So I will have to make most of my decisions on my own. . . . But I also look forward to that. I'm glad about that.

L. If there's no structure that you can put faith in, . . . where do you look to place your faith and trust?

J. I look to better examples than what is going on right here. You can look to other countries, you can look to other communities. For instance, what you said about jobs. There are people who are satisfied with their jobs and really love it. Like, in factories that are beginning to be controlled by the workers. There are a lot of workers who really love their work. The same with education. There are a lot of people who really like going to school. You have to look for those examples and find out, you know, what the

differences are. I mean it's not *all* going down-hill. There are lights.
(Recorded April 26, 1976.)

Based on the old saw, "Every cloud has a silver lining," Roz and
Jan find hope in the future in terms of the individuals who are
able to carve out happy, meaningful lives within the system or as
active participants in changing it. They see alternative models of
existence emerging from other societies that may provide the
solution to some of America's seemingly insoluble problems. Yet,
Roz and Jan are unusual people. Roz aspires to be a poet and
rejects the notion of a conventional career. Jan is a talented
musician who is going to study in Paris next year. Their optimism exists in their own efforts to transcend the system. They see
themselves as architects of their own futures, not a widespread
view, even though most students hope that they will be able to
live autonomous lives.

The views of the future presented by the students of Utopia
High are centered around the contradiction between desire and
necessity. They all realize the necessity of earning a living, but
they would like to pursue the kinds of labor that have intrinsic
rewards—work that is meaningful, contributes to the social good,
and provides a measure of autonomy. We are reminded of Roger's
question, "Do you want to work for someone else the rest of your
life?" The overwhelming answer is "no," but only Mary admits
that for her, there is no alternative. Sarah's critique of future
opportunities seems to summarize the problem well, so she will
have the last word on the future:

LARKIN. Do you want to pursue a career, or be a housewife?

SARAH. I would *love* to pursue a career. It's just that right now all
the hassle of getting good grades and so on are driving me up a wall
and I don't think I will make it into any college that will give me
what I really want. I'm very interested in philosophy. I'd love to be a
lawyer, I really would, but you need a lot of money. We don't have a
lot of money. And I am incredibly lazy. I happen to be a very lazy
person. I don't think I could do all the work. It would probably be
worth it, but I don't even know, then, because what are you going to
do? Get a job as a philosopher? There's no such thing. I mean if

you're interested in philosophy, you have to do something to make money. Everything, no matter how you circle around it or beat around the bush about it, it comes down to money. How much money are you going to make in a year? How are you going to support yourself? And I don't like that system at all. (Recorded May 3, 1976.)

CONCLUSION: WHO GIVES A DAMN?

In this chapter, our main concern has been the subjective experiences of the students at Utopia High. They experience "institutional reality" as unreal. Their lives are pervaded by a lack of purpose and meaning. They have difficulty in making sense of what they do, and feel themselves coerced and "hemmed in." Yet this subjective awareness occurs in a setting that is far more liberal than that in other schools and in other communities around the nation and is certainly more liberal than the educational context that was experienced by high school students of the 1950s and 1960s. This means that the students of the 1970s have sensitized themselves to the repression of their behavior to a much higher degree than students prior to the youth movement of the 1960s.

Since they are acutely aware of the arbitrariness of their lives, much of their behavior is a reaction to this pervasive sense of oppressiveness. Most choose the line of least resistance: they withdraw emotionally from the school experience, accept it as a necessary part of existence, and live for "free time," in which they can indulge in pleasures and experience themselves as "authentic" beings. Most "free time" is spent on the weekends or during vacations. Their lives are pervaded by a sense of boredom and they yearn to participate in non-coerced activities. They look forward to "getting blasted" or "getting wasted" on the weekends and to partying; however, such events merely function as release valves so they can get through another week. The high they obtain on the weekends is only high in comparison to the grayness of the rest of the week. As we found in chapter 4, the highs generated through pot and sex tend to be merely physical and emotional releases from otherwise humdrum lives. They are primarily attempts at warding off the abyss of everyday life.

This sense of absurdity is heightened by virtue of the fact that the administration has instituted "student input" channels in the decision-making process, but when push comes to shove, the mechanism is exposed as a sham and student powerlessness is laid bare. Since there is no student movement and since the acts against the system, such as vandalism, work against the students, political activism is seen as futile. Even though student politics is incorporated into the structure of the system, the students have learned to take what is given to them and realize that there is little that can be done about what is taken away.

Because of their powerlessness, students find that "purposive action" in the institutional world is not worth the effort. Instead, they withdraw into themselves as the refuge of last resort. The self is the one thing that is their own. They have power over their own thoughts and feelings. The self is the last bastion of autonomy and is cherished by many students at Utopia High as that which is truly "theirs" and which supplies, meaning to their lives. Friends—intimates with whom they can share essentially private experiences—are another source of meaning. The affinity group of like-minded peers provides a bulwark against the formalized world of adults. Yet, friendships are often subject to change and the ephemerality of life at Utopia High serves to undermine the cohesiveness of friends and the meaningfulness of their relationships.

Because their lives are subject to social forces over which they have no control, Utopia High students view the future with uncertainty. They are optimistic, in that they feel that somehow things will get better. They all realize that sooner or later, they will have to encounter the "real world" out there and begin supporting themselves. Nobody particularly wants to work in a hierarchical structure: the working-class students want to operate their own businesses (usually automotive repair shops), while students from a middle-class background want to become artists or free professionals. There is a sense among them that seems to question the necessity of routinized labor, and few are willing to

admit that they will probably have to work in a highly bureaucratized structure.

School life is, for the most part, boring and unrewarding. The
students are putting in time, hoping that the next phase of their
lives will be happier. They participate in social structures in
which they don't really give a damn, and they suspect that the
teachers and administration don't either, beyond doing what is
necessary and collecting their paychecks. School has changed
from a pasture to a corral. No longer is its main function to
nurture the young and prepare them for community life. It has
become a holding pen for superfluous people who are segregated
from significant community participation. Because of this shift,
the community of the school has been divested of life and spirit. It
is just another hurdle in a long line of hurdles to get over in the
progression of existence. As such, the school contains little to
enrich the lives of Pleasant Valley youth.

NOTES

1. The term *bourgeois ego* refers to those aspects of the self which conform to the
   expectations of bourgeois culture, which raised the demands of productivity to
   ideals of virtuous behavior, called *values*, a term derived from classical
   economics (e.g., use value, exchange value) that presupposes rational calcu-
   lation on the part of the valuing individual. The values of bourgeois culture
   are dominated by the reality principle: postponement of pleasure, work as its
   own reward, sexual restraint, deference to hierarchy, punctuality, rationality,
   and compulsive orderliness. For details on the characterology of bourgeois
   culture, see Riesman's discussion of the "inner-directed" personality in *The
   Lonely Crowd* (1955) or Erikson's discussion of the anal-retentive personality
   in *Childhood and Society* (1950).
2. The erosion of student privileges recorded in 1976 have escalated over the
   following year. An editorial entitled, "Stagnant Council," in the February
   1977 issue of the student newspaper, scores the student leadership for not
   acting to protect student "rights":

   > In this year of increasing restrictions on students' freedoms, one would think that the
   > Executive committee would have its hands filled with resolutions designed to improve
   > the plight of the student. . . .
   >   The only resolution which is of any value to the students is the "open campus
   > resolution" which was not even suggested by the Executive committee.
   >   We feel that the Executive committee should have no trouble in coming up with
   > meaningful resolutions directly affecting the student body, given the drastic curtail-

ment of students' rights this year. When and if the Executive committee ever resolves the issue of open campus, it should address itself to such issues as cutting penalties, increased commons flexibility, and greater student access to resource areas and materials.

To the Executive committee:

. . . Be it resolved that the Executive committee work with the students instead of around them.

6

THE OTHER SIDE
OF THE BARRICADE

Don't you give me no dirty looks,
Your father's hip, he knows what cooks.
Just tell your hoodlum friend outside,
You ain't got time to take a ride.
Yakety-yak.
Don't talk back.

The Coasters, "Yakety-Yak," 1958

It's getting better all the time
I used to get mad at my school
The teachers that taught me weren't cool
You're holding me down, turning me round
Filling me up with your rules.

The Beatles, "Getting Better," 1967

Wednesday morning at five o'clock as the day begins
Silently closing her bedroom door
Leaving the note that she hoped would say more
She goes downstairs to the kitchen clutching her
    handkerchief
Quietly turning the backdoor key
Stepping outside she is free.
She (We gave her most of our lives)
Is leaving (We gave her everything money could buy)
She's leaving home after living alone
For so many years. Bye, bye.

The Beatles, "She's Leaving Home," 1967

The students' views of adults are not particularly flattering. The police are "punks" and are resented for heavy-handed enforcement of drug laws. There are some "good" teachers, but most are seen as boring plodders more interested in getting from 9 A.M. to 3 P.M. than in turning students on to intellectual pursuits. The principal is seen as a remote figure who commits himself to a position on an issue as little as possible in an attempt at self-protection. Counselors are distrusted and accused of either attempting to inveigle the confidences of the students or not caring. Finally, parents are graded on their ability to understand their teenagers and allow them autonomy to live their own lives as they see fit. Few measure up to the criteria.

What are the adults in the students' lives like? How do the adults view this generation of young people? What do they see as the problems of these students? In an attempt to find out how the significant adults in these students' lives feel and think about them, I interviewed some teachers, a counselor, the principal, the juvenile officer in the community, and several parents.

THE TEACHERS: A SENSE OF LOSS

The teachers, like the students, are gritting their teeth and weathering the changes at Utopia High. However, they are more stoic in their toleration. They view the decline in resources and the increased class sizes with dismay and see their ability to instruct students undermined by the erosion of support services. Older teachers have watched the motivation and pleasure of students with school gradually decline over the years and remember the "good old days" in which students really wanted to know what teachers had to teach them. Increasingly, they are being called upon to police resisting students. The teachers see themselves caught in the middle of a crossfire of expectations. The community wants them to enforce a more highly regimented curriculum upon the students, while the students want greater latitudes of freedom in choosing and executing their own studies. No one is happy.

Apart from the changes in the students, the teachers were most upset about the cutbacks in the educational program wrought by the financial crisis. The cutbacks increased class size and reduced the amount of available resources. One teacher related the following:

LARKIN. What are the effects of the cutbacks? . . .

FEMALE TEACHER. Everything is going to be marred by it terribly. I mean, when you put thirty or forty kids in a class you are not going to have what you would have had when you had sixteen or twenty. And that's 'big tragedy number one. It's above and beyond what you can do well. And we did very well. We had very individualized instruction in this school. They closed the language labs and found within a couple of weeks, out of desperation, they had better open it. So we had parents come and take more menial, er, trivial jobs so that the language experts could get up there and do something about these materials that would be waylaid. You bought all the material and you have the experts to handle it. And now you close it and ask the experts to be . . . policemen, perhaps. You're not saving money there. You're paying me for the lab work and having me do police work. You're *wasting* money. (Recorded May 19, 1976.)

The teachers, like the students, see themselves in a situation where it is increasingly difficult to do what they want in the context of the school. The teachers, who are there to instruct students, are finding it difficult to do so in the face of reduced resources and community support. However, they view themselves as responding positively to the crisis by honoring their commitment to the students in their attempts to overcome hardships generated by the tightened economy. A young teacher employed in the school for the past three years said:

As far as [Utopia], compared to other districts I have taught in, if you cut back everything in this district, the teacher here would probably be doing just as good if not a better job than they are now. I'm convinced of that. I say, "When you cut back money, let's refuse to teach that subject." They won't do that here. The people are too . . . damn professional. I think you could smack them in the face and they would still come back and want to teach the kids. It's unbelievable. The other school district I was in, man, at a quarter to three everybody is out of the building. . . . If you didn't have paper, you would refuse to give a test. They don't do that here. Teachers bring paper from home, they recycle things. . . . Our department will moan about a cutback and say, "Gee, this is going to hurt the kids." But the teacher will turn right around, go back into that classroom and give 110 percent. (Recorded May 19, 1976.)

However, another teacher, after hearing the above teacher, stated that the increase in class size made it impossible to teach; and the teacher quoted above admitted he was not the type he had described. Even with the attempts to do one's job despite the adversities, the teachers feel discouraged and beaten. Underlying the brave words of the teacher fighting the odds is a sense of futility and loss. Not only are the teachers getting pressured from above, but also from below.

A teacher who had taught at Utopia for thirty years was disheartened when she talked of the changes in the student-teacher relationships:

LARKIN. How have student-teacher relationships changed over the past twenty to thirty years? . . .

TEACHER. The subject was very important to [a student twenty to thirty years ago]. He was dedicated to learning. He wanted to learn. He had a zest for learning. . . . They worked *beyond* what you wanted them to. It seems incredible, but it was there. It was *there*. Then, slowly, through the years, the student changed. He'd not ask you to do this, . . . but he would begin to *tell* you what to do. And he was not qualified. . . . Today, a student thinks he can tell you how to teach Spanish, even though he hasn't studied any Spanish or learned any yet. They're ready to give opinions on things without any background at all. That's a big change. (Recorded May 19, 1976.)

This teacher sees herself as an expert and the students as novices. She is disturbed by their resistance to being defined as such and their attempts to equalize the relationship. She focused herself on the subject matter and they were concerned with the hierarchical relationship. The conflict between this teacher and her students concerned the definition of classroom reality. She assumed that she was there in her role as expert and expected the students to respect her dominance because of her superior knowledge. Yet the students did not seem to acknowledge expertise as a legitimate criterion for classroom control and were continually trying to wrest it from her. In the 1960s, the notion of the superiority of experts was undermined, as "freakified" youth and their academic counterparts declaimed them as inherently hierarchical, linear, and co-opted by the "establishment" (see Foss, 1972, chapter 4; and Roszak, 1969, chapter 7). This delegitimation of the role of the expert has continued throughout the 1970s to the point where this teacher said that students are audacious enough to claim that they know how they should be taught Spanish better than she does. The students are suspicious of her expertise and her institutional superiority. As institutions decline in their legitimacy, the authority of the office holders is questioned. This same teacher laments:

> **TEACHER.** Today, [the students] ask, "Why are we doing this lesson?" So you have to give ten minutes, perhaps I am exaggerating slightly, but you've got to give them ten minutes to convince them that this lesson is worthwhile because if you achieve it, these are the things that will come. [I say,] "Trust me. I know that it is worthwhile for you. Let's not waste ten minutes of today on telling you why we should learn this."

> **LARKIN.** So you are saying that there is a decline in trust between students and teacher.

> **T.** Perhaps that's it. They don't trust anything. I wouldn't say that it's less trust for me than anything else. There's a sick distrust in general of everything. (Recorded May 19, 1976.)

Another teacher commented that students were continually asking, "Why?" when assignments were given. He suggested that this part of a shift in student orientation from cognitive to affective interests:

> When I started teaching, the thrust at the training schools, also where I first began [teaching] . . . was subject-oriented. Kids did come to learn a subject. At the end of that, they wanted to know the subject. Now I venture to guess that a lot of students choose personalities, rather than the subject. I get a lot of kids that don't care what you're teaching, just so it's you. There are other kids who avoid me like the plague even though they think the course might

be worthwhile. So here we are talking about personalities and feeling rather than what is being taught. (Recorded May 19, 1976.)

The teachers seem unanimous in their agreement that students are more concerned about the teachers than the subject matter. On the one hand students are suspicious of authority, while on the other, they search for teachers who satisfy more affective requirements. In line with the rise of subjectivism of the 1960s, the students of the 1970s search out teachers who "turn them on." In the previous chapter, Gary told of searching out classes that offered him something and then he went after it. He also said that such classes were rare in Utopia High.

The teachers were also saddened by the decline in student motivation and spirit. They agreed that students are less happy in school in the 1970s than they have been during previous decades. The teachers saw the students as less motivated to do school work, less skillful in basics, poorly informed, and generally less involved in school as a social institution. The changing attitudes of students compound the sense of loss of the teachers. The Spanish teacher retells the decline of the club she sponsored.

SPANISH TEACHER. The Pan-American Club dissolved itself in the 1960s because it was established [unintelligible]. And I saw that thing disintegrate. It was one of the most beautiful things we had. (*To the nurse*) You remember that.

NURSE. We had a future nurses club that disintegrated, too. Nobody was interested.

S.T. And then, suddenly, "Oh, no. [We're] against the establishment! This is an established thing, we'll do it without organization." And without organization, I saw it disintegrate.

N. That's what happened with my group.

S.T. I could have stopped it. I saw the young teachers come in and help it disintegrate. They were against the establishment. Well, you couldn't learn Spanish. (Recorded May 19, 1976.)

Even though the temper of the times eroded the club structure and the insurgencies of the 1960s was an irresistable force in the school, the teacher blamed herself for the failure of the Pan-American Club. She felt that she had allowed it to happen. Yet, she refrained from asserting herself on behalf of her conception of how the club ought to be run, since she felt that the students may be right. She felt guilty, while at the same time, she felt powerless in the face of forces over which she had no control. Her sentiments were echoed by the nurse, who had been at the school for the same amount of time as she.

If this wasn't depressing enough, the fact that many students did not seem even to like or care for teachers was the crowning blow.

> **NURSE.** I think that what I see as a difference is in the give and take. They don't give.
>
> **SPANISH TEACHER.** Yes, that's right.
>
> **N.** I used to have students willing to come and help in my office. Help me, help other students. Now even if you ask for help, they'll shake their heads. (Recorded May 19, 1976.)

The older teachers consoled themselves with the fact that at Utopia High about fifty percent of the students are academically motivated and want to learn. The Spanish teacher remembered when almost all the students were that way. The younger teacher saw the students as responding to economic realities imposed by declining family spending power.

> **LARKIN.** You mentioned that students don't seem as willing to give as much as they used to, but they seem less committed to school—
>
> **YOUNG TEACHER.** I'll agree with that maybe to the school, but the student who could give up his time years ago when he could stay after school or maybe take time off during school, [the Alternative School] kids have to cut out at 12:30 to make those bucks! To compete in the world on the weekend, keep that car. I mean, we have kids who are working and have to put money in their own homes. . . . As far as that kid being dedicated, boy, he is dedicated to that job. If we give him time in class to help out, for instance to help me out or fix my car or work on a puppet show, if you give them time in school, yeah, they'll work hard. But I don't think he is going to give his time after school, before school, . . .

maybe he doesn't have that time because he wants to get all of his subjects in and [get] *out* [of school]. (Recorded May 19, 1976.)

This same teacher stated that students viewed school as a part-time job. By defending the students, he admits that they seem more dedicated to labor which pays, reinforcing the observation that students tend to view schooling as unpaid labor.

Paradoxically, the teachers' attempt at finding solutions to the problems of student motivation and their own legitimacy was to become more authoritarian. They interpreted the students' loss of motivation and trust and their demands for autonomy as evidence of a need for structure to be imposed by the teacher.

LARKIN. I was wondering if you had any idea why [the loss of trust, increasing vandalism, and demands for autonomy] have occurred?

NURSE. Maybe we have gotten too far away from the structure. Perhaps they need [more structure].

SPANISH TEACHER. The students don't know what they want. The pendulum has gone all the way the other way and now they come back for—they need more direction.

N. I think they really do. I think some of them miss it.

S.T. I know that with my stronger classes, when I give them direction, and they're, they are capable of doing more on their own, they seem to prefer—"How many paragraphs [do] you want?" "I really don't care. Just get the information in there." But if I'll say ten, they're happy. They want a number. They want direction. They *want* you to direct.

L. Could that be interpreted as the students trying to establish the minimum of necessary work to get the job done? Do you understand what I am saying?

S.T. Yes, but I don't think so. They were against the establishment, yet they want me to establish the framework. "Tell me how many. How many pages shall I make it?" . . . They're very happy if I tell them eight pages. Then they're ready to do the work.

YOUNG TEACHER. . . . I feel the kids need, want, direction. They may resent it once the guidelines have been drawn—

S.T. In actuality, they want it.

Y.T. They are more at ease. Maybe they don't want it but they are more at ease with it.

OTHERS. Yes.

Y.T. Given the option, they'll hate them both. But then they'll ask you. It has to be their initiative, though, [they'll ask,] "What do you want me to do?" But I *do* think they want, they need. What was the word I used?

S.T. They *want* it.

Y.T. I don't know whether they really want it, but—

S.T. They ask for it.

Y.T. Yeah, but it's a different feeling. They don't really want . . . that direction. But, uh, . . . they need it. They won't come out and say they need it. But they're more comfortable with it. They're at ease with it. (Recorded May 19, 1976.)

The teachers seem genuinely confused about the demands of the students. They feel that the students need structure imposed upon them, even though they resent it. They also feel that even though students resent such imposition, it apparently simplifies the classroom situation, so the students feel at ease because the expectations have been clarified. However, if students attempt to seek out enjoyable teachers as opposed to instructive courses, then where does the imposition of teacher demands fit in? The suspicion is also aroused that the teachers' assertion that students want or need imposed structure (even if they resist) is a self-serving argument in which the desires of the teachers are projected onto the students. The teachers are at a loss to explain the decline in their legitimacy and the students' disaffection with school. Since they tend to view the problems as organizational rather than cultural, they explain them in terms of the students and themselves without analyzing larger social and cultural forces. This encapsulation of the problem has two consequences which affect the student-teacher relationship. First, the teachers blame the students and/or their families. Second, they blame themselves. The prior leads to estrangement and the latter leads to guilt. The teachers feel both guilty and resentful about the loss of the underlying motivational structure of schooling. They are confused because they see themselves as conscientious persons, no less committed to the task of educating students than in the past. Times have changed—and for the teachers it has been for the worse. Authority which in the past was unquestioned is now suspect. The teachers see hostility where there used to be enthusiasm, even though they feel they are the same teachers as always. The Spanish teacher consoles herself with the fact that there are still some students who are as eager as in the old days. The nurse is a month from retirement and has given up. The young teacher sympathizes with the students and tries to do what he can within the constraints of the position.

Another problem raised in the teacher interview was, "What is to be imposed and what is to be negotiated?" What kind of structure are the students demanding? What areas of autonomy are they demanding? What are their expectations of their teachers? It seems appropriate at this time to speculate that the students desire to be stimulated within the framework of the classroom, to learn exciting, new, and "important" material. They want to be "turned on." In a sense, they want to be entertained as well as taught by the teacher. Teachers cannot compete with the media to entertain youth. However, there is the possibility that within the confines of the classroom exciting things can happen. Above all, there is a more reality-based concern: admission to college and success in the world. Students must achieve, get good grades, and impress their teachers if they are to have any hope of getting ahead. Therefore, they must "psyche out" teachers expectations. It is in their self-interest to force teachers to specify *exactly* what is expected on a given assignment. Once the students know what the expectations are and have a concrete statement of what the teacher wants, they can choose to meet, not meet, or exceed those expectations. Thus, if a teacher can be pinned down to a statement that he or she expects eight pages, no matter how substantively irrational this expectation might be, students may assume that a five-page paper will get a lower grade than a ten-page one. Teacher responses such as, "As many pages as you need to make your point," are viewed as an attempt by the teacher

to veil expectations in vagueness. Without knowing what the
teacher expects, students are seized by anxiety over the amount of
time and effort needed to be allocated to the task at hand. On the
one hand, they could far exceed the expectations of the teacher
and waste time and effort when it wasn't needed. On the other,
they could underestimate the teacher's expectations and end up
with a poor grade. Since the work is coerced in the first place, it
makes sense to the students to establish minimal acceptable
criteria for their assignments. It is obvious that this is the kind of
structure that students want—not for the reasons that some of my
more cynical colleagues have proffered, that students want to
know what the minimum is that they can get by with, but, rather,
to establish the parameters of acceptability of the assignment so
they can allocate the time and effort to put forth to satisfy or to
exceed the amount of work required.

That the teachers misread the students' desire for structure is
attested to by their own words. The students want to know that
what they are being taught is worthwhile. In questioning the
value of the classwork, they are becoming sharp consumers.
When students ask why they are doing a particular assignment,
they are voicing concern over the efficacy of what is being done in
the classroom. Students have mentioned throughout this investigation that classwork is frequently boring and uninspiring. They
figure that if they are going to be coerced into doing work that is
intrinsically dull, it is legitimate that they should find out
whether or not it is worth doing. It seems only natural that if a
student is faced with a distasteful task, he or she should rightfully
expect that some good may come from it.

In defense of the teachers, it must be pointed out that it is more
difficult to teach these students than those of the past. Today's
students have been raised on television which propagandizes
instant gratification through commodity consumption, deni-
grates craft, and reduces attention span. (For more information,
see the proceedings of the Consumer Subcommittee of the U.S.
Senate Committee on Commerce, Ninety-Third Congress, Second Session, 1973.) The food most teenagers eat is full of carbo-

hydrates, sugars, and preservatives, which alter the chemistry of the body and may lead to hyperactivity and lack of concentration (Kenniston, 1977). But most of all, teachers must confront students who are deeply afflicted by the cultural crisis. Students do not see the effort that they put forth in school is leading them in a rewarding direction. Once it becomes apparent that there is a disjunction between what they do in school and the rewards that are supposed to accrue from their efforts, they become depressed, cynical, and suspicious. Many have decided that school is not worth the effort, but they ritualistically attend because there are no other options. The classroom experience for such students and their teachers is not likely to be satisfactory.

THE COUNSELOR:
SAVING INDIFFERENT LIVES

Unlike the teachers, who were depressed, the counselor was angry. The counselors are viewed with suspicion by the students, and are used as psychological fire-fighters by teachers who expect instant results. They are caught within an administrative web that requires them to schedule students into classes and hamstrings their attempts to give psychological aid to them, who, for the most part, do not request help until a crisis has been reached. The counselor saw himself as the recipient of conflicting demands and impossible expectations. The crowning irony was that despite all his efforts at helping people, he felt unappreciated. At the end of the interview, he gave an eloquent and impassioned defense of the counselors:

COUNSELOR. I think kids use counselors as semi- or quasi-psychiatrists, and they sit here and expect some answers for free. . . . When you're wrong, you are told you're wrong. There's no two ways [about it]. You're told by everybody: parents, kids, teachers. Where a psychiatrist can say, "If you don't like me, go see somebody else," I am forced to take whatever is given to me. Here is your hundred kids. Here is your two hundred kids. [Because of the budget crisis, counselor case loads had increased.] They're yours. Be their counselor. They don't even have the opportunity to pick us. How in the hell can you expect them to trust me, when all of a sudden I became a person who is to guide them in their life?

LARKIN. It's by a quirk of the computer.

C. Absolutely! [Students] come out of a junior high school [and] don't even know what a counselor is. Poor junior high counselors who really mean well and are loving people don't have the opportunity to sit with kids. They're doing some other stupid work. The kid comes over here [to Utopia High] and, sure, maybe I ran down the hall after a kid [this is in reference to my telling him that one student complained of a counselor running after her in an effort to gain her trust], maybe I could be that person, maybe I am really being honest about it! And I really don't give a hoot—well, I *do* give a hoot—about how I do it. And it may take two or three years to switch somebody's mind around. That's fast, two or three years! Teachers want it done in two or three days. They want immediate *change* in a kid when they call you up on the telephone and say, "Johnny Jones was *bad*. Do something!" Ha! "He's not doing his work in school. Do something. *Tomorrow*, do something." The principal throws a kid out or a teacher throws a kid out of a class, "He's a lousy kid. Do something, now! Change it! I'll give you three days."

L. So you are responsible for also maintaining discipline.

C. In essence, yes, Yeah, really. Helping them careerwise, planning their life, [and] if you do it wrong, you're lousy. You made the wrong selection. Can you believe that? Did you ever want anybody [to] make the selection in your life? "You made the wrong selection, you're lousy." If you don't make any selection at all, you [are thought not to] have the guts to make a selection. You know, I could go on and on about this being a counselor in a school, because, boy, I think they are the *most!* Not only because I'm a counselor. [Counselors are] the most overworked, underrated people alive! They do more help quietly than you could believe goes on. Because kids would have *died*. Literally died. Left. Not have done anything at all if it hadn't been for a lot of people who are in this business of counseling. I wish they would get more positive responses. I wish the paper would put some nice things in there about them. I wish kids would *really* tell you the truth and say, "Hey, it was really great knowing you," because they don't say that about their psychiatrists either, even if they *are* helping them. They don't admit the fact that that psychiatrist is really doing a great job. It's not the thing to say that they are doing a great job. "He's taking my fifty bucks, man, and he's not doing anything for me." But when the problem really comes down to it, they pick up that phone and call, man, and they're there. The same thing here. Everyone of those kids knows, they *know* that we're *here* when they need us. (Recorded May 19, 1976.)

The counselor bridles at the conflicting expectations and lack of appreciation shown for counselors by those people who use their services. Counselors are treated as servants by those who use them. The teachers and principal hand them their "dirty linen" and tell the counselors, "clean it." The students treat them as unwelcome snoops, and they are on the lowest rung of the psychotherapy status system.

The counselor performs a complex series of roles, many of which are contradictory. For example, the counselor is supposed to help the students resolve personal problems and be a student advocate among the adults. However, the counselor is also supposed to "solve" discipline problems. Such contradictory expectations demand the counselor to be on both sides of the fence at the same time. When a student is removed from a class, it is automatically assumed that the removal was the student's fault. The student is sent to the counselor to be "shaped up." The counselor has no control over the classroom situation, no authority over teachers, but does have authority over students. Regardless of the counselor's personal feelings, he or she is an agent of the school. Even if the counselor attempts to deny the relationship, the students are aware of it and wary of counselors who try to gain their confidences. That is why the students only go to the counselors as the last resort.

It is interesting to note that the counselor quoted above equates dropping out of school with death. The counselor sees himself saving souls by keeping them in school and believes that the school makes people human, while the students seem to believe exactly the opposite. Just as the counselor sees dropping out as a cause of psychic death, Jennie sees believing in what the school rewards as equally deadly (see p. 128).

The students call the counselors "guides," a shortening of the term *guidance counselor*. Although the counselor I talked to did not like the term, it reveals an underlying reality. The students use the counselors to guide them through school. The counselor quoted above, reacting to the designation of "guide," tells students, "A guide wears a hat that says 5 & 10 and says, 'We'll take you on a trip,'" Yet this is exactly what guidance counselors do. Most of their time is spent with scheduling, program selection, testing, and adjustment problems. The role of guide, then, consigns the counselor to routine work.

The counselor at Utopia High was a sage observer of the students in the school. He was aware of the negative view the students had of counseling. He also was aware of how the students felt about school and of the changes in student attitudes that had taken place over the years.

LARKIN. I was wondering how you would characterize the kids of the seventies as compared to the kids of the fifties and sixties? . . .

COUNSELOR. I think kids hate school more now than they did then. And I mean the word *hate* and underline it. And they use the term *bored* more today than they did then. . . . The reason for the attitude change from then to now, I think—probably the biggest problem is that politics have taken over the school systems. Policies are being run by politicians. Schools are being run down, downgraded by the community by that some process. Budget problems, which may or may not really be true. . . . Boy, I think there is a political football. And I think there is a disgust with what they are supposed to be taught in school about the democratic process. They haven't really seen it functioning properly since Watergate, which was probably the beginning of the end. . . . What it did was it killed the belief that anyone who was in charge of—an administrator, a president, a principal—really isn't in it to help anybody but himself. (Recorded May 19, 1976.)

The counselor was aware of the gulf that existed between parents and children, since he was often called upon to mediate between them. He saw as indicative of the antagonism of adults toward children the adults' decision not to have any children:

COUNSELOR. I can make a kind of cartoon out of it. I see this picture of a group of kids talking to one another, saying, "We're going to fix you, you adults." And then the adults turn around and say, "We won't have you any more." So it's kind of a combination of overbirth—too many children being born. And it's been advertised, "Stop having so many children," to "We can't stand it!" because kids are going into drugs, they're misbehaving, there's a tremendous amount of vandalism taking place, very serious crimes that kids are committing, then "Why the hell should we have kids any more?" "Why should we perpetuate this any more? We'll stop it. We're not going to have any more." So that's where the cartoon takes on an inner reality. "We'll fix your wagon, kids. We're not going to have any more." (Recorded May 19, 1976.)

The counselor quoted above is a lonely person. His sympathy for the students makes him suspect by the teachers. The constraints of the job force him to be more of an administrator than a counselor, and his position as a school official with offices near the administrators makes him suspect among the students. He sees the gulf between young and adult, but is helpless to do much about it, except when he is able to successfully resolve a crisis. He sees himself as a student advocate and because of this resents the students' indifference or negative views of the counseling function. He wants to help people who do not want it, and he is forced to discipline people he does not want to discipline. He sees himself as a good person in an unjust world.

THE JUVENILE OFFICER: THE PROBLEMS OF SPOILED KIDS

The two juvenile officers of Pleasant Valley are very busy men. They handle the majority of crime in the community since it is perpetrated by juveniles. Our interview took place in their office in the basement of the police department; it was punctuated by phone calls and was abruptly ended when duty called. Although both officers were present during the interview, the higher ranking answered most questions while the other took the phone calls and typed reports.

The chief of the juvenile bureau presented an anomalous picture. He looked like a recent graduate of an Italian street gang. His speech patterns reflected working-class origins, sounding like the protagonists in such ethnic movies as *Rocky* and *Mean*

Streets. He possessed street wisdom and a keen intellect, disguised by his dialect. He was tough. It seemed incongruous that he could talk about counseling young people whose psychological problems led them into conflicts with the law, while wearing a snub-nosed .38 pistol tucked under his belt! He sees his duty as enforcing discipline on young people who have been allowed to grow soft in affluent America:

> **LARKIN.** One of the major things I've been concerned with is the contradiction between the availability of facilities and the opportunity for participation [in school and community activities] and [the fact that young people] don't take advantage of them. [What] I've been trying to do is to find out why they don't take advantage of [the opportunities], yet they complain about being bored. . . .
>
> **JUVENILE OFFICER.** I just think the American people are a soft people physically. I really feel that way. I feel that our needs are so catered to that we're lost without what we take for granted. I really think that if another country wanted to come and get us, [unintelligible]. But I think if part of our country was bombed, people just couldn't exist without air conditioning, running water, conveniences, I don't think we could make it. . . . I feel that all the luxuries we have, have taken away from us as a people. We've got too much, too many comforts in this country. We got 'em too quick. (Recorded May 26, 1976.)

The loss of vigilance and the dependence on modern conveniences by the American public has led to a moral flatulence as well. The juvenile officer sees the problems of Pleasant Valley youth rooted in permissiveness:

> **LARKIN.** Why do you think there has been an increase in juvenile crime in the seventies?
>
> **JUVENILE OFFICER.** I think there has been an increase in juvenile crime in the seventies in particular because our society is very liberal and permissive. There is a definite lack of discipline by the family, . . . by the courts, and by the people. That's what I attribute it to. (Recorded May 26, 1976.)

The permissiveness experienced in the wider society has eroded the family to such an extent that they no longer have control over their youngsters. He sees the increase in his work closely tied to the deterioration of the family. What they can't control, he must:

> **LARKIN.** I was wondering what is the nature of the family problems that you are called upon to intercede in?
>
> **JUVENILE OFFICER.** Incorrigibility. Lack of parental control over their children, due to a number of reasons. There are a lot of executives in this community, and they have pressures. Their time is taken up due to executive—whatever executives go about and do—you see, they don't have enough time. This may have something to do with that. Alcoholism—
>
> **L.** Parental alcoholism?
>
> **J. O.** Oh, yeah. We've had a lot of that. Juvenile alcoholism [has] become more prevalent than the drug problem. . . . Incorrigibility [and] lack of parental control probably comes from those reasons. . . . The parents don't have the time, maybe they have a problem between themselves, and it's reflected on the children.
>
> **L.** So the . . . parents aren't able to control the kid, or—you mentioned runaways, too.
>
> **J. O.** Well, that would be included if they don't want to stay in that condition by running away, or failing in school because lack of interest because the family pressures are bothering that child, and it just adds up until they run away or drop out of school and hang around and maybe go to alcohol or drugs themselves. (Recorded May 26, 1976.)

Of course, the juvenile officer sees the family situations at their worst and young people at their most troubled times. Because he is an agent of social control in its most overtly coercive form, he sees the problems of the young in distinctly political terms. Over and over in the interview, the term "incorrigibility" occurred. An incorrigible youth, as defined by the juvenile officer, is one who is beyond adult control. Children who are beyond their parents' control are first "counseled" by the police. However, the term "counsel" is suspect, since the counselor is armed. If the child does not respond to police counseling, efforts may be made at incarceration.

This is not to denigrate the views of the juvenile officer. After all, his job is to control those youths who are not controllable by other community institutions. It is also true that many illegal acts of the young could and sometimes do result in serious injury or death to others. However, the question of the proper relationship between the police and the young people of Pleasant Valley remains unanswered. The students related story after story of illegal searches, harrassment, and heavy surveillance by the police. When I confronted the juvenile officer with their testimony, he stated:

> I don't even know what they are talking about. I really don't. . . . Some congregate in the Reservation. . . , now that's a well known spot for the sale, transfer, and using of drugs. Mostly marijuana, but there are other drugs. That's where you go. Our police do make an effort, especially in the spring and early summer, to keep it as clear and as clean as they possibly can. If that's what they mean by harrassment, I'm not sure, but we don't go out and indiscriminately search people. (Recorded May 26, 1976.)

The police are agents of adult authority and are called to enforce the laws. In the state where this study took place, it is against the law to sell or use marijuana. However, as the students noted, it is the juveniles who get busted on marijuana possession charges, not adults, even though, according to the students, there is a sizeable number of adults in the community who use pot. This is, in part, due to the fact that adults are more likely to use their marijuana more discreetly than the young; however, the activities of the young, especially public activities, are more likely to be surveilled by the police. The enforcement of drug laws, then, become *de facto* laws against use by the young. Both young and adult pot users consider their drug indulgences as their own business. The enforcement of drug laws is seen by the young as an encroachment on their own private behavior, even though it may be done publicly. If youths continued to smoke pot publicly and were not arrested, the police would have to face a reaction on the part of a large segment of the adult population who would accuse them of being derelict in their duty. Consequently, the laws are strictly enforced against the young.

The juvenile officer sees in the consumer society a weakening of internal constraints on behavior. Not only has society become permissive, but it is failing to induce the young to develop internal discipline as well. He scores the school on this issue:

> . . . I feel that without discipline, including personal appearance and whatnot, I feel you have difficulties. We have children going to [Utopia] High School, who leave the premises at will and wander about and return when they want. I don't feel this is right. I feel that they're there to learn, and they should be kept in that environment in the school and they should have rules to guide them by. As a matter of fact, I think they *beg* for rules to tell them what to do. Once those rules are removed, these kids only have young brains, they don't know what to do or where to go. And this is how they adjust to that. They have an awful lot of freedom, and they have no investment. They have no investment in this society, I feel. Other than bein' here taking up space. Not that they're not good kids. Don't get me wrong. They have no investment—no family, they don't contribute to any job, they have no real investment at all, yet they are afforded all the freedoms you and I are afforded. (Recorded May 26, 1976.)

The juvenile officer confuses the desire of young people for attention and caring with need for discipline, which is more or less self-serving; however, he quite succinctly describes the problem of youth in America as well as any sociologist. They are surplus people. They have no purpose other than to "take up space." Excluded from the labor force, neglected by parents who are too busy, and corralled in schools, they have no "investment" in society. In addition, television and ready made toys stunt their ability to create their own pastimes. He notes:

> . . . They are used to being entertained by TV, movies, and the different media. Very seldom are they called upon to use their own skills to entertain themselves in their peer groups. I can see that in my own [children]. I can see where my child can turn on the TV and be entertained for an hour or two rather than take a toy or take *nothing* and make something out of it, or go out in the yard and pick up a couple of pieces of wood and imagine something. That's very important and there should be more self-independent values rather than [dependence] on others. (Recorded May 26, 1976.)

It is interesting that, on the one hand, the juvenile officer advocates the imposition of authority on the young, while at the same time contending that they need to be more independent of adults. He assumes that somehow adults can impose independence upon the young through the maintenance of strict discipline. He sees young people who are left on their own without internalized senses of discipline wandering through aimless lives. The situation is confused, since lack of parental presence not only leaves the child without a sense of belonging and caring, it also leaves the child without internal resources upon which to draw to give life direction. Since television is an omnipresent narcotic in the home, it becomes a place where passive dependence is nourished. It is this syndrome that the juvenile officer sees that leads young people into trouble with authorities. He is right. They have no investment in society, but are merely pacified into acceptance of their state, while the future is dangled in front of them as is a carrot in front of a mule. For those who rebel against their oppression ("incorrigibles"), the juvenile officer supplies the stick. His main complaint is that the stick does not hit hard enough.

PARENTS: THE GATEKEEPERS OF CULTURE

The parents I was able to interview were the community activists. The interview group consisted of five women and two men. Upon entering the interview room, some remarked on the fact that the collection looked like a PTA Committee meeting. Two of the women described themselves as "professional volunteers." Although the various ethnic groups of the community were represented and the group was distinctly ecumencial, they all came from white-collar backgrounds: a sales manager, physician, lawyer, housing specialist, and two prosperous owners of their own businesses. They were all closely tied to the community, with only one person living in it for less than ten years. One person had lived there for seventeen years, another for twenty-eight years, and the other four had lived in the immediate area all of their lives. They ranged in age from late thirties to mid-fifties. One woman had two children; there were three families represented that each had three children; and two families that had five children each.

All of the parents expressed a close identity with the community and a fierce loyalty to it. They saw it as the closest approximation to the ideal in which to live and raise children. They spoke of Pleasant Valley with a genuine sense of pride and pleasure. Even their criticisms of the school and community were couched in the notion that nothing is perfect. For example, the following transpired in a discussion about the schools:

MRS. ARBUTHNOT. [*To Mrs. Gold*] I heard you questioning . . . the schools before and I didn't know whether you [were expressing your] children's reaction, or—

MRS. GOLD. No, it has nothing to do with my kids. Really, it's nothing to do with my kids. Right off the top, I'm not the least bit concerned. I *am* concerned! I'm *not* concerned. I am, I'm not concerned about them. I don't feel cheated, if that's what you mean. But I think certainly [Pleasant Valley] has sat, to some degree, on its laurels for awhile, being that it always was—that everyone moved here for the school system, and got a rude awakening.

MRS. A. Going downhill every since.

MRS. G. I still think we can improve in many, many ways. (Recorded April 26, 1977.)

The "rude awakening" was in reference to the elementary schools, not the secondary schools. Mrs. Arbuthnot found the elementary schools had the reputation of being mediocre. She blamed their lack of quality on a weak administration. Apparently the elementary school district attempted to keep costs down by maintaining a high turnover of beginning teachers. The improvements that Mrs. Gold wanted to see were the end of teacher tenure and the removal of a particular teacher from an honors senior biology class.

The parents are somewhat defensive about the school system. They suspect that its reputation has diminished over the years, while at the same time, they understand that it is still one of the best systems around:

MR. STOUT: I think the center of a great number of people in the community is the school system itself. We *used* to say that this particular institution was one of the most outstanding in the country. Today, I think we say that it is one of the better systems in the state.

MRS. ARBUTHNOT: It's getting harder to measure success. (Recorded April 26, 1977.)

Regardless of the competitive rankings of the school district in the state or the nation, the parents are pleased with the results. Several of the parents have older children who have gone on to college and have had no trouble adjusting. Their academic preparation not only helped them get into elite schools, but provided them with the internal mechanisms for success:

MRS. ARBUTHNOT. I think students leave [Utopia] who are terrifically ready for further education. But it is *more* than academic, because they have developed into a human being, a person, and are open to education from all facets, not just academics. That's what *I* want from education. I don't want only academics. (Recorded April 26, 1977.)

These parents are community minded, "responsible," and have a stake in the area. Their children are also members of the elite. They apparently do not have academic problems, they conform to parental expectations without great difficulty (for the most part), and they make the transitions between phases of life without serious problems. Both parents and children are involved in organized activities, such as scouting, camping, and church youth groups. Being successful and having proud parents, they do not represent the vast majority of students at Utopia High.

When it was mentioned that the universal dynamic of student life at Utopia High was boredom, the parents reacted strongly. Probably no other issue reveals the gulf between the reality of the students and the parents. The following discussion was heated, and, in many cases, more than one person was talking at a time:

LARKIN. One of the things that struck me [about the students] was that boredom was a dynamic in the life of almost every student. They were either bored or hyperactive, trying to fend it off.

MRS. ARBUTHNOT. Now I want every adult to own up. You never felt this as a teenager?

MRS. GOLD. Oh, yes. But "bored" is a very vague, nothing word to me.

MRS. A. See?

MRS. G. I was not bored at [Utopia] High School [when I was a student].

MRS. JANES. Was it the type of person who just doesn't want to do anything outside of school?

MRS. A. (*To Mr. Stout*) And you? Weren't you bored, dissatisfied?

MR. STOUT. Periods of dissatisfaction. But it had nothing to do with boredom. Six month periods of boredom [every so often].

MRS. A. That's different, though. (*Several start talking at once*)

MRS. A. That's just an excuse.

MRS. J. What do they participate—what do these bored kids do after school?

MS. BLOOM. (*Simultaneously*) See, I think that boredom—

MRS. G. (*Jumping in*) Boredom is a word I don't particularly like.

MRS. A. (*In answer to Mrs. J.*) They hang out. They don't have anything to do.

L. (*Also in answer to Mrs. J.*) They don't do anything.

MRS. J. —I remember sitting in class listening to the teacher drone on and on.

MRS. G. But that can't be in every class. In my house, that's the one word I don't like. That and "interesting." (*Laughter*) They're meaningless to me. I mean, they have to explain themselves. Why are you bored? What does "bored" mean to you?

MS. B. I have a similar lack of [sympathy]. I can't tolerate "bored." Bored is up to you. If you are bored, you have decided to hang around like this. (*Makes a face and slumps*)

MRS. G. (*Punctuating Ms. B.'s remarks*) Yes. Right. Correct.

MS. B. Then you're bored. But I remember saying when my kids were really little, they wanted to read, both of them, "As soon as you can read, you'll never be bored again, because you don't have to be alone and you don't have to be without someone to listen to or to communicate with."

MRS. A. I wasn't bored outside of school, but I remember sitting through classes going on and on—

MS. B. Yes, but—

MRS. G. But that is part of living, part of growing up or part of life. I don't think that's so terrible.

MS. B. Yeah, if it is boring while you are washing diapers, when you think about it, you will go out of your mind.

MRS. G. Yes, that's right.

MR. G. I don't think that the professor's [Larkin's] connotation is with the class per se, but boredom with general life. (Recorded May 26, 1977.)

The parental response to the fact that the young are bored is both varied and complex. Their reaction is one of anger, guilt, moral condemnation, and dismissal. To them, boredom is evidence of internal weakness. The bored child is one who does not have the internal resources to occupy his or her time constructively and autonomously. It is evidence of dependency and helplessness. It is also indicative of powerlessness and lack of external resources. Ms. Bloom stresses reading as a resource to fend off boredom. Books are easy sources of diversion. The television is an even easier source, which, by the way, no parent mentioned. The parents operate on the assumption that the external resources are present. If children are bored it is their fault. The only exception, from the parental point of view, was the boredom of the classroom, which is a necessary evil of growing up. We have returned to the politics of everyday life. The young are provided by the adults with a set of alternatives and resources through the establishment of adult-run youth groups and such. Yet the young claim boredom and fail to participate. The adults react by asserting that it is the fault of the young if they are bored, since there are a myriad of activities in which they could participate. The anger of the parents is directed at youth's refusal to (1) participate in adult-directed activities, or (2) occupy themselves without adult supervision with the resources that are available within the community. However, as was indicated in chapter 5, boredom was the consequence of the repression of the impulse to rebel, and, while manifested as a psychological malaise, it is also a type of guerrilla warfare, since they are refusing to participate on the adults' terms. The parents are subliminally aware of this, since their own responses were quite strong. Boredom can evoke guilt on the part of the parents, since they are responsible for instilling such self-reliance. When a child evidences despair and boredom, the parent is likely to ask him or herself, "Where have I gone wrong?" Thus, the blaming of the child for his or her own *angst* is something of a reaction formation on the part of the parent.

Guilt may be part of the reason why the parents attempted to dismiss or trivialize the problem of boredom. Mrs. Arbuthnot claimed that boredom was a natural part of growing up. By asking the other adults whether or not they were bored during their youth, she was trying to minimize its importance. I know that during my own adolescence, there were times of excruciating boredom. This is not to denigrate its importance, but to show that it is something that this generation shares with past ones. Mrs. Gold claimed that boredom was meaningless to her. Yet to the students of Utopia High, boredom and meaninglessness go hand-in-hand. Boredom is the result of the lack of "meaningful" activities. It is the psychological consequence of alienated activity. It is interesting to note that the parents are aware that their children are having problems with "meaning in life." When asked whether or not their children had the same pride in their community that their parents did, the following transpired:

LARKIN. Do you think this community pride is reflected . . . in young people? Do they have this pride?

MRS. ARBUTHNOT. I don't think that young people are inclined to admit anything so pedestrian.*(To the rest)* Do you think?

MS. BLOOM. Not today.

MRS. A. No, that's uncouth. *(Laughs)*

MR. STOUT. Admit? Do they talk about it? Do they think about it, do you mean? You know, our guys, do they look back and say—

MRS. A. No, I don't think that is one of the questions they ponder, really. They may ponder "life—the meaning of" or something. (Recorded April 26, 1977.)

Though Mrs. McKee stated that, as a relative newcomer to the community, her children had indicated that they liked it, the consensus was that the children did not share the adult feelings of pride. Mrs. Arbuthnot seemed to feel that their lack of expression was due to adolescent ingratitude more than anything else. When she stated that it would be "uncouth" to admit such "pedestrian" feelings, she seemed to indicate that on the part of the young it was "uncool" to admit to such sentimentality.

Even though they are well aware that the youth of Pleasant Valley is powerless, despite the "input mechanisms" into the "decision-making process," they see the alienation and cynicism of the young as developmental as opposed to structural. That way, it can be trivialized as a phase that the young pass through on their way to maturity, rather than generated by the structural position of youth as a powerless underclass in Pleasant Valley. The symptoms of dependence such as boredom, aimlessness, and despair are written off as a universal experience of the young independent of their status. These parents can soothe themselves on two counts: first, their own children do not seem to be strongly affected by such debilitation, and second, most will outgrow it. Finally, none of these parents indicated that they were having trouble with "meaning in life." They were all well integrated into the formal structure of the community: active in civic events, school, and church groups. They tended to treat the problem of meaning as developmental also, assuming that, sooner or later, it would be found. Yet it is this very problem that seems to be plaguing the middle classes of America in the 1970s and the finding of meaning is the prime commodity of a good many therapies, religions, and cults catering to the middle classes.

For these parents, the sexual behavior of their children was not a serious problem, even though in several cases, they knew that their children were sexually active and they didn't particularly approve. The discussion of the sexuality of their children provided a certain amount of good-hearted banter and stories of children asking parents questions that made them blush.

LARKIN. How do you deal with the sexual maturation of your children?

MRS. ARBUTHNOT. Ignore it. *(Laughter)*

MRS. JANES. Hope it will go away. *(More laughter)*

MS. BLOOM. Oh, no. We get to talk about it. My little one asked about it very early in the game and I started with a preliminary discussion. I was prepared to deal with certain narrow areas, but she asked a lot more questions and they were very intelligent questions, and we had a long discussion. (Recorded April 27, 1977.)

This led to Mrs. Gold's description of her son's inquisitiveness:

MRS. GOLD. My fourteen-year-old, I don't remember what television program we were watching together—sometimes you get stuck in the room and you have no choice and can't leave—it was all over and he started asking me questions about different feelings he had and already I was dying. "Where is it going from here?" [she asked herself]. And then he did ask. He said, "Do you and Daddy do it?" And those were the terms he used. And I said, "Yes." And I [was thinking], "Dear God, what is coming next?" And I was ready to kill my husband because he wasn't in the room and there was nobody to save me! And then he asked me a very interesting question, he said, "Isn't it *boring?*" *(Laughter)* And I mean to tell you, oh, now I feel myself blushing, but I didn't know where to go from there.

MR. STOUT. Since then the word ["boring"] has been taboo in your house. *(Laughter)*

MRS. G. Right. . . .

MS. BLOOM. Did you tell him it was boring or not? *(Laughter)* (Recorded April 27, 1977.)

It was Ms. Bloom and Mrs. Gold, the two Jewish women, who talked about the sexual curiosity of their children. Mr. Stout, a Unitarian, described how his sons had brought the girls they lived with into the house and slept in the same room which was equipped with double beds. He and Ms. Bloom were obviously the most liberal parents in terms of tolerating the sexual behavior of their children. Mrs. Janes, Mrs. McKee, and Mrs. Arbuthnot were silent about the sexual development of their children. Mrs. McKee was a Catholic and Mrs. Arbuthnot and Mrs. Janes were Protestants. Although Mrs. Gold was conservative in her sexual attitudes and claimed that no child of hers was going to bring a lover into her house and have sex with her knowledge, she and Ms. Bloom were obviously conscious of their sex appeal, both dressing in high fasion, maintaining model figures and youthful looks. The other three women, though each had an attractive face, were obviously out of the sexual marketplace: they dressed down, maintained a minimum of jewelry, and were well beyond advertisers' portrayals of ideal weight. Mrs. Gold and Ms. Bloom portrayed themselves as sexual beings, with all the feminine trappings. The other women played down their sexuality. Part of this may be due to religious and cultural emphases on sex. American Protestantism originates from Calvinism and tends to be sexually repressive, as is the Catholic Church. Among Jews, sexual attitudes tend to be less repressive and more fatalistic: it is inevitable, so you might as well enjoy. Thus, we have the phenomenon of the two Jewish mothers squirming as their children ask them questions about sex, but enjoying the process at the same time.

The pre-marital sexual behavior of their children is not seen as a problem unless the parents are forced to confront it. They generally consider their children's sexual behavior to be in the realm of their children's own private affairs. However, they do not want to be put in the position of having to condone or encourage it. The Golds, Mr. Stout, and Mrs. Arbuthnot have older children who are away at college or out earning a living who are not married, but living with a member of the opposite sex. Mr. and Mrs. Gold's son is living with a girl at college; however, they do not allow cohabitation in their own house, as does Mr. Stout. One of the issues raised by cohabitation is the double standard. Mr. Gold claimed that it didn't matter to him, but Ms. Bloom said that she felt that parents of girls tended to be more restrictive than the parents of boys.

Although sexual behavior was treated jocularly and light-heartedly, drugs was a much more serious topic and generated much greater parental anxiety. Whereas, parents tended to take pride in their openness with their children in reference to sex, they often relied on scary misinformation to keep their children from smoking pot. For example, Ms. Bloom told of allowing her child to think that the smoking of pot led to lung cancer:

> **MS. BLOOM.** [Pot smoking] is not something I have observed among my own youngsters, nor among their closest of friends. However, some of their friends have gone through—their less close—the next circle of friends, in concentric circles out, there are kids who occasionally smoke pot. They've mentioned it. I've said that I would appreciate it if they wouldn't smoke here, and I think that so far as I know, it has never been violated. I could be very naive.

> **LARKIN.** Do you know whether or not your own children smoke or have smoked, or have experimented?

> **MS. B.** I consider myself lucky. I don't know whether it will last. My kids watched TV . . . when those cigarette commercials came out and talked about cancer and they were very impressed by them. Particularly when a nurse we had at that time who stayed with my children each time we went away, whom they knew very well, who smoked a great deal and was always sending them out for cigarettes or when a person would come into the house, would send them out, died of lung cancer. It was the most fantastic message! I mean if you are going to get a message, my kids got that message! And if anyone they know or feel strongly about has anything to do with smoking they are . . . very concerned. So I assume that my kids don't smoke less because they are afraid of pot, than they are afraid of smoking. . . .
>
> My little one once said she smoked a cigarette. She'd gone off to someone else's Sunday school. And I came up to her room to say good night and she was very agitated. And she was sitting with this for twelve hours and she was beside herself. And she said they had gone off somewhere and one of the boys had a cigarette and she tried one. She had taken one deep breath and was beside herself.

> **MRS. ARBUTHNOT.** *(Laughing)* Talk about guilt.

> **MS. B.** It really preyed on her mind. (Recorded April 26, 1977.)

It sounds like Ms. Bloom's child was not feeling guilty so much as she was experiencing the terror of the prospect of her own death. The parents were relieved because they were being told that pot smoking had leveled off and declined in the last few years while alcohol abuse has increased. Even though pot is less physically harmful, in Pleasant Valley it was associated with a decline in striving and achievement. However, since "drugs" were in plentiful supply in Pleasant Valley it remained a serious threat. Mrs. Gold testified that the junior high school was loaded with "drugs":

MRS. GOLD. I think there is more pot or as much in the junior high as there is in the high school.

MRS. ARBUTHNOT. *(Agreeing)* Uh-huh.

MRS. G. I really hear more about it in the junior high. I hear so much about it in the junior high it's unreal. Now my ninth grader wouldn't touch a cigarette if he came within 100 feet of it. He is so afraid of dying. He really is. He is afraid he is going to die. He and my little one. They are really afraid they are going to die if they smoke cigarettes.

MS. BLOOM. That is the same age that my kid was—

MRS. G. She'll tell you. She'll come right up to you and tell you you're going to die if you smoke. That's it . . .

MRS. JANES. When I asked my eighth grader if there were drugs at the junior high, he said, "What kind of drugs?" Smart alec.

MRS. G. He [her son] says you can get anything. And he's a straight ninth grader. Naive, maybe a little bit. Sweet. And he says you can buy anything. (Recorded April 26, 1977.)

The fear that was generated by the drug problem lead the parents to a variety of tactics. Mrs. Arbuthnot said that she didn't want to know about it. Mr. Stout believed in a strong drug education program. Mrs. Gold and Ms. Bloom allowed their children to be terrorized by the specter of death. Yet the interesting fact is that probably as much as thirty percent of the student body at Utopia High have begun smoking cigarettes. Why, even though cigarette smoking is allowed at Utopia High, is the fear of pot so high among parents? The answer seems to lie in the tie-in between pot smoking and non-achievement.

The symbolic significance of pot is much stronger to these parents than the reality of pot smoking. Pot, to them, is a much greater threat to the lives of their children than premarital sex. Ms. Bloom sums it up:

> I think there was an anxiety among my friends when the oldest ones were in junior high because [pot] was all over school. It was all over [Utopia] as well. We were not at [Utopia] yet, but we were concerned about it. There was a great deal of anxiety. I know I even made a pact with my very dearest friend that if she heard it about my kid or I heard it about hers, we wouldn't play any games. We'd come out straight and talk about it, because we *would* want to know, we *would* want to talk to the kids about it. We'd want to know what to do if there were any problem. It didn't materialize and it seems that for the seniors now the interest really fell off. Even for those kids who were really into it. I'm thinking of those kids whose parents I knew for many years who were involved in it as late as the sophomore year. By the time they were juniors, it didn't seem to be there. . . . I had a feeling that they were more involved in non-boredom around here: they were more involved in the newspaper or the yearbook or a team of some sort. All of a sudden they weren't bored. And I am thinking of one particular kid who was into smoking pot and also into not achieving. And all of a sudden the whole thing turned around. He began to do better in school, he supposedly gave up pot and he really shaped up. (Recorded April 26, 1977.)

Premarital sex can be integrated into conventional life, since, in the seventies, it is practiced in conventional form. However, pot smoking is associated with a behavioral syndrome that is anti-establishment: boredom, non-achievement, and hostility toward adults. Thus, we have come full circle. For these parents, the fear is that their child will hit the reefer and give up: he or she will stop striving, fall into failure, and regress into non-achievement. *They fear that their children may try to escape the struggle to maintain middle-class respectability*. In this, their fears are quite rational, since the big fantasy among the young at Utopia High is letting go and getting out.

CONCLUSION: THE POLITICS OF AGE

The incontrovertable fact of the relationship between youth and adult is that it is class-based. The adults control the life conditions of youth. Regardless of the intentions or leniency of adults, they dominate the lives of the young. Because of their physical and social dependency on adult society, such sub-dominance is a universal experience. Only within the last ten years have children been legally defined as persons in their own right, not merely the property of the parents. As the young are consigned to more and more age-segregated institutions that are outside the mainstream of society, they are assuming an identity outside the family as a separate status group. Yet this status group is basically a sub-dominant group within adult-dominated bureaucratic institutions.

The domination of children by parents, until recently, has been characterized as a caste relationship: traditional, ascribed, eternal, and non-rational. Even into adulthood, the child was subject to the authority of the parent. However, with the onset of capitalist society, the parent-child relationship became more class-based, temporary, and defined in terms of property relations. As children were consigned to bureaucratic institutions such as schools, camps, institutes, reformatories, and the like, they increasingly became a client population to be served by adult authorities. As such, they are certainly not the property of such structurally rationalized organizations; but caught between the sometimes conflicting claims of family and formal organization, they assume statuses of "people." As people, however, their lives are still not their own to live, because they are dependent both developmentally and structurally.

The problem of the middle-class youth is that the family is isolated and the breadwinner is involved in an intense struggle for status. The family, as the repository of status, assumes the external manifestations of the status of the breadwinner. However, the more the breadwinner(s) involves him or herself in the struggle for status, which occurs in the world of work, the family becomes merely a material adjunct of the status struggle. The internal workings become harnessed to the strivings of the adults and the emotional tenor of family relationships are attenuated and subsumed by the necessity to maintain or increase status. Children becomes fetters on status strivings, since they require time out from labor in the world of work. The juvenile officer stated that the big problem in Pleasant Valley is that children are neglected by their parents who, in the struggle for accumulation (of both material possessions and status), have no time for them. Such families are emotionally and socially immizerated and provide little or no basis for the healthy development of children. They must depend upon paid professionals for their children's rearing, whether nannies, teachers, psychiatrists, or counselors.

The developmental dependence of the young is used as the legitimation for adult domination. The teachers and the juvenile officer state that children *want* to be dominated, even though they may resent it. The bureaucratization of the adult-child relationship has politicized it. Of course, there has always been a political side to the adult-child relationship. However, it has only been in the last hundred years that such politicization has taken the form of participation in formally organized structures in which the children constitute a client population. As the family has become tied to the formalization of economic life as the maintainer of the symbolic attributes of status, it has become important as the prime provider of the motivational syndrome for striving and status maintenance.

Parental fear of pot, the privatization of student problems until they reach crisis proportions, student demands for specific expectations from teachers, parental loathing of boredom all attest to the importance of status striving in Pleasant Valley. The teachers, counselors, parents, and police are dedicated to keeping the kids moving, competing, working, and striving toward the goals of middle-class respectability. Parents are not afraid of instilling even the fear of death in the struggle to "make it." The police are also the agents of fear. The counselor consciously equates the quitting of the competitive struggle with death. If the testimony of the teachers and parents is correct, it is becoming more difficult to get these young people to strive at the necessary levels. They have become truculent and show signs of rebellion against the whole idea of the competitive struggle. Parents in whose children is incorporated the desire to "make something of themselves" thank their lucky stars. The young who hang out and refuse to achieve are a threat to one of the most cherished virtues of the community: that purposeful, goal-directed striving is what makes a person good. The specter of failure hangs heavy over the high aspirations in Pleasant Valley, and the young who wear the badge of disillusionment with the competitive struggle are threats to the adult definition of reality, which equates success with virtue.

The tension between adults and young is generated around two interrelated arenas of activity. In the microcosm, it is the structural dominance of young by adults, which results in a muted class struggle (e.g., students trying to put something over on a teacher; hiding nefarious activities from adults, but bragging of them to peers; theft; vandalism; etc.). In the macrocosm, it is the necessity to struggle for power and status, which results in invidious competition, cultural immizeration, and despair. This dual domination of the young by adults, *even when it is not overtly violent and is carried out in the name of love and caring*, has disastrous consequences for the young. The young are a dominated class, which, of course, provided the basis for youth dissidence in the 1960s and allowed the category of youth to be the status around which a "youth consciousness" could be generated, so that they could act for their own class interests. However, with the resurgence of dominant institutions and the regeneration of the status competitive struggle as an important parameter of their lives, the necessity for inter-peer competition breaks down the ability of youth in the 1970s to act as a class *for* itself, as young people are fragmented into various competing groups at different status levels within the community and school. The adult interpretation of reality reigns, and, since the young are not able to generate an alternative, they must either accept or reject it. Those who reject the adult reality and attempt to drop out of the struggle, must admit failure, since the non-competitive ideology of the 1960s is obsolete, and they are living out of joint with time. For those who are successes, there is fear of failure; for those who have failed, there is despair.

7

YOUTH AND
THE DEGRADATION
OF EVERYDAY LIFE

Last thing I remember, I was
Running for the door
I had to find the passage back
To the place I was before.
"Relax," said the night man,
"We are programmed to receive.
You can check out any time you like,
But you can never leave."

The Eagles, "Hotel California," 1976

REPRESSIVE DESUBLIMATION AND
THE EROSION OF EVERYDAY LIFE

Throughout this exploration into the lives of affluent suburban youth, we have found a basic contradiction between the wealth of the surroundings of these young people and their internal immizeration. In this final chapter, I will analyze the contradictions generated by contemporary capitalist culture, the place of the young in it, and the psychic consequences of these contradictions. Since the satisfaction of basic needs comes from the economic sector of society, we must begin at that point. There are three economic processes which we must consider: production, consumption, and reproduction.

As noted in chapter 2, in order for monopoly capitalist economy to maintain its vigor, it must continually expand for social as well as economic reasons. It must be able to provide places for an increasing labor force, or else be disrupted by social unrest created by the disparity of the distribution of wealth and the danger of having idle masses in the streets, as in the case of Italian youth in the mid-1970s. At the point of post-scarcity, though, the self-expansion of the economy becomes increasingly irrational, as labor becomes less productive and more an excuse to consume (see Braverman, 1974). The building of the corporate state was necessary to maintain the social relations of capitalism, while at the same time providing nonproductive labor for a bureaucratically dominated *consuming* middle class. Social class relationships are codified and rationalized within bureaucratic structures, and those persons who are left over are organized as client populations and kept in a state of dependency until such time that they can be absorbed into the hierarchy at a level that provides a modicum of income which allows an individual to become "independent," although he or she is still dependent on organizational position. Consumption, at the time that Marx wrote *Capital* (1867) was primarily that necessary consumption which was required to maintain and reproduce the labor force, which, for the most part, lived precariously perched on the edge of subsistence. However, as productivity and material wealth increased, consumption became ideologically important for the maintenance of the discipline of the labor force. In the early twentieth century, capital became increasingly concerned with controlling the social relations of production through the consumption process. Ewen (1976:18) notes:

> Arguing for an implementation of a social capitalism, Bloomfield [Meyer Bloomfield—businessman and Director of the Vocational Bureau of Boston in 1915] stated that "wise business management recognizes the good sense of organizing the source of labor supply" beyond the immediacy of the factory. This perspective was linked to changes in the productive capacity of American business—the fact that for the first time it appeared that the industrial machine might be able to transform the nature of consumption among a broad sector of the population.
>
> It was within such a context that the advertising industry began to assume modern proportions and that the institution of a *mass* consumer market began to arise. Up to that point, much of indigenous working-class culture had resisted capitalist growth in general, and the invasion of capitalism into their work and lifestyles in particular. . . . The imposition of factory discipline, characteristic of American industrialization up to that point, had not been an entirely effective means toward confronting the unrest born of its routines. As a result, the business community now attempted to present an affirmative vision—a new mechanism—of social order in the realm of daily life to confront the resistance of people whose work lives were increasingly defined by the rigid parameters of industrial production and their corporate bureaucracies.

Thus, capital could buy off the revolution through the generation of a consumer ecomomy, in which the labor force participated in the form of mass markets. For capital, then, two birds were killed with one stone: labor insurgencies could be minimized through the introduction of shorter work weeks and increasing prosperity. Also, increasing demands created by mass marketing would keep the economy expanding.

In order to maintain an expanding economy, population expansion was necessary. However, the mere physical reproduction and expansion of the labor force was no longer sufficient. Preparation for the labor force participation was an essential part of the socialization process, requiring the reproduction of the necessary attitudes and skills (Bowles and Gintis, 1976). Even more recently, it has become necessary to instill in the younger generation the proper characterology for consumption. The world of work has significantly altered since the beginning of the century, from primarily an arena of material production to an arena of coerced consumption as non-productive white-collar labor has expanded to half the labor force. In addition, private life has become dominated by efforts to consume.

The culture of monopoly capitalist society is organized around consumption. It is necessary, then, that the individual psyche be molded to conform to the necessities demanded by an economy driven by expanding consumption. It is in this sense that Marcuse (1955:viii) stated that

> . . . in the contemporary period, psychological categories become political categories to the degree to which the private, individual psyche becomes the more or less willing receptacle of socially desirable and socially necessary aspirations, feelings, drives, and satisfactions.

The characterology of the volatile consumer is forged by commodifying the world and selling it back to the individual in its alienated form. On the one hand, the individual is taught to desire more than he or she has, while on the other, he or she is warned of the social consequences of poor consumption. As human needs are transformed into desires, which are manipulable through the process of advertising and the sponsoring of individualized competitive struggles, the psyche of the individual becomes an arena for colonization. Compliance, though necessary, is no longer sufficient for the purposes of domination. Domination must be made palatable and even pleasant. It is through the process of tying desires to commodity consumption and generating fears over performance adequacy by which this is accomplished. Therefore, the attitudes promulgated through the advertising media serve distinctly political purposes. The conquest of the "unhappy consciousness" through "repressive desublimation" (Marcuse, 1964) is the process by which the individual psyche, through the inculcation of insatiable desires, becomes tied to commodity consumption and thereby subject to external control through ideological means. Contradictions are blurred and all problems become potentially solvable. In Freudian terms, the pleasure principle is "desublimated" for the purposes of maintaining the repressive dominance of the reality principle. Thus, pleasure becomes a realm of competition for status and is subsumed under the reality principle in the form of the performance principle. As the consumption of pleasure becomes the basis for competitive "lifestyles," people are coerced into believing that they cannot perform properly without the right equipment. This rule applies equally to the ski slope and the bed. (In the August 1977 issue of *Eros Magazine*— subtitled "The Magazine of Decadent Sophistication"—an advertisement appeared by the Stamford Hygenics Dept. claiming that women need more sexual stimulation than most men can provide to achieve orgasm. This "natural" orgasm gap, as they call it, is remediable by their "kit" which contains an instruction book, rubber "stimulators" driven by an electric motor, and oils—all for only $25.)

Marcuse (1955) termed the dominance of the performance principle surplus repression. That is, given the existing state of hierarchical arrangements, excess repression is needed to maintain the *status quo* the face of the possibility of liberation of the impulsive "free play" of libidinal energy made possible by the *material wealth* generated by capitalist economy which could possibly be used to reduce toil. The psychic toll of this form of surplus repression is reflective in the problems of the upper-middle class: fears of inadequacy, loneliness, meaninglessness, futility, and apathy. Notes Marcuse (1970:17):

> As productivity increases, the taboos and instinctual prohibitions on which social productivity rests have to be guarded with ever greater anxiety. Might we say . . . that this is so because the temptation to enjoy this increasing productivity in freedom and happiness becomes increasingly strong and increasingly rational?

For the students at Utopia High, it is *feelable,* if not thinkable that routinized toil should be reduced in their lives. However, they are tied to routine and see no reason for it. As opposed to

Marcuse's notion that the unrepressed pleasure principle sub-limates itself and the world becomes eroticized (infused with love), commodities are tied to all sorts of supposed need-satisfiers, which make it impossible for the commodity to satisfy the needs for which it is proported. As advertising loads commodities down with symbolic values, actual consumption of the commodity leaves the purchaser dissatisfied, since it does not deliver the irrational desires to which it has been attached. Love, freedom, autonomy, and belonging are high on the list of wants of Utopia High students, but, because these concepts are mystified, reified, and used to manipulate desires, they haven't the slightest idea of how to achieve them. All they know is that they want them very badly.

YOUTH AND NEEDS

Abraham Maslow (1954) theorized that human needs exist in a hierarchy: basic physiological needs constitute the base, and then in order of necessity are the needs of safety, belongingness and love, esteem, and self-actualization. Whether these needs exist in a hierarchy is debatable—it seems that all the others rest equally upon the physiological needs—but nevertheless, it is self-evident that these needs exist within human beings.[1] Put simply, capi-talism, for the students at Utopia High, has solved the problems of physical maintenance (though not too well, judging by their dietary habits, which emphasize fats and sugar) and safety (to the point of cloistering). However, in the struggle to maintain physi-cal security and social status, the other needs have been ignored. Thus, the struggle of the students is around the need for be-longing, love, esteem, and self-actualization. The world around them is not so much hostile as it is veiled, "unreal," and im-penetrable. They are isolated by hidden curtains. They feel that adults are holding out on them, both emotionally and intel-lectually. Adults, for the most part, maintain their distance and have a tendency to mystify social relationships.

Students' relations with their peers are not much better. A few trusted friends are the most one could possibly ask for. They are competing with each other for certain scarce resources, which, on the one hand, the level of scarcity or future scarcity is unknown. On the other, no one is sure that even if a scarce position could be obtained, whether it would really be what was wanted in the first place. The governments of the Western nations, at the writing of this book, are busy wringing their hands over what to do with the children of the baby boom in stagnating economies that are increasingly unable to absorb the younger part of the labor force. Yet, these children of post-scarcity society do not necessarily want routinized labor. In addition, since they have been brought up in a televised world, they have been repeatedly told that pleasure is something that commodities provide.

Contemporary institutions are attempting to forge these students into perfect consumers: estranged, isolated, confused about their identities, dissatisfied, and desirous. A good consumer must have insatiable desires, and this is achieved by continually dangling new temptations in front of his or her eyes. The family and school maintain conformity through privilege structures and sometimes outright bribery. The family and the school are also gateways to the world of work, which provides the necessary income for independent consumption. Despite these forms of control, the young are concerned about love, skill, community, and emotional expansiveness. They are cynical and quick to see the political side to their relationships with adults. They hide the problematic sides of their lives from adults, question teachers on the efficacy of their methods, grouse about administrators who hide behind the formal structure of the school, despise the police, and distrust professional psychology. They see their lives as tied by invisible strings—they not only feel suppressed, but repressed as well, which leads to a certain amount of self-blame for their depressing way of life.

Their basic needs satisfied, higher order needs emerge. These needs are unmet because of the necessity to maintain the social relations of waste production through the generation of a consuming class which will take its place in hierarchy of relationships that reproduce existing social class alignments. Because unmet needs assume primacy despite attempts to mystify them through the mechanisms of popular culture and advertising, the dissatisfaction of the young transcends the desire for status. They desire to be authentic in an unreal world. However, because of the mystification of the self that is generated in contemporary society, these young people are not exactly sure what "authentic" means, apart from "busting out" from their existing patterns.

> The great contradiction which undermines the consumer society results from the fact that cumulative production has unleashed forces which destroy the economic necessities. The internal rationale of the system requires an infinite economic development, and only the quantitative and consumable are actually supplied to the individual. Once primary needs have been fulfilled to saturation, new, pseudo-needs are "manufactured" (a second car, a better refrigerator, down to the ultimate gadget which is no use for anything [this was written before "Pet Rocks" hit the market]). This process causes an accelerating degradation of everyday life. But at the same time, tremendous technical strides give a glimpse of new worlds, of unsuspected means of gratifying unknown desires. Consequently the critique of everyday life is initially carried out from the *inside*—it is the critique of the "real by the possible." (Gombin, 1975:63-64.)

The critique of the world around Utopia High students is not stimulated by a vision of the possible, but generated by the hope-against-hope that life has more to offer then what they're getting. Perhaps this point of view was best expressed by Roz when asked how she would change the school. She responded by saying that she didn't know what she would do, but it wouldn't be run like Utopia High.

Let us return to the Maslovian hierarchy of needs. The needs of physical preservation and safety are ego needs subsumed under the program of the reality principle. The needs of social belonging, love, and esteem are id needs, subsumed under the pleasure principle. The need for self-actualization is a need for unity within the self, between self and other, and between self and nature. It is characterized by acceptance, emotional depth, rationality, spontaneity, egalitarianism, and the ability to love. The satisfaction of the need for self-actualization, according to Mar-

cuse (1955:193–94), occurs when sexuality is liberated and sublimated under the free play of Eros, which in turn, allows for the
development of a non-repressive culture:

> . . . The culture-building power of Eros *is* non-repressive sub-
> limation: sexuality is neither deflected from nor blocked in its
> objective; rather, in attaining its objective, it transcends it to others,
> searching for fuller gratification.
> . . . The pleasure principle reveals its own dialectic. The erotic
> aim of sustaining the entire body as subject-object of pleasure calls
> for the continual refinement of the organism, the intensification of
> its receptivity, the growth of its sensuousness. The aim generates its
> own projects of realization: the abolition of toil, the amelioration of
> the environment, the conquest of disease and decay, the creation of
> luxury. All these activities flow directly from the pleasure princi-
> ple, and, at the same time, they constitute *work* which associates
> individuals to "greater unities"; no longer confined within the
> mutilating dominion of the performance principle [the form of the
> reality principle in this historical period], they modify the impulse
> without deflecting it from its aim. There is sublimation and,
> consequently, culture; but this sublimation proceeds in a system of
> expanding and enduring libidinal relations, which are in them-
> selves work relations.

The students at Utopia High experience a two-fold alienation:
from adult society wherein the power lies, and from each other as
invidious competition and mobility undercut authenticity and
understanding of each other. They are isolated as a class and as
monadic individuals. Most lives are characterized by lack of
depth: in their family ties, friendships, skills, and commitment to
any organizations. They live life at the surface, fearful yet desirous of what might happen should they "bust out" of their not
quite Edenic existence. With the exceptions of those successful
students who have had the fortune to live the "good life,"
students at Utopia High School are terrorized by their fears. Their
impotence and timidity generates self-hate and despair. Yet the
pervasiveness of the power of the world-out-there leads to a
helpless apathy. Despite their relatively privileged condition,
Henri Lefebvre (1971:146) would claim they live in an overly
repressive society, which is

one that, in order to avoid overt conflicts, adopts a language and an attitude dissociated from conflicts, one that deadens or even annuls opposition; its outcome and materialization would be a certain type of (liberal) democracy where compulsions are neither perceived nor experienced as such; either they are recognized and justified, or they are explained away as the necessary conditions of (inner) freedom. Such a society holds violence in reserve and only makes use of it in emergencies; it relies more on the self-repression inherent in organized everyday life; repression becomes redundant in proportion to the performance of its duties by (individual or collective) *self-repression*.

Since their own self-repression and suppression by the dominant society is not recognized as such, they are at a loss to explain why they feel as badly as they do. Also, since they lack the requisite skills for assessing their own situation in a comprehensive way, they are left with their discontents and no visible solution.

Thus, it is no wonder that their major problem is "the meaninglessness of existence." *Meaning* and *means* are tied together. In order to engage in purposeful activity, one must have a purpose. If life is reduced to random nothingness, means and purposes have no place. On the one hand, this could be a source of joy. Life would revolve around the total experience of the moment, the experience of the "oceanic feeling" the first Freud (1961 [1930]) and then Maslow (1954) talked about as the center of the authentic experience of the self. However, for Utopia High School students, it is a source of acute pain and despair. They are not autonomous, and immersion in the present is an attempt to ward off fears of the future. Ecstasy is determined by its temporality and its fleeting nature. Instead of the present being integrated with past and future, it becomes an escape from them. When the "freaks" on the back lawn of the school say, "Live today," the assumption is that today must be isolated from the worries of tommorrow.

American culture lionizes a successful elite and their accomplishments, while at the same time presents to the young a degraded packaged experience of ersatz success. Take, for example, something as mundane as model airplanes. The mental skill and physical dexterity required to put together an inexpensive model plane is much lower now than it was twenty years ago. In addition, since the process is reduced to essentially assembling fitted plastic parts and then glueing them, the young person learns nothing of the structure of an airplane while constructing it, only its outer form. The construction of an airplane out of balsa wood and tissue paper was a much more complex process. While constructing a plane, one learned how to construct wings so they would give proper lift, fusilages that were not too heavy, tails that provided proper stability, and so forth. Thus, in contemporary model kits, the structure of the object and the process of construction are mystified in such a way as to prevent one from knowing anything about how the real item was built. While it is true that a child assembling a plastic plane may feel success at the conclusion of his labor, such feelings are short-lived since the process was a short cut in the first place. Because the majority of the work was done by a machine at a toy factory, the attachment to the model is ephemeral and is soon outlived. There is little of the self which can be infused into such a model; whereas, in a model that one constructs "from scratch," there is a much greater involvement of self and a more justified sense of accomplishment.

By degrading the process by which one can attempt to reconstruct the world, external reality assumes a facile and, at the same time, a mystical quality. Prepackaging allows young people to believe that problem solving is essentially a process of selecting the correct combination of alternatives. The construction of the alternatives, being a political process that occurs in places which are well-shielded from unwanted eyes, is hidden and mystified. Because of this mystification, the young person learns to assume the superiority of those processes over his own. In addition, the emphasis is altered to focus on quantity rather than on quality. Since the construction of model airplanes has been degraded, and advertisers emphasize collections to enhance sales, instead of the young person learning to construct a small number of complex models. Of course, once a hobby or any other endeavor becomes easily quantifiable, it becomes the basis for the accumulation of status and psychological dominance ("I have bigger——than you."). The degradation of the process of labor teaches the child at an early age to participate in a competitive struggle surrounding commodity consumption. Such invidious competition, in school and out, generates a fear of inadequacy tied in with one's ability to consume. Therefore, volatile consumption becomes necessary for status among and dominance over one's peers. Such alienation of the peer group leads to an impoverishment of the psychic life of the young.

Once a person accepts the superiority of the mystified process of the production over his own abilities, he is reduced to a mechanical entity who chooses among preset alternatives. The same process is revealed in human relations. National talent is continually present on television, in the movies, on recording, and so forth. The disparity between the young person's own rudimentary skills and those of a star may stimulate the emulation of a few, but discourages the many; especially since most young people are taught to desire instant gratification. Contemporary American culture discourages the learning of a discipline, as the average person is reduced to a spectator viewing professionals who are paid for participating in activities which might be intrinsically satisfying to the amateur. The images of success are so far out of reach for most young people, they are defeated before they start.

Consequently, they adopt a "what's the use?" attitude toward trying new things, since the exemplars of our society tend to intimidate more than inspire. When the school and community dangle alternatives in front of these young people's faces, the apathy that results is generated by a deep distrust of adults (what are they getting out of it?), resentment of adult judgments (usually in the negative), and a fear of failure (meeting adult standards). Everything is offered to them on adult terms, in adult dominated organizations. Yet they are incapable of sustaining any effort at formal organization. First of all, they don't like formal organization, since they are at the bottom of the ones with which they are familiar. Second, they prefer less coercive, voluntary modes of organization. Third, they have not seen democracy work very well, from elementary classroom school elections to the

Nixon Administration. They see adults abuse power and deny them participation. To them, democracy is a hoax and student government is a sellout. Adult authority is so pervasive that the best one can hope for is to avoid it as much as possible. As a matter of fact, it is the very students who are willing to cope with adult authority that are in the student political elite. The student political elite chide their peers for lack of responsibility, while at the same time they realize that without power, there is not really much to be responsible for. Thus, "responsibility" essentially means doing what the adults tell you to do. The apathetic majority want to avoid being told what to do at all costs. Their gripe is lack of power, with which the student political elite agrees. The politicos maintain that if students want power, they must confront the adults. To engage the adults in direct conflict makes one vulnerable to adult sanctions and judgments. They see it as a quixotic act in which there is little to gain and much to lose, and chances are that they'll lose. It is no surprise, then, that the most vicious method of fighting back is vandalism, which takes place when nobody is around. It is a type of guerrilla tactic in which one never has to face the enemy directly.

The barriers erected between youth and adults lead to a vitiated learning environment. Not only is the teacher the sole arbiter of what is to be taught, student apathy requires the teacher to "motivate" the students to learn the subject matter. It is a rare occasion in which a teacher asks a class what they want to know. Attending class is merely a way of taking up time under the supervision of an adult. For most, the subject matter is secondary to the fact that *one must put in time*, do the necessary labor, and achieve at a pre-determined rate in order to pass through the massive educational sorting mechanism at levels acceptable to one's (or, more likely, one's parents') aspirations. It all seems like a meaningless game that attains a dreamlike quality about it as one drifts through the mechanism letting off steam during "free time."

Now let us address the problems of "youth" in our society. First, we must recognize that "youth" as a status in contemporary society has evolved as a result of economic and cultural changes. Therefore, the "problem" of youth is a problem of social structure, and requires structural change. Second, it has only been recently that young people have been legally defined as "persons." However, in contemporary society they are treated as second-class persons, deprived of any real power over their own lives. Youth, then, is primarily a *political* status in which a person has the body of an adult and the economic dependency of a child. Youth is mainly a client population for educational bureaucracies; thus, the most common role in the youth status is student, which, for all intents and purposes, can be referred to interchangeably with youth.

The way to eliminate youth as a problem is to eliminate youth as a status. Of course, this requires a complete restructuring of society: Non-productive, non-essential labor must be eliminated; waste consumption must be ended; bureaucracies must be abolished; the market mechanism must be eliminated as the basis of distribution of wealth and income; all hierarchies must be made temporary and task-specific; necessary labor must be distributed on the bases of equity and ability; and everybody must be considered equal participants in the social enterprise until such time as they determine differently. In all social systems, there are going to be invidious differences and status hierarchies. However, there is no reason that such differences cannot be based on personal qualities of the individual apart from the attributes of material wealth, and that such status differentials can be minimized and be sources of inspiration for those less gifted or dedicated. Certainly such difference should not be the basis of access to material goods. Such a society would eliminate childhood, adolescence, youth, adulthood, and old age as *political* categories. Obviously, there would continue to be developmental differences and biological and emotional dependencies of the younger upon their elders. However, in an egalitarian society, the elders would need the young as much as the young their elders. A true mutuality of interests could emerge in which the relations between people in different parts of the life cycle could non-coercively come together as equals. Instead of the cannibalistic relationship that presently exists between adults and the young, in which the young are the food for the adult-dominated systems, there would be mutual need satisfaction.

THE END AND THE BEGINNING

The conclusion of this study is similar to that of Christopher Jencks, et al. (1972) in their study of inequality: education cannot be adequately reformed without restructuring society. Jencks suggests income equality as a solution, but avoids the question of wealth distribution. It has been the thesis of this book that the major function of education is the absorption of economically generated waste. Whether it absorbs it in the form of "humanistic" education, compensatory education, "back to basics," "value clarification," or "free schools," makes no difference so long as the products are consumed. As long as this is the case, educational reform directed toward the rejuvenation of the commitment of its members is impossible. We are now able to ask, given the present state of technology, whether people, given a computer and video system, can develop their own education without the intervention of a state bureaucracy.

The tax revolt that began in California and is sweeping the country as this book is written, indicated that bureaucracy (especially in the form of the state—which is *supposed* to waste money) constitutes its own critique. Of course, the surplus absorbing middle classes may be slitting their own throats by cutting waste consumption through reduction of taxes, thereby increasing unemployment among their own ranks: teachers, social workers, public administrators, and so forth. The taxpayers' revolt constitutes an attack on bureaucracy from the right, led by those who claim that the money can be better used in the private sector. However, the attack upon educational bureaucracies is clear. A national poll taken by *Newsweek* magazine[2] following the California referendum on taxes (Proposition 13) indicated that 25 percent of the respondents felt that too much was being spent on schools. The only other government service to have a greater percentage of public animosity was "social services," which included welfare (42 percent). Also, the Gallup Poll released the 1978 edition of its poll on confidence of American institutions. Most institutions lost confidence from the 1973 polling. Schools were especially hard hit. In 1973, 58 percent of those polled stated that they had a "great deal" or "quite a lot" of confidence in education. In 1978, that percentage had dropped to 45 percent (*The New York Times, June 18, 1978*).

The major problem in capitalist America is social control. If personal spending is allowed to rise rapidly, then a revolution of expectations is generated, as witnessed by the social unrest of the 1960s. However, if personal spending is held constant and bureaucratic spending is increased as in the 1970s, then the state is attacked as a parasitic blood-sucker. Underlying both these phenomena is the contradiction of monopoly captialism: the economy must expand by virtue of its own internal logic, while such expansion unleashes forces that undermine its legitimacy. Employment must be held as the normal mode of social participation at all costs, while employment becomes an excuse to consume. The stratification that is generated by such a structure becomes undermined as the state's ability to simulate scarcity that is presupposed by capitalism becomes more difficult, and the social hierarchy makes less and less sense, not only to the office holders, but to those over whom they are supposed to exercise authority.

In order to resolve the crisis of contemporary capitalism, we must end stratification. Socialists (such as Jencks, et al. 1972.) believe in income redistribution. This is not sufficient. *We have arrived at the point in the development of society where labor no longer has to be tied to status accumulation.* That is, given the technical possibilities of our productive capacity, people need not work for a living. (As chronicled in the Bicentennial Edition of the *Detroit Fifth Estate* (July 1976), one of the surviving underground newspapers, "Workers of the world, relax!") The implication of this is that the amount of time spent in coerced production and consumption, on the part of any given individual, will be radically less than at present. Obviously, while we commit our social resources to ridding ourselves on onerous labor, we will have a certain amount of coerced labor, which will have to be distributed equally and equitably. Some readers are going to ask who is going to run the trains, who is going to pick up the garbage? The former can be automated. As for the latter, the question should be asked from the other side that is, "Why is there so much trash?" Of course, waste production presupposes waste consumption: planned obsolescence, coerced consumption (e.g., the use of elaborate packaging and the American habit of bagging sold commodities), and, of course, consumption for consumption sake.[3] If there were no need for waste, the amount of trash in our society would drop dramatically, necessitating less commitment of time, energy, and resources to its collection and disposal.

In the unstratified society, labor will not be for sale. The social order will operate on the assumption that if work is not needed, it won't get done. This is not to say that collective enterprises will not occur, nor the differences in skill and talent will not be recognized. It will mean that collective enterprises will not be coerced through the withholding of the means of existence from one class by another. Rubenstein will not have to play the piano for a living. Everyone will share in the social wealth equally.

It is obvious that the issues raised herein raise more questions than they answer. The formulation is fraught with contradictions. However, given the diagnosis of the problem, there must be a possibility of a solution. Human life has only been recently harnessed to capital. It is short sighted to assume that capital will dominate the lives of humans for eternity merely because this is the case at present. The problem that has been focused upon is that of youth, which leads us to the problems of schools, and, hence, society. As has been said elsewhere, the problem of youth is their existence as a category of stratification. It is a societal problem and, as such, demands a societal solution. However, the presentation of an alternative to present society can only be done in broad strokes, giving only a crude hint of what is possible.

The means by which we achieve the unstratified society is

through "liberatory" technology. From the invention of the first tool, technology has helped to liberate the human species from the toil of onerous labor. This is true in capitalism as well, where living labor has been supplanted by congealed labor in the form of machinery. However, the "labor-saving" aspects of technology have been used by the capitalist class to extract ever-increasing amounts of unpaid labor from workers and to increase capital's control over the conditions of labor. Thus, the development of technology has been one-sided, and its development, since it has enhanced the dominance of one class over another, has been alienative. The liberatory aspects of technology have been advanced only insofar as they have benefitted capital. For example, the federal government, until very recently, has heavily subsidized nuclear energy to the detriment of solar energy. Nuclear energy requires a large, centralized, bureaucratic structure, massive capital investment, and large servicing agencies; whereas, solar energy, with the exception of investment in the original phases of research and development, does not.

Not only does technology have the possibilities of liberating us from onerous labor, but it also contains the possibilities of liberating us from stultifying bureaucratic control. Technology is an extension of the senses. Incorporated under the term, "media," there are a vast array of devices that contain the potential for revolutionizing social relationships in general, and schooling in particular. The possibilities presented by our *existing* communications technology offers staggering possibilities for the development of alternatives to schooling. In 1977, Warner Communications Corporation began hooking subscribers up to the first interactive television network in the country, called QUBE. Even though QUBE is a very primitive system and locked into the requisites of corporate necessities, it contains the possibilities of revolutionary change. The 26,000 subscribers each have a rudimentary computer attached to their television. The computer gives them two options that regular television users do not have: access to 30 stations, and interactive capacities. Of course, cable television has been around for awhile, so the increased access is nothing new. However, it does allow for alternatives to

network television, such as instructional channels, local programming at very low levels of capital investment, and coverage
of local events. The interactive capacity of QUBE is only two-
way, between the viewer and the station. Each viewer has five
buttons on his or her terminal which allows the viewer to choose
between up to five alternatives to respond to the questions. Even
though QUBE does not allow the viewer to respond directly to the
televised content in complex fashion, or to communicate with
other viewers, such capabilities are already in use in more advanced computerized systems.

The merging of the computer and the television set generates
possibilities for restructuring communications within our society. With the onset of videotape recorders, videocassette
recorders, portable VTR's, video discs, interactive console
systems, sophisticated computer programs, community cable
systems, computer communication via telephone lines, citizens'
band radio, micro-processing chips, etc., the nation can be
hooked up into a vast computerized system allowing for instan-
taneous communication between any number of individuals and
groups. Each community could have its own computer termi-
nals, recording systems, input/output devices, and television
screens. Huge amounts of information would be available to all
equally. The democratization of access to communal resources
would have a leveling affect on human relationships. Communities would become redefined along axes of common interests, concerns, issues, desires, or anything else. Information
could be shared among all interested parties, without exclusion
by virtue of lack of resources, since all resources would be
communal and easily accessible. The true individuation of social
relationships would then be possible, as people would participate in collective enterprises on the basis of uncoerced choice.

Some people may wonder if the extensions of media will make
us slaves of technology. This does not have to occur as long as
the media are used to facilitate the development and evolution of
free communities. The possibility exists for people to interact
with other like-minded people from all corners of the country (or
hemisphere or world). Although such interaction may be medi-

ated, there is no reason why it cannot actually facilitate face-to-face relationships. For example, a woman sees a tape about ham radio operators, finds it very interesting, and wants to know more about it. There are many options open to her, including gaining access to books, pamphlets, license directories, etc. about ham operations from the computer. However, she would like to actually see a ham station in operation. She goes over to her computer terminal, gets on the system, and types out, "Are there any ham operators nearby?" The computer would then print out a list of all the ham operators in her area code, beginning with those nearest. She might wish additional information on the complexity of the nearby stations, supposing she wants to see a relatively simple operation. She finds a station within a mile of her and sends the operator a message that she would like to see the station in operation. On the operator's console, an asterisk would appear in the lower left-hand corner of his screen indicating there is a message for him. Upon receiving the message, he could call her and invite her over while he is operating the station. While admittedly oversimplified, the example indicates that the new communications technology does not have to be a barrier between people, but can actually encourage social relations that might not have occurred if equal access was not possible.

As mentioned above, a certain minimum of coerced labor will be necessary to maintain necessary services and production. It is obvious that the provision of necessary services will generate status hierarchies and will require levels of expertise. Given that technology can relegate necessary labor to the periphery of our lives, such status hierarchies will be functional rather than dominating forces in the status hierarchy. For example, a doctor will not have any greater access to the means of existense than a plumber, even though he may have more status by virtue of the nature of the labor he performs. (Of course, one could argue, "Who needs a doctor when your pipes are leaking?" However, having leaking pipes is less serious than a leaky heart valve.) People must be trained for jobs that require high levels of skill. Professional communities will certify people at various skill levels in necessary labor. They will provide practicum, laboratory and tutorial work, and provide a center for face-to-face inter-action between those of higher skills and novices, the intellectual content and prerequisites could be done by computerized video-instruction.

As necessary labor declined as a result of innovation, the boundaries between school and society would diminish. The school would "wither away," as intellective functions would become the province of communities, family, peer group, and the self-directed individual. There would be no need to segregate the young from the rest of society. As they would grow and develop, they would assume responsible roles as providers of necessary labor on the basis of social need and level of skill. Schooling functions would be returned to the community as a whole, the family and the peer group. Rather than cloistering the young in artificial bureaucratized environments, children would be exposed to *real* learning by doing. As Ivar Berg (1971) has pointed out, education in its present form has very little to do with job training. There is plenty of evidence to indicate that the best way to learn most tasks is to perform the particular task *in situ* with proper guidance and instruction.

At present, educational institutions have incorporated communications innovations in an alienated and fragmentary form. Every major American university has a sophisticated computer system. Many mathematics and hard science courses are taught by computers at the secondary and collegiate levels. Videotapes are often used in more "topical" courses in the humanities and social sciences. The incorporation of films, radio programs, audio tapes into course content are old hat by now. Most of these incorporations of media are used to lessen the load on the teacher or professor. A film means one less lesson plan, a computerized course means more research time for the professor, or perhaps a reduction in faculty by the administration. The impetus of behavioral objectives and programmed instruction that characterized the late 1960s, served mainly to further circumscribe the student's behavior to lock-step mechanized sequences that channelled the student's subjectivity to the demands of the programmer as the ends justified the means. All these innovations were used to enhance the dominance of the bureaucratic mechanism over the individual learner. The system is out of their hands and they are passive recipients of prepackaged programs.

The technology is now available to liberate the young from their deadening days in the school house consuming various newfangled educational products in alienated forms. The walls of the schoolhouse must be broken down and the students must be reintegrated into the community. Children love to play with computers, even if it is in the extremely primitive form of computerized television games such as "pong." It has been said that the problem of computerized instruction is the fact that the "software" is poor. Computerized programs that do a good job of teaching basic skills are not readily available. However, there are programs that can teach elementary principles of physics and logic through the use of games. One wonders what could be possible if the 2.4 million elementary and secondary teachers in the United States were replaced by a mere 240,000 computer programmers dedicated to developing games that taught basic skills to the young. As the young would be introduced into computer programming, there is no reason why they could not develop programs for each other. There have been many successful experiments where young people have made their own videotapes, movies, etc. that could, in the future, be available to others who are interested.

As necessary labor is reduced to its minimum, the necessity for segregating the young into baby-sitting institutions would decline. The young could then be integrated into the community as socially necessary persons who would contribute to the social wealth along with everyone else, commensurate with their level of skills. The family, community, and peer group would assume reciprocal responsibilities for the socialization of the young and they, in turn, would have the right of self-determination to follow their own dictates outside the provision of necessary services from all to all.

The psychic immizeration that is experienced by the students at Utopia High School is a consequence of the fact that they experience their encapsulation in bureaucratic institutions as senseless. Their lives are devoted, in one way or another, to consuming capital. They feel that there must be something more.

Shortly after the onset of puberty, a prospective Sioux brave would be sent onto the plains along with a minimum of protection to survive until he received a vision which would be used to guide him through the rest of his life. Once the vision had been received, the Sioux would dedicate his life to the realization of his vision. For all our innovation and technological tinkering, we seem to have a society that is incapable of bold vision. It is understandable to try to hold onto what one has; perhaps we grasp too much that is not worth the effort in the face of the possibilities of our own liberation.

NOTES

1. Michael Maccoby (1977), a student of Eric Fromm, has criticized Maslow's notion of a need hierarchy on the basis that it ignores conflict, the relationship between the rational and the irrational, and views impulse and discipline as opposed. He also scores Maslow's theory on the basis of its inherent self-congratulatory ideology of the successful (1977:232–33):

   > Despite his conscious attempt to develop a modern humanistic psychology, Maslow ends by supporting, even celebrating some values—hierarchy, mechanistic thought, idealization of success, careerism—that block the development of the heart.

2. June 19, 1978. The question was stated, "Does your community spend too much, too little or just about the right amount for local services?" Below are some selected responses.

	Too Much	Too Little	Right Amount	Don't Know
Public schools	25	33	35	7
Fire department	5	24	59	8
Police department	12	28	52	7
Parks & recreation	16	25	48	3
Sanitation	9	19	58	8
Social services (welfare, counseling, mental health, etc.)	42	19	28	10

3. One wonders how many employees the FBI used in compiling the 70,000 pages of material on the tiny Trotskyite sect, the Socialist Workers Party. How many

agents, secretaries, clerks, and administrators could be justified by the SWP threat to American security? Ironically, the U.S. government violated more laws in studying the SWP than did the Trotskyites. During 25 years of illegal surveillance, the FBI was unable to document a single indictable offense!

METHODOLOGICAL
APPENDIX

You've been with the professors and they've all liked
   your looks,
With great lawyers you've discussed lepers and crooks.
You've been through all of F. Scott Fitzgerald's books,
You're very well read it's well known,
But something is happening here
And you don't know what it is.
Do you, Mister Jones?
                              Bob Dylan, "Ballad of a Thin Man," 1965

THE REVOLUTION OF PARADIGMS

It is my belief that the mission of sociology is twofold: it must both *discover* and *create* truth. As the sociologist attempts to uncover the links between the social order, culture, and personality, he or she participates in the creation of reality. The empirical sociologist either puzzle-solves within an existing paradigm, presents anomalous data which undermines it, or attempts to build a new one which explains social phenomena at a superior level than the preceding paradigm (Kuhn, 1970). The first type of inquiry reinforces the status quo, the second erodes it, and the third revolutionizes it.

The reigning paradigm for sociology in the post-World War II period is structural-functionalism. Nicholas Mullins (1973), in his analysis of the growth and development of schools of sociological thought, aptly termed it "the faith of our fathers." Talcott Parsons, Robert Merton, George Homans, William Goode, Kingsley Davis, Wilburt Moore, Marion Levy, and lesser stars of structural-functionalism dominated professional sociology in the 1950s. The loyal opposition were the symbolic interactionists such as Herbert Blumer and Howard Becker. Functional analysis dominated macro-theory; Parsons and his students were in their hey-day. Institutional studies were concerned primarily with the analysis of functions, structure, dysfunctions, and latent functions. Even the analysis of social conflict was carried out from a functionalist perspective (cf. Coser, 1956). Anomie theory was the paramount model of explaining deviance until Becker (1956) did battle with Merton and labelling theory became an acceptable adjunct to anomie theory. Marxism had no place in the social theory of post-war American sociology, even though it has had important adherents throughout its history (e.g., Albion Small, Robert and Helen Lynd, and both Lewis Coser and Daniel Bell in their early years). Because of the anti-Communist hysteria during that period, the left was driven out of respectable academic circles. All Marxism was associated with totalitarian ideology, and functionalists such as Talcott Parsons and Seymour Martin Lipset never missed an opportunity to declaim Marxism in their writings (see, for example, Parsons's *The Social System* [1956] and Lipset's *Political Man* [1960]).

As Alvin Gouldner (1970) has pointed out, structural-functionalism was closely aligned with the assumptions of capitalism (the "free market economy") and the liberal democratic state. It viewed social conflict as pathological and *prima facie* evidence of the need for institutional reform. Structural-functionalists viewed the system from the top down and, for the most part, did not question the legitimacy of existing hierarchical arrangements. This is perhaps best exemplified by the Moynahan report (1965) which, in response to the civil rights movement, advocated state intervention into the black family.

The insurgencies of the 1960s undermined the idealized view of the corporate state which predominated in sociology. The image of the benign, pluralistic, representative state in which corruption was an aberration was replaced by a view that emphasized class dominance, controlled violence, systemmatic corruption, and monomaniacal neo-imperialism as the Vietnam War was pursued and police-state tactics were used to silence protesters. The core of student radicalism came from the departments of social sciences in the major universities. Students seriously questioned their professors. Marx reemerged in classical theories courses in sociology. (It might be noted that the leading introductory sociology text by functionalists Leonard Broom and Phillip Selznick [1955] barely mentioned Marx in the 1950s. In the fourth edition, published in 1968, they allotted a page and a half to his class analysis followed by four pages of rebuttal.) The younger faculty and their students challenged the established professors as maintainers of the *status quo* and the "value-free" sociology of structural-functionalism was biased in favor of existing elites. Leftist-oriented professors (such as Gouldner) who had been silent during the 1950s came out of the closet and joined the students at the intellectual barricades.

Following the 1960s, structural-functionalism has become moribund. Even Broom (Broom and Cushing, 1977) has questioned one of its fundamental tenets in a recent article. Perhaps the only area that is still alive within the realm of functionalism is social exchange theory which has its intellectual roots in Max Weber. In the wake of functionalism, we find a myriad of competing schools. However, the emergent schools are neo-Marxism and ethnomethodology. These two schools exist in the 1970s as alienated fragments of 1960s movement ideology. Both make claims of radicalism; neo-Marxism because it challenges the basis of existing social class relationships and exists as a critique of capitalism. Ethnomethodology makes its claim on the basis that it questions the assumptions of conventional reality. In line with 1960s subjectivism, ethnomethodologists claim all realities are created equal (Mehan and Wood, 1975:31).

The neo-Marxism of the 1970s is an outgrowth of the political wing of the 1960s youth movement. It emphasizes the politics of domination, the hegemony of the economic sector over the political sector of society, social class relationships, the critique of hierarchy, and the maintenance of false consciousness. Ethnomethodology became popular in the late 1960s and early 1970s as an attempt to make subjectivism a legitimate methodology of social science. Borrowing from its pioneers (e.g., Edmund Husserl, Alfred Shutz, George Herbert Mead, Martin Heidegger), it leap-frogged the symbolic interactionists' concern with learning theory and attitude development, and attempted to study the process of consciousness itself, constituting itself as a critique of social science constructions of reality as a system which is *imposed* upon other realities. Such imposition, they maintain, creates distortions and is inherently *political*, whereby the social scientist becomes the arbiter of what is real by virtue of his superior position vis-a-vis the respondent. Ethnomethodology also critiques standard social science on the basis of the false dichotomy between the researcher and the researched, emphasizing the intrusion of the sociologist into the social situation of data collection.

Freund and Abrams (1976) made the first attempt to bring ethnomethodology and Marxism together. However, such an attempt was at the level of conceptualization. Paradoxically, most Marxist research (e.g., Kolko, Domhoff, Bowles and Gintis) has been strongly positivist in its assumptions and has been methodologically indistinguishable from standard sociological practice. The school which shares most in common with the ethnomethodologists, the cultural Marxists (or critical school), do not engage in empirical research at all, but write treatises on capitalist culture (e.g., Habermas, Lefebvre, Brown, Lukacs). Ethnomethodology, on the contrary, is distinctly empirical and has devised ingenious methods to study the process of consciousness through qualitative research.

This study represents, to the best of my knowledge, the first attempt to integrate critical Marxian theory with some ethnomethodological techniques. Insofar as this syntheses has occurred, a new paradigm has been constructed which combines elements of disparate models into a new view of social reality. It combines macro-theory with the study of intentionality and subjective awareness; combines the negative critique of the social order with postivistic empiricism; and merges two antagonistic schools into a unity. Critical theory lacked an empirical base and ethnomethodologists attempted to investigate reality with no conception of society. The merging of these two paradigms generates an alternative to functionalism that has possibilities for incredibly strong explanatory power.

METHODOLOGY AND MESSODOLOGY

The research reported in this book links the problems of suburban youth of the 1970s with my prior interests in youth culture. During the 1960s, youth culture took the form of a social movement, generating visions of social change in which Westerners would be liberated from the onerous burdens of coerced labor and the constraints of bourgeois culture. This movement was unique in several ways: it diverged from the trend toward increasing rationalization and bureaucratization of movements during the period of industrialization (e.g., the Labor Movement), it was subject to kaleidoscopic changes and cultural shifts in a matter of weeks, the basis of cohesion was a shared subculture of dissidence, and it occurred among the most affluent and privileged groups in the social order (see Foss, 1972).

Because of the nature of the phenomenon of the "youth revolution," sociologist Daniel Foss abandoned standarized notions of sociological "methodology," which attempts to impose a rationalized, standarized plan on the study of social phenomena. He correctly noted in his book, *Freak Culture* (1972), that the youth movement of the 1960s caught the sociological profession completely off guard. Nobody predicted it. Of the important writers on youth in the late 1950s and early 1960s, James Coleman (1961) claimed that what youth needed was more academic competition, which was something they rebelled against. Kenneth Kenniston (1960) made a plea for commitment to utopian ideals. Edgar Friedenberg (1959) openly admitted his pessimism concerning the ability of youth to shape a new world. Jules Henry (1963), in discussing the cultural binds that are placed on Americans, claimed that he saw no hope for change. Yet two years later there was a full-scale attack on the cultural contradictions he had been describing. Even as the youth revolution struck, sociology tended to fragment it into its various manifestations, while ignoring the whole. Monographs began to appear about "the Hippies," "the student movement," "the Anti-War movement," "the generation gap," and so forth, which led to the trivialization of a much larger phenomenon. Foss, proclaiming that "it is better to be completely wrong than to be insufficiently right" (1972:17), waded into the mess in an attempt to rationally and systemmatically analyze "what the hell is going on" (1972:16).

Noting that society has come unhinged, Foss abandoned standard notions of sociological methodology for what he called "messodology." Messodology begins with the construction of a Macro-theory which lends itself to a coherent interpretation of seemingly disparate phenomena. The theory makes heavy demand upon the sociologist, since it requires him or her to know a great deal about many areas of knowledge: it must account for economic, historical, cultural, and psychological forces. It must also be able to account for changes, and the sociologist must be sensitive to the catalytic moment at which quantitative changes become qualitative and assume a reality of their own. For example, it is the central thesis of this book that the economic function of surplus absorption has become the dominating force in the process of education and has radically undermined the motivational patterns of students and educators. Until sociologists and educators understand the master forces, they continue to analyze fragments of the problem (e.g., deviance in the schools, declining SAT scores, accountability, etc.) without seeing the basic cause. Oftentimes, such research leads to blaming the powerless for their own situation. Students are being blamed for the drop in SATs, school officials are being blamed for vandalism in the schools, parents are blamed for the loss of motivation of their children. Although this may have a certain cathartic value for the accusers, it hardly sheds light on what is rightfully a societal problem. In linking abstract theory with research interests, messodology allows the sociologist to enter a seemingly chaotic or confused situation with a sense of what and where to look. If the thesis is correct, data will begin piling up to support it, since it will be *overdetermined.* If the thesis is incorrect, it fails *completely,* and the sociologist is forced to look elsewhere for master trends. Yet the research findings become the basis for forging the new grand theory.

For the purposes of example, let us assume that the major function of education is the distribution of rewards and the allocation of the young to various positions in the social status hierarchy. Such a theory would infer that student unrest would occur among those students who were allocated a disproportionally small amount of rewards, or that changes in the reward structure which created relative deprivation for any segment of the student population would stir reactions from the affected higher status levels. Yet the experience of the 1960s invalidates such a hypothesis, since the middle-class youth rebellion did not encompass relative deprivation vis-a-vis other segments of the student population, but an all-encompassing critique of capitalist society, bureaucratic hierarchy, and the structure of all reward systems. Messodology assumes a dialectical relationship between theory and data *within the research process itself*.

At the time, youth culture was punctuated with a myriad of weird events that defied the scrutiny of standard sociological analysis: be-ins, love-ins, sit-ins, mill-ins, LSD tripping, Tarot divining, public sexuality, "freak outs," public goofs, etc.. Messodology was appropriate for the times. Not only was the youth culture inventing new social forms and discarding them before they could be co-opted by the establishment, but sociology, bound by cumbersome "methodological requirements" and tied to rationalized granting procedures, was unable to understand such innovative behavior since the phenomenon often disappeared before it could be studied using conventional means. Youth culture, always shifting and ephemeral, had reached new levels of innovation which were completely ignored by standard sociology. Even sociologists who were sympathetic to movement could not break the mold of positivism. One is reminded of the story of Marshall Meyer asking student radicals to rank themselves on a conservatism-liberalism scale and being admonished by his own respondents (Meyer, 1971). Messodology, then, became necessary to understand a social phenomenon from the outside in and the inside out. Its purpose is to enable the sociologist to formulate the subjective experiences of the participants in a coherent form and tie such changes to the macrostructural forces that generated the phenomenon. However, it is most important that the *content* of the experience shape the form. If the form is allowed to shape the content of the study, then violence is done to the subjective experiences of the participants. We will deal with this problem below.

Although messodology was conceived during a period of social upheaval, it has been useful beyond the frame of social movement periods. Foss and I used messodology to study youth culture phenomena during the post-movement period that lasted from 1970 to 1975. Again, youth culture had manifested quite weird events: the rise and fall of the Symbionese Liberation Army, the Weatherunderground, the rise of unorthodox religions such as the Hari Krishnas, Children of God, Guru Maharaj Ji and The Divine Light Mission, the Process Church of the Final Judgment, and so forth. We studied the followers of Guru Maharaj Ji over the three year period from 1973 to 1976, documenting the activities of the believers of a most unlikely God. This allowed us to understand the problems of ex-movement participants in a period of especially painful transition back to normalcy (see Foss and Larkin, 1976; 1979).

Now that youth culture has moved back into a period of normalcy, it offers a different set of problems. No longer are there underground newspapers that report the *geist* of the community. Dissidence and inventiveness have declined, and the changes in youth culture are more evolutionary and subtle. There is no new vision that has to be apprehended by the researcher. Yet, the divisions between young and old are as compelling as ever. The only way to understand the young today is to hang out with them and "mess around."

Most research on youth, especially youth who are below college age, are carried out through standard sociological data gathering devices, such as the questionnaire and the structured interview. These types of data gathering devices are fraught with problems. First, they require the sociologist to define all the concepts by which these people are measured. Second, it requires minimal interaction between the sociologist and the subjects (who are really "objects" of study, since their subjectivity is totally ignored beyond the parameters of the sociologists' requirements). Third, whatever is defined as "real" must conform to the pigion-holes the sociologist has determined *a priori*. Because the sociologist becomes the sole arbiter of reality and provides the form in which the information must be supplied, the consciousness of the so-called respondent is denied so long as it does not fit the Procrustean bed of the questionnaire. When sociologists study "culture," this is especially true, since culture necessarily encompasses form. Style is central to culture. For example, it is not enough that a ritual be performed, but it must be performed in accordance with cultural imperatives and normative strictures.

Most sociological investigations ignore such important aspects of subjectivity, assuming the awareness of the sociologist is superior to that of his respondents. Thus, sociologists like to think of themselves as "debunkers," who explore what is "really" happening beneath the ideological fog.

The problem posed by standard sociological methodology is political. When studying sub-dominant groups who are relatively powerless, the politics of the methodology take on added importance. There is an element of cultural imperialism involved, since sociological definitions are imposed upon the data *prior* to data collection and responses are forced into the sociological mold. The experience of the participants becomes distorted. Nuance is destroyed. Radicals in the 1960s did not see themselves as on a continuum between conservatism and liberalism. They saw the Communist Party as conservative. Likewise, they saw thieves as radicals. How does a sociologist put that on a scale? Sociological imperialism trivializes the phenomena under investigation. Such an example, among many, was an article published by Raymond Eve (1975), in which he asks, "Is 'adolescent culture' a convenient myth or reality?" His first trivialization was defining culture as synonymous with "values." He then defines values as attitudes toward cheating, mischief, sports, fighting, selling marijuana, partying, buying marijuana, drinking, and automobile use. If there had been no difference between teacher and student mean scores on these attitude scales, he would have been ready to conclude that there was no adolescent culture. That was the second trivialization. (As a matter of fact, as is argued in chapter 2 of this book, there may not be an *adolescent* subculture, but not for the reasons Eve proffered.) As it was, Eve did find differences on several dimensions. His conclusion landed him squarely on the fence:

> Taken as a whole, this study has provided evidence that although students do maintain a statistically distinct value system, this system is primarily conventional in its orientation and differs only to a relatively small degree from the value system of the adult world. (1975:165)

The problem with Eve's study is that, given his methodology, there is no possible way to find a qualitative difference between adults and the young. When is a significance statistic large enough to indicate a qualitative difference? Never. Therefore, it is *inevitable* that Eve would conclude that "adolescent values" would vary from "adult values" only quantitatively.

Such distortion and trivialization flattens culture to the point of unidimensionalty. The sole virtue of the concept "values" is that it is operationalizable. As has already been mentioned, the concept itself is loaded with ideological trappings and was abstracted from bourgeois economics. The term "value" was originally used to denote the quantity of labor a commodity could command. When applied to human morality, it tends to "objectify," commodify and quantify qualitative beliefs. By posing hypothetical questions to their subjects, sociologists can use the concept to order a "hierarchy of values"—or at least a hierarchy of espoused "values." The ultimate realization of the concept of values is contained in social exchange theory, in which each individual is viewed as a rational calculator who is trying to maximize psychic profits while minimizing psychic losses (cf. Blau [1964] and Homans [1966]). "Value realization" (the acting out of the values of the community) leads to the accumulation of social capital in the form of esteem.

Once the total of the symbolic realm is reduced to a quantifiable entity, culture as a concept is negated. Of all the concepts in the realm of social sciences, culture is the most difficult and complex. It has depth and texture; these are qualities that are not easily measurable. It is imbedded in every action of human beings. We, as humans, cannot act without a meaning being attached to what we do. Even to have an act declared meaningless is demonstrative of the cultural imbeddedness of human behavior. The sociological tendency to trivialize culture destroys the most important bases of understanding human action.

In gathering and reporting the research herein, the cultural ramifications of larger social phenomena have been emphasized. I have tried to portray the dimensionality of culture and keep the *texture* of experienced reality alive.

THE CONDUCT OF THE STUDY

The study of Utopia High School youth began quite serendip-
itously. Daniel Foss and I were collaborating on developing a
theory to explain the continuing decline of legitimacy of American social institutions beyond the insurgencies of the 1960s into
the mid-1970s. Polls had indicated that "trust in institutions"
which had declined during the 1960s showed no abatement as late
as 1976. We focused on the decline and fall of bourgeois culture
and the economic requirements of monopoly capitalism, which
provided the basis of the theory in chapter 2. We had noticed that
"functioning" seemed to be emerging as an important social
problem. Therapy cults arose claiming to be able to help people
function more easily in their social roles, fantasy movies that
portrayed disasters where normal functioning was no longer
possible were grossing huge profits (e.g., *The Poseidon Ad-
venture, Earthquake, The Towering Inferno*, etc.), Valium prescriptions had reached epidemic levels, and the psychic problems
of the upper-middle class focused on the problems of "meaning
in life" and getting through the day.

Meanwhile, as college professors, we noted that the student
population had collapsed into a collective funk. They, too, were
having problems getting through the day. They were cynical,
distrustful of anyone in authority over them, and extremely
closed-mouth about their feelings. The 1970s generation of youth
was keeping a low profile. However, the gains in the liberalization of school policies were being chopped away by faculty and
administrations, who, once the insurgencies of the 1960s had
died, felt new confidence to reimpose more restrictive regulations
on student prerogatives. Only a very small student minority
protested. Apathy reigned.

During the winter of 1975–76, a colleague began talking to me
about the school district in the town where she lived. The school
board, for years dominated by liberals, was the focus of a challenge by conservatives who wanted to institute a "back to basics"
program. The conservatives swept the election and began putting

pressure on the administration to reinstitute controls over the behavior of the students and return to the three Rs. In addition, they were having budget problems that were creating a great deal of difficulty in the school system. As we talked, I became fascinated with the school district, which had been a place of dissident activities during the 1960s. The high school provided the perfect laboratory to study the youth of the 1970s.

My colleague showed me copies of the school newspaper that reported the turmoil in the school. She gave me the name of the principal and acted as my entree into the community. Through the principal, I secured permission from the school board to study the school. Once I received permission, I began to draw up a set of questions that I thought were important, and incorporated them into a questionnaire. The questionnaire was not used in the conventional manner. It provided a framework that allowed me to check off the various topics I wanted to cover with the students. My intention was to get them talking with the tape recorder on. The questionnaire functioned as a "front" (to use a Goffmanesque term) to establish that I was indeed a serious researcher doing serious sociological research. This allayed the fears of those who were worried about having a stranger walking around a high school campus recording students' thoughts. As a matter of fact, one student, Roz, found me in the hall one day and quizzed me about the problem of data control. She claimed that Utopia High was not a typical school and that she was concerned that the picture that I would get would not typify the national high school experience. I replied that I knew that the school was not typical, but it was atypical in a way that suited the purposes of the study.

Even in the more formalized interviews, the questionnaire was used more as a prop than anything else. Once the students began talking, the interview session would assume a conversational cast, which was what I wanted. The interview sessions were designed to get students to interact with each other as well as myself. Even though the presence of the researcher altered the reality, once people became relaxed and began to enjoy talking about topics that were central to their lives, they opened up and the conversation flowed. I saw my role as more of a facilitator of discussion than anything else, although a review of the tapes shows that sometimes I could be argumentative. However, the students were not in awe of me and would argue back. For the most part, though, I tried to remain neutral and interested.

The interviews with the adults were much more formal than those with the students. We met at appointed times, I explained the purpose of the study and conducted an informal interview. Again, the questionnaire was used as a prop and a guide. Of all the data collected on the students, there were only two formally scheduled interviews. The rest were gathered "in the field." Some of the most startling revelations were given under the most informal circumstances.

The process of data collection began with the presentation of a proposal to the principal who, in turn, relayed it to the Board of Education. I discussed the proposal with the principal and the chairman of the social studies department and told them what I wanted to do. They gave me carte blanche and left all research decisions up to me. The principal gave me a tour of the school and we scheduled a meeting with the student leaders. There were two immediate problems: (1) we had to secure parent permission, and (2) we had to grant absolute confidentiality. The parent permission requirement presented a hurdle in that my major method of gaining information was to hang out and record what students said to me. It was impossible to gain parent permission for such spontaneous occurrences. It also could not be gathered after the fact. Parent permission generated a political problem as well. These young people's right of free speech would be abridged. If parent permission had to be secured for the study, it would be impossible to carry out, not only because it eliminated the most important method of data collection, but it created a situation where I would be forced into acting as an agent of adult authority. The problem was resolved by maintaining strict confidentiality and asking the students *not* to reveal their surnames to me while the tape was in motion. In addition, I have written the book using pseudonyms for first names and have not mentioned the exact location or real name of the school district.

Obviously, within Pleasant Valley, such personages as the principal and the juvenile officer will be known. There are enough people in the community who know the study has taken place so the book will be of interest. However, it will be extremely difficult for any student to be identified, unless by positional status. For example, the editor of the yearbook was identified as such when he talks of matters concerning the yearbook. However, when he discussed other topics such as sex, a separate identity was given him to protect his privacy.

Once the problems of confidentiality and parent permission were solved, I began collecting data. It was my policy to always identify myself as a sociologist and state my purpose. The students usually accepted my word at face value. There was only one instance in which a student refused to talk to me. He was a member of the greaser subculture and was extremely suspicious of me and the questions I asked. His friend attempted to encourage him to talk while giving me a "stoned rap" for about fifteen to twenty minutes.

The data was collected between March and July 1976. Interviewing was done during class time, and the majority of informal observations were made either during the lunch breaks (commons periods) or after school. The best time to collect data was between 10 A.M. and 2 P.M. since the school had staggered lunch periods. I varied the days of the week I appeared in school, averaging one day a week. Upon completion of the data collection, I had about twenty hours of tape. I have returned to the school district several times since the formal data collection ended to keep track of what has been going on and to complete the study.

As I collected data, I began to generate a sense of the social structure of the student population by asking students their views of the types of various student subcultures. I attempted to verify my own views by testing them out on the students. They were always glad to help. After a day of interviews, I would review what had been said, analyze what had been missed, and make a note as to what topics or what groups I had to cover in the future visits to the school. Quite frankly I was frightened to talk to the "greasers," fantasizing myself being attacked by a gang of them and having my tape recorder stolen. Such are the prejudices we bring to the field.

Concomitant with the interviewing, I built up a file of documents. I kept a file of the year's publications of the school newspaper, read the annual yearbook for the preceding year and the year of the study, compiled a set of school publications for the students and their parents, and read through the issues of the local weekly newspaper. In addition, I read documents on the history of the town and the area and collected what I could from regional and national publications when Pleasant Valley was catapulted onto the national scene.

The data collection ended when I found myself covering the same ground with the students that I had done previously. I reviewed my list of questions and found that they were answered. I then listened to the tapes and outlined their content, noting the footage. I reread the documents I had collected and began to develop an outline for the study. I needed more information on the community and examined census tract data. In the case of Pleasant Valley, the census tracts were coterminus with the town boundaries, making an accurate collection of data easy.

While the study was in progress, I was reading in the fields of economics, youth culture, contemporary history, and modern culture. From my readings, I pieced together a ninety-five-page theoretical document in two sections. One section was entitled "The Decline and Fall of Bourgeois Culture," which chronicled the erosion and destruction of bourgeois culture by the necessities of monopoly capitalism to maintain labor force discipline and generate an expanding economy through the development of a consumer culture. The second section was concerned with the development of youth as a status in modern industrial society and the universality of the experience of being in a position of social subordination. This section was entitled, "Beginning at the Bottom." I decided that two theoretical chapters were too much and condensed the arguments into what is now chapter 2.

As I wrote, I read the chapters aloud to my wife, who criticized them and helped with some of the editing. I then gave copies to colleagues and friends who read and critiqued the drafts. I was also lucky to find three students who had attended Utopia High School who were willing to read the manuscript. One was a sophomore, one a senior, and the other was a recent graduate at the time of the study. Each student was able to give me a slightly different perspective. The recent graduate told me what changes had occurred between her tenure and the study (e.g., declining support for student activism). The senior passed the study to her friends and they all thought that it was an accurate picture of Utopia High. The sophomore, while offering additional information on the relations between the politicos and intellectuals was able to chronicle the decline in student privileges following the study.

CONCLUSION

This study was carried out "loosely." The design was not rigid. There was no attempt to randomly select students. There was no structured questionnaire to be adhered to. Interviewing was done under uncontrolled conditions, sometimes with heavy distractions; they were conducted while I was standing up, sitting down, and lying around. I do not see this as a weakness of the study; but, rather, its strength. I was able to use any technique I considered necessary at the time to get information. Students saw me in a great many contexts. I tried to communicate my respect for them, and I truly think that they trusted me to the point of revealing to me thoughts and feelings they would expose only to their nearest and dearest friends.

I believe that sociological research should be an extension of what C. Wright Mills (1959) called "the sociological imagination." The best sociology is found at the intersection of personal problems and historical conditions. Data collection depends on the informed judgment of the sociologist, and no amount of rationalization or pre-punched data cards can remove that from the calculus. I felt that the best way that I could study the consequences of the cultural crisis on the young was the way described above. I had to live *with* them and talk *with* them, even if it was for just a little while.

There are weaknesses in the study. The major weakness is insufficient data. I should have talked to more students, especially from the jock/rah-rah crowd. I talked intensively with only three teachers. There should have been more. It took me almost a year to figure out that I needed to talk to parents. The parent interview took place a year after the rest of the data collection. I also should have made an effort to hang out with these young people beyond the school. However, every study has its weaknesses, and I stand by the conclusions in this book.

also two sisters, Tina Gross, [...] then and [...] Christmas even

If it was [Ottimiste]. It if was said.

[...] or weakness in the subject. The major weakness is its

insufficient data. I should have taken a more systematic way

profile from the look with his crowds to find them richer with

so many more teachers. There should have been more. It does the

allows one to figure out that I needed to talk to parents. The

conflict interviews took place a year after the end of the data

collection. I also should have made an effort to hang out with

these young people behind the school. However, given my time

constraints, and I wanted to do the broadcast, and this was

REFERENCES

Baran, Paul and Paul Sweezy
    1966   Monopoly Capital. New York: Monthly Review.
Barnet, Richard and Ronald Miller
    1974   Global Reach. New York: Simon and Schuster.
Beck, Rochelle
    1973   "White House Conferences on Children: An Historical Perspective." Harvard Educational Review 43: 653–68.
Becker, Howard
    1956   Outsiders. New York: The Free Press.
Bell, Daniel
    1976   The Cultural Contradictions of Capitalism. New York: Basic.
Berg, Ivar
    1971   Education and Jobs: The Great Training Robbery. Boston: Beacon.
Blau, Peter
    1964   Exchange and Power in Social Life. New York: Wiley.
Bookchin, Murray
    1971   Post-Scarcity Anarchism. San Francisco: Ramparts.
Bowles, Samuel and Herbert Gintis
    1976   Schooling in Capitalist America. New York: Basic.
Braverman, Harry
    1974   Labor and Monopoly Capital. New York: Monthly Review.
Brookover, Wilbur and David Gottlieb
    1964   A Sociology of Education. New York: American Book.
Broom, Leonard and Robert Cushing
    1977   "A Modest Test of an Immodest Theory: The Functional Theory of Stratification." American Sociological Review 42:157–69.
Broom, Leonard and Phillip Selznick
    1955   Sociology. New York: The Free Press.
Brown, Bruce
    1973   Marx, Freud and the Critique of Everyday Life. New York: Monthly Review.

Castaneda, Carlos
    1968   The Teachings of Don Juan. New York: Balantine.
    1970   A Separate Reality. New York: Simon and Schuster.
    1972   Journey to Ixtlan. New York: Simon and Schuster.

Chinoy, Eli
    1955   Automobile Workers and the American Dream. New York: Random House.

Clark, Burton
    1962   Educating the Expert Society. San Francisco: Chandler.

Coleman, James
    1961   The Adolescent Society. Glencoe, Ill.: The Free Press.

Coser, Lewis
    1956   The Functions of Social Conflict. New York: The Free Press.

deMause, Floyd (ed.)
    1974   The History of Childhood. New York: Psychohistory.

Domhoff, G. William
    1970   The Higher Circles. New York: Vintage.

Durkheim, Emile
    1956   Education and Sociology. New York: The Free Press.

Erikson, Erik
    1950   Childhood and Society. New York: Norton.

Eve, Raymond
    1975   "'Adolescent Culture.' Convenient Myth or Reality? A Comparison of Students and Their Teachers." Sociology of Education 48:152–67.

Ewen, Stewart
    1976   Captains of Consciousness. New York: McGraw-Hill.

Flacks, Richard
    1971   Youth and Social Change. Chicago: Markham.

Foss, Daniel
    1972   Freak Culture: Lifestyle and Politics. New York: Dutton.

Foss, Daniel and Ralph Larkin
    1976   "From 'The Gates of Eden' to 'Day of the Locust': An Analysis of the Dissident Youth Movement of the 1960s and Its Heirs in the Early 1970s—The Post-Movement Groups." Theory and Society 3:45–64.
    1979   "Roar of the Lemming: Youth, Post-Movement Groups and the Life Construction Crisis." In Harry M. Johnson (ed.), Religious Change. A special issue of Sociological Inquiry 49. San Francisco: Jossey-Bass.

Freud, Sigmund
    1961   Civilization and Its Discontents. New York: Norton.

Freund, Peter and Mona Abrams
    1976   "Ethnomethodology and Marxism: Their Use for Critical
            Theorizing." Theory and Society 3:377–94.

Friedenberg, Edgar
    1959   The Vanishing Adolescent. New York: Dell.

Galbraith, John
    1958   The Affluent Society. Boston: Houghton-Mifflin.
    1967   The New Industrial State. New York: Mentor.

Gallup, George, Jr.
    1973   "Confidence in Key U.S. Institutions." Gallup Opinion
            Index 97 (July):10–17.
    1975   The Gallup Poll: Public Opinion 1935–1971. New York:
            Random House.

Gillis, John
    1974   Youth and History. New York: Academic Press.

Goldstein, Richard
    1968   The Poetry of Rock. New York: Bantam.

Gombin, Richard
    1975   Origins of Modern Leftism. Harmondsworth, England:
            Penguin.

Gordon, C. Wayne
    1957   The Social System of the High School. Glencoe, Ill.: The
            Free Press.

Gouldner, Alvin
    1970   The Coming Crisis in Western Sociology. New York:
            Basic.

Grogan, Emmett [pseud.]
    1972   Ringolevio. New York: Avon.

Habermas, Jurgen
    1973   Legitimation Crisis. Boston: Beacon.

Henry, Jules
    1963   Culture Against Man. New York: Vintage.

Hoffman, Abbie
    1968   Revolution for the Hell of It. New York: Dial.
    1969   Woodstock Nation. New York: Vintage.
    1971   Steal This Book. New York: Pirate.

Homans, George
    1966   Social Behavior: Its Elementary Forms. New York: Har-
            court, Brace, and Jovanovich.

Jencks, Christopher, et al.
    1972   Inequality: A Reassessment of the Effect of Family and
            Schooling in America. New York: Harper and Row.

Kenniston, Kenneth
1960   The Uncommitted. New York: Dell.
1968   Young Radicals. New York: Harcourt, Brace, and World.
1975   "Prologue: Youth as a Stage of Life." In Robert Havig-
       hurst and Philip Dreyer (eds.), Youth. The 74th Yearbook
       of the National Society for the Study of Education, Part 1.
       Chicago: University of Chicago.
1977   All Our Children. New York: Harcourt, Brace, and Jo-
       vanovich.
Kohn, Melvin
1969   Class and Conformity. Homewood, Ill.: Dorsey.
Kolko, Gabriel
1962   Wealth & Power in America. New York: Praeger.
Kuhn, Thomas
1970   The Structure of Scientific Revolutions. Chicago: Univer-
       sity of Chicago.
Lefebvre, Henri
1971   Everyday Life in the Modern World. New York: Harper
       and Row.
Lipset Seymour
1960   Political Man. New York: Doubleday.
Lukacs, Georg
1971   History and Class Consciousness. Cambridge: MIT.
McFadden, Cyra
1977   The Serial: A Year in the Life of Marin County. New York:
       Knopf.
Maccoby, Michael
1977   The Gamesman. New York: Simon and Schuster.
Marcuse, Herbert
1955   Eros and Civilization. New York: Vintage.
1964   One Dimensional Man. Boston: Beacon.
1970   Five Lectures. Boston: Beacon.
Marx, Karl
1967   Capital, Volume I. New York: International.
Marx, Karl and Friedrich Engels
1970   The German Ideology. New York: International.
Maslow, Abraham
1954   Motivation and Personalty. New York: Harper and Row.
Mauss, Armand and William Garland, Jr.
1971   "The Myth of the Generation Gap." Unpublished paper
       presented at the 1971 American Sociological Association
       Meeting, Denver, Colorado.

Mehan, High and Houston Wood
    1975   The Reality of Ethnomethodology. New York: Wiley.
Meyer, Marshall
    1971   "Harvard Students in the Midst of Crises." Sociology of
            Education 44:245–69.
Mills, C. Wright
    1951   White Collar. New York: Oxford.
    1956   The Power Elite. New York: Oxford.
    1959   The Sociological Imagination. New York: Grove.
Mitchell, Juliet
    1971   Women's Estate. New York: Vintage.
Moynahan, Daniel
    1965   The Negro Family: The Case for National Action. Wash-
            ington, D.C.: U.S. Printing Office.
Mullins, Nicholas
    1973   Theories and Theory Groups in Contemporary American
            Sociology. New York: Harper and Row.
Musgrove, F.
    1965   Youth and the Social Order. Bloomington, Ind.: Indiana
            University.
Parsons, Talcott
    1951   The Social System. Glencoe, Ill.. The Free Press.
    1959   "The School Class as a Social System: Some of Its Func-
            tions in American Society." Harvard Educational Review
            29:297–318.
Peterson, Richard and John Biloursky
    1971   May 1970: The Campus Aftermath of Cambodia and Kent
            State. Berkeley, Cal.: The Carnegie Commission on
            Higher Education.
Phillips, Joseph
    1966   "Appendix: Estimating the Economic Surplus." In Paul
            Baran and Paul Sweezy, Monopoly Capital. New York:
            Monthly Review.
Reich, Charles
    1970   The Greening of America. New York: Random House.
Reich, Michael
    1972   "The Evolution of the U.S. Labor Force." In Richard
            Edwards, Michael Reich, and Thomas Weisskopf (eds.),
            The Capitalist System. Englewood Cliffs, N.J.: Prentice-
            Hall.
Remmers, H. H. and D. H. Radler
    1957   The American Teenager. Indianapolis: Bobbs-Merrill.

Riesman, David with Nathan Glazer and Reuel Denny
    1955   The Lonely Crowd. New York: Doubleday.
Roszak, Theodore
    1969   The Making of the Counterculture. New York: Doubleday.
Rowbotham, Shiela
    1973   Woman's Consciousness, Man's World. Harmondsworth, England: Penguin.
Rubin, Jerry
    1970   Do It! New York: Simon and Schuster.
Sale, Kirkpatric
    1973   SDS. New York: Vintage.
Turner, Victor
    1969   The Ritual Process. Chicago: Aldine.
U.S. Department of Commerce
    1974   Statistical Abstract of the United States. Washington, D.C.: U.S. Printing Office.
    1975   Statistical Abstract of the United States. Washington, D.C.: U.S. Printing Office.
Veblen, Thorsten
    1899   The Theory of the Leisure Class. New York: Mentor.
Weber, Max
    1958   The Protestant Ethic and the Spirit of Capitalism. New York: Scribner's.
Weil, Andrew
    1973   The Natural Mind. Boston: Houghton-Mifflin.
Wolfe, Tom
    1976   The "Me" Decade. New York Magazine, August 26.
Yablonsky, Lewis
    1968   The Hippie Trip. New York: Pegasus.
Yankelovich, Daniel
    1972   The Changing Values on Campus. New York: Pocketbooks.

INDEX

Abortion, 108, 122

Absurdity. *See* Meaninglessness

Abzug, Bella, 21*n*

Administration. *See* School administration

Adolescence, 39–45, 48, 78, 100–102, 111, 118, 120, 192; culture, 91, 237; rebellion, 47

Advertising, 31, 35–36, 116, 205, 209

Affluent society, 28, 45

Agnew, Spiro, 4, 22*n*

Alamo Foundation, 56

Alcohol, 75, 105, 115–18, 153; abuse, 20, 118, 127, 196; alcoholism, 27, 121, 183; drunkenness, 80. *See also* Drugs

Alienation, 205; de-alienation, 53; in education, 222–23; parents' perception of, 192; sexual, 113; of youth, 47–48, 78, 148–52, 213

Allen, Dwight, 11

Alternative school, 11, 13, 15, 172

American Civil Liberties Union, 17

American dream, 5, 155

American Grafitti, 78

Anarchism, 74

Anomie theory, 229

Anti-communism, 46, 229

Apathy, 135, 142, 239; causes of, 144, 206, 210, 213; student complaints of, 76, 93, 132, 140, 147, 151. *See also* Boredom

Asexuality, 109

Athletics, 18–19, 46, 69, 87, 94*n*, 132, 237

Attitudes, 205, 237; toward adults, 167; development of, 231; toward Pleasant Valley, 129–30, 145, 187; political, 46; toward school, 180; sexual, 100. *See also* Parents; Sex, attitudes toward; *specific topics*

Authority, 60, 81, 87, 171, 175, 185, 217; of adults 41, 44, 70, 198; in school, 7–9, 12, 97; structures of, 9, 132. *See also* Hierarchy

Basic skills, 17

Beard, Dita, 21*n*

Becker, Howard, 229

Beer. *See* Alcohol

Berry, Chuck, 111-12

Black power, 80

Blackboard Jungle, 76

Blacks, 3, 5, 72, 91, 93; in school, 79–80, 82–86, 147; status of, 40, 76

Blumer, Herbert, 229

Bobos. *See* Greasers

Boredom: and marijuana, 197; parents' attitudes toward, 188–93; among students, 60, 129–35, 148, 160, 180. *See also* Apathy

Bourgeois culture. *See* Culture, bourgeois

Bourgeoisie. *See* Social class

Bowles, Samuel, 231

Bribery: congressional, 4, 22*n*; corporate, 4; Korean, 4, 22*n*

Brown, Bruce, 232

Bureaucracy, 30–31, 44, 64*n*; corporate, 5, 57; government, 5, 31, 216; school, 5–10, 151, 215

Bureaucratic: context, 37; domination, 142, 203; existence, 35; hierarchy, 234. *See also* Hierarchy; institutions, 45, 198; rationality, 127

Bureaucratization, 59, 162, 199, 232

Butler, Francis, 124*n*

Capitalism, 57, 62*n*, 230; monopoly, 29–32, 38–39, 58, 61*n*–62*n*, 64*n*, 203, 205–6, 217, 243. *See also* Economic